Andrew Wallace

Popular traditions of Glasgow

Historical, legendary and biographical

Andrew Wallace

Popular traditions of Glasgow
Historical, legendary and biographical

ISBN/EAN: 9783337153298

Printed in Europe, USA, Canada, Australia, Japan

Cover: Foto ©Andreas Hilbeck / pixelio.de

More available books at **www.hansebooks.com**

Popular Traditions

of

Glasgow:

Historical, Legendary and Biographical.

Edited by

Andrew Wallace,

Author of " A Popular History of Glasgow," &c.

" And such is human life, so gliding on,
It glimmers like a meteor and is gone!
Yet is the tale, brief though it be, as strange,
As full, methinks, of wild and wondrous change
As any that the wandering tribes require,
Stretched in the desert round their evening fire;
As any sung of old, in hall or bower,
To minstrel-harps at midnight's witching hour!"—*Rogers.*

GLASGOW: THOMAS D. MORISON.
LONDON: HAMILTON, ADAMS & CO.
1889.

PREFACE.

—o—

THE City of Glasgow has a history which is not only intensely interesting and instructive to its own citizens, but which ought to be almost equally interesting and instructive to many others in the kingdom of which the city forms an important factor. From a small and insignificant hamlet situated on the banks of a petty rivulet—the Molindinar Burn—it has grown to be one of the largest and most powerful cities in the world, and the history of that growth must carry with it such lessons of truest wisdom, and display such vivid pictures of the lights and shadows of human life, as should not only arrest the attention and rivet the interest of the merely casual reader, but also convey solid instruction to the thoughtful and earnest student. Having for its early founders a holy and renowned minister of God, and an earnest religious and ecclesiastical community, who have given a tone to its whole subsequent career, and having for its earliest motto, "Let Glasgow flourish by the preaching of the Word," it may safely be said that the foundations of Glasgow were established in Righteousness, and we might venture to add that never since its foundation has Righteousness departed from its gates. True, the city has been to some extent favoured by its situation beside the banks of a noble river, and by its contiguity to rich fields of mineral wealth. But it was not more favourably situated in those respects than other towns and villages which were at one time larger and more important than itself, though these have remained practically but towns and villages to this day : and the conclusion is forced upon us that the wonderful growth and importance of Glasgow, are due more to the character and enterprise of its founders and citizens than to any mere external advantage of situation or circumstance.

In the following pages we have endeavoured to collate from almost every source available to us, a few of the more graphic and striking sketches of life and character from the History of Glasgow, at its different stages, partly with the view of stimulating our readers to a more systematic and consecutive study of that History, and partly with the view of exhibiting some of the essential principles and underlying forces of the city's progress and prosperity, so that our young readers especially may not become bewildered with the multitudinous and ever increasing details of our city's life and interests, but come into living contact with its heart and spirit, and thus become partakers of its inner life, and conduct their own lives in harmony with its best and noblest traditions. We make no pretence to originality of research. The only merit we claim is that of careful selection and combination; and of having kept steadily in view, the elucidation of what we consider to be the leading and guiding principles that have gone to make Glasgow what it now undoubtedly is, the Second City in the United Kingdom.

Like the *Popular History of Glasgow*, published seven years ago, the present work is chiefly intended for the rising generation of our citizens, and to those others who have not had the opportunity of perusing the larger and costlier works that have been written; and to these classes we trust the book will afford some pleasure and instruction.

GLASGOW, *March, 1889.*

CONTENTS.

CHAPTER I.

THE STORY OF SAINT MUNGO.

	PAGES
Saint Mungo and King Morken—The Queen of Cadzow—Other Legends—The Long Interregnum, . . .	9-20

CHAPTER II.

THE CATHEDRAL AND ITS BISHOPS.

The Erection of the Cathedral—Sketches of its more Celebrated Prelates—The Old Bridge of Glasgow, . . 20-35

CHAPTER III.

THE BISHOP'S CASTLE AND MANOR HOUSES.

Earlier and Later Conditions of the Castle—Manor Houses at Anderston, Partick, Lochwood, Carstairs, &c., . 35-40

CHAPTER IV.

THE UNIVERSITY AND SOME NOTABLE PROFESSORS.

Foundation of the University—Sketches of Zachary Boyd—David Dickson—Robert Baillie—Robert Wodrow—Robert Simson—Adam Smith—Thomas Reid—Modern Professors—Anecdotes, ... 41-65

CHAPTER V.

DISTINGUISHED STUDENTS OF GLASGOW UNIVERSITY.

Sketches of Sir William Alexander—George Buchanan—Sir William Hamilton—John Wilson—Francis Jeffrey—James Smith—Archibald Smith—Tobias Smollett, **65-77**

CHAPTER VI.

SKETCHES OF NOTABLE POETS AND LITERARY MEN.

Mrs. Grant—Michael Scott—Dougal Graham—Rev. James Grahame—Thomas Campbell—Robert Macnish—Wm. Motherwell—John Strang—William Glen—John D. Carrick—Dugald Moore—John Gibson Lockhart—Hugh Macdonald—Sir Arch. Alison—Henry Glassford Bell—James Hedderwick—William Black—James H. Stoddart—William Freeland—Minor Poets—Anecdotes of Authors, **77-123**

CHAPTER VII.

COACHING AND THE POST OFFICE IN OLDEN TIMES.

Express Postal Despatches—A Ship Insurance Anecdote—Mail Coach Adventures—Newspapers at the Tontine—A Love Story, **123-133**

CHAPTER VIII.

TOBACCO LORDS AND EARLY MERCHANTS.

Early Traders—Glasgow Privateering—Anecdotes of Bailie Mitchell—Rise of the Tobacco Trade—Cunninghame of Lainshaw—Speirs of Elderslie—Glassford of Dugaldstone—Ritchie of Craigton and Busbie—Campbells of Blythswood—James Finlay & Co.—Monteiths of Anderston—Anecdotes of David Dale—Tennants of St. Rollox—Prosperity of Modern Merchants—Anecdotes, **133-167**

CHAPTER IX.

ON THE MANNERS AND HABITS OF OUR FOREFATHERS.

Dinner Parties in Olden Times—The Fashions and Local Manufactures—Police Establishment—"Jaikey" Brown and the "Eerish"—John Douglas of Barloch—Religious Orthodoxy and Bigotry—Anecdotes of Rev. Mr. Thom, &c., **168-179**

CHAPTER X.

A MEDICAL CHAPTER.

Faculty of Physicians and Surgeons—The Andersonian University—University Faculty of Medicine—Short Sketches of Glasgow Medical Men—Peter Low—Robert Hamilton—William Hunter—Matthew Baillie—Joseph Black—William Hamilton—Allan Burns—John Moore—Colin Douglas—Alexander Stevenston—Dr. Drumgold—William Mackenzie—Geo. C. Monteath—Andrew Buchanan—Medical and "What you Please" Clubs—The Resurrectionists—A Doctor and his Fee, ... 179-198

CHAPTER XI.

MODERN RELIGIOUS LIFE IN GLASGOW.

Sketches of Thomas Chalmers—Edward Irving—Robert Gillan—Norman Macleod of Barony—William Anderson—David Stow—Mary Ann Clough—The Foundry Boys' Society—Anecdotes, ... 199-242

CHAPTER XII.

SKETCHES OF SOME ODD CHARACTERS OF GLASGOW.

Samuel Hunter of the *Herald*—Robert M'Nair, Jean Holmes & Co.—Stirling of Keir—Anecdotes of "Hawkie"—William Dunn of Duntocher, . . 242-255

CHAPTER XIII.

MISCELLANEOUS STORIES AND ANECDOTES.

Romantic Story of Governor Macrae—Jenny Geddes outdone—Another Shawfield Riot—A Deputation to London in the Olden Time—Two Remarkable Coalpit Adventures—The Wail of the Old Canal, . . 256-272

BY THE SAME AUTHOR. Pp. 196. PRICE 3s. 6d.

A Popular Sketch of the History of Glasgow,

FROM THE EARLIEST TO THE PRESENT TIME.

OPINIONS OF THE PRESS.

Glasgow Herald:—"A bit of fair historical work is worth a ton of poor novels; and in that light, Mr. Wallace's *Sketch of the History of Glasgow* is of very considerable value. . . . We very heartily commend it to all lovers of their native city. It is cheap and good."

North British Daily Mail:—"Mr. Wallace merits unstinted praise for the satisfactory style in which he has performed a seasonable bit of work, and supplied a long felt want. If the reception of his book corresponds with its deserts, it will find its way into thousands of Glasgow homes."

Evening Citizen:—"Orion," in "Tangled Talk," says—"I cordially recommend Mr. Wallace's most readable and racy, yet accurate and valuable *Sketch of the History of Glasgow*, to the inhabitants of the second city in the Empire."

Glasgow News:—"We can cordially commend the book as a clear, well arranged, comprehensive, and enjoyable account of our city's history. Embodying all that is generally interesting about its past career, its historical associations and its individual celebrities, with the part which the citizens have taken in public movements, in commercial enterprise and scientific discovery."

Paisley and Renfrewshire Gazette:—"Mr. Wallace takes his readers along very pleasantly, beguiling the way by the narration of many curious events, so judiciously intermingled as to give one a good deal of insight into not only the political but the social life of the centuries. This compact little history will be found very useful and most interesting."

Hamilton Advertiser:—"We have enjoyed the book thoroughly, and advise all who are interested in Glasgow to make its immediate acquaintance."

PUBLISHED BY

THOMAS D. MORISON, 225 INGRAM STREET, GLASGOW.

POPULAR TRADITIONS

OF

GLASGOW.

CHAPTER I.

THE STORY OF SAINT MUNGO—THE LONG INTERREGNUM.

> " But if some pilgrim through the glade
> Thy hallowed bowers explore,
> O guard from harm his hoary head
> And listen to his lore ;
> For he of joys divine shall tell,
> That wean from earthly wo,
> And triumph o'er the mighty spell
> That chains his heart below."
> —*Beattie.*

No book relating to Ancient Glasgow would be considered at all satisfactory that did not contain some reference to its worthy and holy Founder, Saint Kentigern or Saint Mungo; and although it may be to most of our readers a thrice-told tale, we cannot refrain from relating briefly the half mythical story of his life and the wonderful legends attached thereto.

There are two different accounts of the date of this holy man's birth. One gives it in the year 514, the other in 527. The latter is the more probable. He is said to have been born at Culross on the Firth of Forth, and to have been the illegitimate son of a British prince variously named Owen ab Urien Rheged and Eugenius or Ewan Eufurien, king of Cumbria, and of a British princess named Dwynwen or Thenew. He was educated under the kindly and judicious care of Servanus or St. Serf who presided over a monastery on the banks of the Eastern Firth, and is reported to have been greatly beloved of that holy father. Hence his name of Mungo or *Mungu*—dear friend.* He found his way to Cathures—an ancient name for a place at or near Glasgow—about the year 550 when he was about 23 years of age, and it is supposed that he was consecrated as Bishop of that See about two years thereafter. A halo of sanctity appears to have surrounded the youthful priest from an early period of his life, for there is a legend attaching to his appearance on the banks of the Clyde which bears some faint resemblance to the story of the aged Simeon who waited for the coming of our Lord. The legend is to the effect that on the same night on which Kentigern left Servanus, he lodged in the house or cell of a holy man named Fergus, who lived in a place called *Kearnach* to whom it had been revealed that he should not die till he had seen the holy Kentigern. He expired immediately after the Saint entered his house, and Kentigern having placed the body on a car to which were yoked two wild bulls, he commanded his friends to carry it to the place ordained by the Lord. This order they meekly obeyed, and followed by the Saint and a great multitude, carried the body to Cathures, where they buried it beneath some ancient trees, near a forsaken cemetery that had been consecrated by Saint Ninian, a famous man of God in those early times. On that very spot it is said was afterwards reared the transept of our noble Cathedral, and the aisle or crypt of which was dedicated to Fergus. On a stone in the roof over the entrance to this aisle there is carved a rude inscription of the dead monk extended on the car with the inscription "*This is the ile of Car Fergus.*"

The people of Scotland at that time appear to have been only partially converted and they were—in Clydesdale—under the reign of a wicked king named Morken who conceived a great dislike to the holy Kentigern, and at last succeeded in driving him from his See and compelling him to take refuge in Wales where he founded a Monastery afterwards named after one of his disciples, St. Asaph.

* While the above is the popular tradition regarding the birth-place and training of Kentigern, it is proper to state that the present Marquis of Bute—who has given a good deal of attention to ancient Ecclesiastical history—throws doubt upon the assertion that Kentigern was born in Culross; while according to several other authorities of note, among whom may be mentioned Mr. Skene and Mr. A. Macgeorge, it would appear that Servanus lived two centuries later than his supposed pupil.

Referring to the persecutions of St. Mungo by the apostate prince Morken, there is a legend told which curiously illustrates the superstitions of these ancient days.

Saint Mungo and King Morken.

It happened at one time that in the monastery of the good Saint Kentigern there was a great dearth of provisions, and the head of the Confraternity went to King Morken and informed him of the sad straits into which the brethren had fallen. "Cast thy care upon the Lord, and He will sustain thee;" Scripturally, but mockingly replied the king. Mungo pleaded for human assistance, and Morken tauntingly told him that he could have the contents of his barns at Cathures, which had been newly filled with the harvest proceeds, if, by his power, he could transport them to Deschu (Glasgow). The suppliant retired from the royal presence, and by means of his miracle-working gifts he caused the waters of the Clyde to sweep the barns and their contents up the Molindinar to the Convent or College.

This story has been converted into verse by an anonymous rhymer of modern times, as follows:—

Saint Mungo sat in his old oaken hall
    In late autumn time of the year:
The bleak winds howled round his convent wall
    And the rain fell dismal and drear.

His brow was dark and o'ershadowed with care,
    And sorely he mourned his sad fate;
For his barns and stores were all empty and bare
    No harvest had come to his gate.

And Morken the king had treated with scorn,
    The Saint's humble prayer for food;
A valley of oaths he sent 'stead of corn,
    And a message blasphemous and rude.

"Go say to your master" the king had replied,
    "Neither corn nor wine need he crave,
Unless on the wings of the wind they can ride
    Or sail on the boisterous wave:

"He has thriven full well for many a day
    On his legends of heaven and hell,
But Morken has cast all such fables away,
    And broken the priest's lying spell :

"If God there be as Saint Mungo has said,
    Who rules in the earth and the sky,
Then let Him provide His servants with bread,
    Or let them now curse Him and die."

So the worthy Saint sat in his oak hall,
    His spirit all burdened with care,
While the wild winds raved round his Convent wall,
    And the black clouds darkened the air.

He went to his knees and called on the Lord,
    To come to the help of his child ;
But the rain fell fast and the hurricane roared,
    And the night grew more stormy and wild.

It seem'd as if Heaven had turned a deaf ear,
    To the cry of His people for bread ;
And the heart of His Saint was stricken with fear,
    His hopes were all scattered and dead.

But in man's darkest hour the Master draws nigh,
    He rides on the wind and the wave ;
He hears 'mid the storm the child's feeble cry,
    And His arm is stretched forth to save :

The rain fell fast and the wind blew strong,
    And loud was the tempest's uproar,
While the great ocean tide came swelling along,
    And swept all the lands by the shore.

And the barns and stores of Morken the king
    Were carried away by the "spate,"—
Borne high on the wave, while the wind's strong wing
    Wafted them to Saint Mungo's gate.

And deep in the hearts of the people around,
    This lesson of wisdom was stored,
What time darkness reigns and troubles abound,
    Is bared the strong arm of the Lord.

The legend goes on to show that Morken, though literally taken at his word, was furious when his loss was made known to him, and he went in a rage to St. Mungo, whom he denounced as a magician and a sorcerer. Becoming more exasperated, he lifted his kingly foot, and made the saint measure his length on the ground. In addition to that, one of Morken's servants, a man who had never shown much respect for Mungo, spoke insultingly to him, and roundly abused him. But the hour of retribution was at hand. While the royal company was riding away to the king's country residence at Pertnet, believed to be the old name of Partick, this man's horse became restive and threw the rider, causing immediate death. No sooner, also, had the king arrived at his palace than he was attacked with gout in the foot he had applied to Mungo's person; and from this disease, in an exceedingly acute form, he died shortly after. As Morken's death was thought to be clearly traceable to the power of St. Kentigern, the deceased king's relatives desired to be revenged. They endeavoured to lay hands on the holy man; and so much did he fear their rage that he set out on a visit to St. David in Wales. (*Macgregor's History of Glasgow*, page 13.)

It should be explained that before the advent of Kentigern to Glasgow, four kings of the Britons were engaged in conflict with the Saxons. One of these kings, Rhydderich or Rederchen, was at the head of that party among the Britons who were termed Romans, from their supposed descent from Roman soldiers or Roman citizens, and this king appears to have embraced Christianity after its introduction by St. Ninian. The other kings belonged to a party which, though it also embraced Christianity, had apostatized, and reverted to a semi-paganism fostered by their bards; and one of these kings having obtained an ascendancy in Strathclyde, opposed and persecuted Kentigern, and obliged him to fly, as we have seen, to North Wales. A great battle took place amongst these kings on the river Esk, near Carlisle, in the year 573, resulting in the victory of the Christian party and the establishment of Rhydderich as King of the Cumbrian Britons. On this event Kentigern was invited to return, and having appointed Asaph, one of his monks to be his successor, he left North Wales.

On the return of Kentigern to Strathclyde he was gladly received by the king, by whom he was protected until the death of the latter in 603. Kentigern took up his residence, with his colony of converts, on the banks of the beautiful stream, "Vocabulo Melindonor," where he had buried Fergus, and where he and his followers maintained themselves by rural industry, and by the practice of the arts of peaceful life. (*Old Glasgow*, Macgeorge.)

As we are writing a book of incidents, and not a history, we cannot quote in full the life of our good patron saint; but proceed to relate the legends connected with him and our city's well known insignia or arms. These, as our readers are all aware, consist of the tree, the bird, the fish, and the bell, and these emblems have been endeared to the hearts of our youthful citizens from time immemorial, by the oft repeated rhyme :—

> "There's the tree that never grew,
> There's the bird that never flew,
> There's the bell that never rang,
> There's the fish that never swam.
> Let Glasgow flourish by the preaching of the Word."

Each of these emblems of our city arms has a legend attached to it.

As for the tree, it was originally only a twig or branch, but through process of time it developed into an oak tree covering a large portion of the escutcheon, very likely because it would be considered more in keeping with the dignity of such a large and noble city. But as a twig it was intended to commemorate a frozen bough which Kentigern, when a boy, miraculously kindled into a flame. He had been appointed by his master, Servanus, to maintain in the refectory the holy fire sent from heaven, but having fallen asleep, some of his companions, out of envy, extinguished the fire, whereupon Kentigern when he awoke broke off a frozen branch from a hazel tree, and breathing on it in the name of the Holy Trinity, it immediately burst into flame.

The legend of the bird is also curious. The bird was a redbreast, and it is so described in the office of the saint in the Breviary of Aberdeen. The second lesson for the day in that ancient office consists of the story which tells how the saint miraculously restored to life, a tame robin, the favourite of St. Serf, which was by chance killed by his disciples, who, to screen themselves, laid the blame on Kentigern. That remarkable youth took it into his hand, made over it the sign of the cross, and thus restored it to life.

The story of the bell is of a more authentic and historical character than the two preceding. It represents a real bell which, although its origin cannot be traced, is known to have been in existence in Glasgow from a very early period till so late as the middle of the seventeenth century. Jocelin, the good bishop and founder of the Cathedral in 1181, says the bell was brought to Glasgow by Kentigern from Rome, where he had received it from the hands of the Pope, but Mr. Macgeorge says that no reliance can be placed on that legend, and thinks the bell was made at home—perhaps in Ireland—and may have been given to Kentigern at the time of his ordination by the bishop who came over to perform that office. The bell appearing on the early seals of our bishops, and also on one of the early seals of the community, is a representation of a bell then in existence in Glasgow, and believed to have belonged to Kentigern. It is a quadrangular bell—a form which denotes a very high antiquity. It was probably made of bronze, was used at the altar services, and was also rung through the streets by the friars, for the souls of the departed, especially of those who had been benefactors of the church. After the spoliation of the Cathedral at the Reformation, the bell came into the hands of the civic authorities who preserved it with commendable care.

On the 23rd October, 1640, an entry is recorded in the Town Council minutes ordering a new bell, the ancient bell, it being presumed, having become worn out and unfit for further service. The minute runs as follows:—"Ordaines ye Dean of Gild to caus mak ane new deid bell to be rung for and before ye deid under hand."

The legend relating to the salmon and the ring is well known by all the citizens of Glasgow, but may be briefly repeated here, for the information of the young and rising generation. The story is thus given in the office for the Saint's day in the Breviary of Aberdeen. "It happened that the Queen of Cadzow had laid herself open to the suspicion of an intrigue with a certain knight, whom the king had taken with him in hunting, and the knight being asleep the king abstracted from his scrip a ring which the queen had given him, and flung it into the river called Clyde (*Cludam*). Returning home he demanded the ring of the queen, threatening her with death if she did not produce it. She having sent her maid to the knight, and not receiving the ring despatched a messenger to Kentigern, telling him everything and promising the most condign penance. St. Kentigern taking compassion on her, sent one of his people to the river to angle with a hook, directing him to bring alive the first fish he might take : which being done, the Saint took from its mouth the ring, and sent it to the queen, who restored it to the king and so saved her life."

This legend has been turned into rhyme after the style of the old Scottish Ballad, and for the sake of variety we present it in this form to our readers :—

THE QUEEN OF CADZOW.

A LEGEND OF ANCIENT GLASGOW.

The Queen o' Cadzow to her chamber has gane,
    An' a sorrowfu' Queen is she ;
In drearie despair she sits a' alane,
    While the saut tear dims her blue e'e.

She dreads the return o' her ain liege lord,
    (An' a crusty aul' carle was he) ;
For he has left her wi' an' angrie word,
    An' a threat that was sair to dree :

"O whaur is the ring," the aul' carle said,
    " The gowd ring I gied unto thee,
On the day that I took ye, a puir countrie maid,
    My gudewife and Queen for to be ?"

" I ha'e lost ye're gowd ring," the Queen she replied,
    " On the banks o' the silverie Clyde,
And meikle I fear, though to find it I've tried,
    It has gane wi' the ebb o' the tide."

" I heed na' ye're fears," quoth the auld carle king,
    " Ye're tears and fair speech I despise ;
But wae be to thee if ye find na' the ring,
    By the morn whan the sun shall rise."

THE QUEEN OF CADZOW.

Sae the Queen o' Cadzow to her chamber has gane,
    An' a sair, sair heart has she ;
For weel does she ken the gowd ring was ta'en,
    By her lover the young laird o' Lee :

The young laird o' Lee her lover had been,
    When a fair countrie maid was she,
He had won her heart on her ain village green,
    'Neath the shade o' the hawthorn tree.

But the aul' carle king in his pomp and pride,
    A-wooin had come to her door,
An' will she or nil she, he made her his bride,
    Tho' her heart was fu' dowie and sore.

Then the young laird o' Lee to be near his true love,
    To the King o' Cadzow straight did ride ;
He vowed that a faithfu' knight he would prove,
    To him and his bonnie young bride.

An' aye by the side o' his fair one he rade,
    Oure hills and through valleys sae green,
A leal-hearted service to her he still paid,
    Wha was baith his true love and Queen.

Yestreen they had met for a moment apart
    Unkent by the aul' carle king,
When the rash young knight in the joy o' his heart
    Took awa' the Queen's bridal ring.

Neist day to the hunting, King Cadzow he hied,
    The young laird o' Lee by his side,
By chance the gowd ring o' his queen he espied,
    An' flang't in the silverie Clyde.

.   .   .   .   .   .

"O what sall I dae ?" cried the fair young bride,
    As she wrung her hands in despair.
"I'll send to the Kirk on yon bonnie burn side,
    The guid priest will answer my prayer."

Sanct Mungo he hearkened her sorrowfu' say,
    Then straight to the Clyde river went ;
A fisher he spied through the dim dawn o' day,
    On catchin' the sawmon intent.

"O cast oot ye're line!" the haly man said,
"An' a guid fish to me quickly bring;"
The man an' the sawmon his order obeyed,
An' lo! in its mouth was the ring.

. . . .

And by the fair Clyde a great city grew
Known all o'er the land north and south,
And o'er its escrol 'neath the bird that ne'er flew,
Is a fish with a ring in its mouth.

It remains but to be added that the good Saint Mungo after spending a long life in labours of love and beneficence, died on the banks of the Molindinar about the year 603, leaving a good memory behind, the fragrance of which still lingers round the precincts of our noble and ancient Cathedral, and even, though it may be unconsciously, in the hearts and lives of the citizens of Glasgow. For we are all proud of our patron Saint, and of the grand old motto bequeathed to us.

The Long Interregnum.

For a period of about five hundred years after the death of Saint Mungo, a cloud of darkness and mystery hangs over the history of Glasgow; and any little ray of intelligence that has been let in upon it seems only to "render the darkness more visible." Still, we think it may be interesting to our readers to collate from various sources, what little tradition or history we can glean, so as to give an appearance of continuity to our illustrative sketches of Glasgow, ancient and modern.

M'Ure, the earliest historian of the city, says:—"After St. Mungo, for many ages, the Episcopal See was overrun with heathenism and barbarity till the reign of Alexander the First." Another writer (Dean Gordon) says:—"Baldredus is said, by some, to have succeeded St. Mungo. He founded a Religious House at Inchinnan, near Renfrew; but how long he lived, or who were his successors, no account can be given. It is a question whether this is the same Saint Baldred, the Apostle of East Lothian, who died in the beginning of the seventh century. He was wont to pass his sojourn in secluded spots and islands. One of his favourite resorts (according to the *Aberdeen Breviary*) was the Bass Rock, in the Firth of Forth. In the churchyard of Preston (dedicated to St. Baldred) an effigy of the Patron Saint was in existence at the end of the last century. There is a Well there also, named after him; and a Pool in the Tyne, which is called *St. Baldred's Whirl;* and on the Tyningham Coast there is a Basin, formed by the sea in a rock, called *St. Baldred's Cradle.*" Dr. Gordon adds, " For the long space of 450 years after this period a veil of impenetrable mystery hangs over the history of the See; and to account for this blank, it is supposed that the Church was destroyed by the Danes during their inroads into this country, who either slew or drove away the religious community from Glasgow. During this period Scotland presented a picture of human nature in its most barbarous form. Civil wars and an utter disregard to laws and property were the distinguishing features of its policy."

From the *Chronicles of Saint Mungo* we learn that "The first mention which we find made of the City of Saint Mungo after this time occurs under the year 1050, in the history of York Cathedral, when it is recorded that three bishops in succession, MAGSUEN, JOHN, and MICHAEL were consecrated to the See of Glasgow by the Archbishop of York. Considerable doubts, however, are entertained by historians whether these records were not interpolated as precedents to support the claim of superiority over Scotland, set up by the See of York. On the reference of the question to Pope Alexander III, his holiness pronounced decision in favour of Scotland; and, when the subject was subsequently revived, the former judgment was corroborated, with a confirmation of the entire independency of the Scottish bishops, by Pope Sextus IV, who, at the same time, erected the See of Saint Andrews into an Archbishopric in 1466 (or 1491)."

Mr. James Pagan, in his *History of Glasgow Cathedral*, says that Saint Mungo " is said to have been succeeded by St. Baldred, but as to how long he lived, or who were his successors, no account can be given. For the long period of nearly 500 years a veil of almost impenetrable obscurity hangs over the See. There is no doubt that the sanctity pertaining to the resting-place of the bones of so holy a man as St. Kentigern kept the establishment together, and drew around it the village which became the nucleus of the future city. There is little doubt that the small community suffered from the incursions of the Danes from beyond the seas, as well as from the semi-barbarian tribes at home, upon whom the mantle of Christianity was as yet very loosely adjusted."

Mr. Andrew Macgeorge, the erudite author of *Old Glasgow, the Place and the People*, says :—" Of the early Church and of the local history of Glasgow during the long dark period between the time of Kentigern's patron, King Rydderch, and the accession of David in the beginning of the twelfth century, during which the kingdom was passing through so many changes, we have almost no record. It was a period of great confusion and change."

The bloody conflicts that were waged between the various petty kingdoms of the Picts and Angles, the Britons and the Scots, were anything but conducive to the religious spirit or to the true welfare of the country at large, although they doubtless were beneficial and perhaps necessary in those rude ages, as a disciplinary ordeal to bring turbulent spirits into subjection, and to teach men by dire experience the blessings of unity, industry, and true prosperity. And when comparative peace was restored, the spirit of Christianity again appeared upon the scene, and exerted its blessed influence in leading the people into the paths of civilization and real progress. The Church of Glasgow was again established on the banks of the Molindinar, and the city began its distinguished career.

CHAPTER II.

THE CATHEDRAL AND ITS BISHOPS.

"But hark ! the portals sound, and pacing forth
  With solemn steps and slow,
High potentates, and dames of royal birth,
  And mitred fathers, in long order go."
  —*Gray*.

As has been said regarding the patron saint of the city, so it may also be said of the Cathedral ; no account of Glasgow would be considered at all satisfactory that did not deal with its history and associations to a greater or lesser

FOUNDATION OF THE SEE.

extent. In our former *Sketch of the History of Glasgow*, we gave a brief account of its construction, and made some reference to those bishops under whose auspices the noble pile had been erected. But we desire, in this chapter, to give a brief narrative of the progress of this religious institution, and a sketch of a few of the more eminent and able prelates who presided over its affairs, and exerted a powerful and, on the whole, beneficial influence over not only the interests of the city, but also over a wide district of the kingdom round about. Of course our narrative must be very concise.

We are told by Chalmers, in his elaborate work, *Caledonia*, that the Diocese of Glasgow extended over no fewer than 240 parishes, and must, of course, have enjoyed much income and influence. On the same authority we learn that, in the time of Cameron, the "magnificent" prelate, there were as many as thirty-one prebendaries connected with the See who had mansions or residences erected in the immediate neighbourhood of his own castle; and that this concentration of important ecclesiastical dignitaries drew together a considerable number of attendants and retainers, and all these combined necessitated the presence and services of merchants and others, who catered to their temporal requirements. In short, the Cathedral and its adherents constituted the nucleus of the city itself, and gave the first start to its great career. The Market Cross, or centre of trade, was in those early times at the "Bell o' the Brae," near the head of the High Street; there the merchants erected their booths, and there also the annual Fairs for the surrounding districts were held.

At the close of the Long Interregnum, already referred to, King David I refounded the See of Glasgow, and appointed as its Bishop his own chaplain, John, commonly called Achaius. John was a man of much learning and energy, and he, about the year 1124, proceeded to erect a church or cathedral for the diocese. He was greatly encouraged in this work by his royal master. Chalmers informs us that, "after he became king, David made a grant to the Church of Glasgow in pure alms of a *tenth* of his *can* in Strathgrief and Cunningham, and in Kyle and Carrick. This grant was dated from Cadihou (or Cadzow) within Clydesdale, where the King had probably a seat. David, moreover, gave to the same church the eighth penny upon all his pleas throughout Cumberland. We may thus perceive that the worthy David was the real founder of the Church of Glasgow."

The new Cathedral was twelve years in building, and was consecrated by John, in the presence of his Sovereign, on the 7th July, 1186. But it was destroyed by fire some forty or fifty years afterwards, a great part of it probably being of wood; and it is believed that not a vestige of it was preserved. Besides founding the Church of Glasgow, Bishop John, out of the funds so liberally supplied to him by the King, established various prebends; and David himself procured the restoration of many other ecclesiastical institutions, and in this way so reduced his exchequer that one of his successors, James I, who esteemed his liberality to the Church as rather excessive, was forced to exclaim that Saint David was "ane sair sanct for the croon." Bishop John, towards the close of his life, undertook a pilgrimage to Jerusalem, and, returning, died at an advanced age on the 28th May, 1147, having held the See for the long period of thirty two years.

His successor in the See was Herbert, then abbot of Kelso, who was consecrated on St. Bartholomew's day the same year, 1147. He died in 1164. During his reign the Church continued to grow in affluence, and the pope enjoined the clergy and people of the Diocese to visit the Cathedral Church of Glasgow yearly.

Bishop Herbert was succeeded by Ingleram who had a papal bull for his consecration, notwithstanding the vehement opposition of the Archbishop of York, who claimed the obedience of the Glasgow prelates as their Metropolitan. Herbert's surname was Newbigging and he was of the house of Dunsyre in the county of Lanark; he had formerly been Archdeacon of Glasgow, and chancellor of the kingdom under king David and his successor Malcolm IV. He died on 2nd February, 1174, at a great age, and he had done much good in the high station which he occupied.*

* As an illustration of the position and wealth of the clergy in those early days it may be mentioned here, that so early as 1170 Ingleram, Bishop of Glasgow, leased to Richard Moreville, the constable, the whole territory of Gillemoriston for fifteen years, and received from him beforehand the sum of three hundred marks as a fine or *grassum*.

His successor in the See of Glasgow was the excellent Jocelinc, Abbot of the Cistercian Monastery of Melrose. He was consecrated at Clairvaux on 1st June, 1175, by Esceline, the Pope's Legate. He also resisted the encroachment of York; and contended that the successors of St. Kentigern were subject to no primate, but were vicars of the apostolic See itself, and took precedence and had power even above kings, so long as Cumbria was a kingdom. When Jocelinc came to the See he enlarged the Cathedral, and rebuilt it in a more substantial manner than formerly. The work was begun about the year 1181, and finished in 1197. This latter event is recorded by Winton, the old prior of Lochleven, in the following lines:—

> "When Joacline the Bishop of Glasgow.
> He hallowed the Kirk of St. Mungo.
> That was a thousand one hundred year
> And seven and ninety to that clear.
> That was done most solemnly,
> That year the fourth day of July."

The Cathedral erected by Bishop Jocelinc however, seems also to have been of a temporary character, and with the exception of a pillar and part of the vaulting in the southwest corner of the Crypt, was superseded by the present magnificent structure, which was begun during the episcopate of Bishop Bondington in 1233.

It was during the time of Jocelinc that Glasgow was made a Burgh of Barony in the holding of the bishops; and he procured many other privileges to the inhabitants to encourage the trade and commerce of the town. After an honoured episcopate of twenty-four years, the good Bishop departed this life on the 17th March, 1199.

In turn he was succeeded by William Malvoisin the chancellor, who was elected in the same year 1199, and consecrated in France by the Archbishop of Lyons in 1200; but before he sat two full years, he was translated to the Episcopal See of St. Andrews. (According to Cleland, a Society of Fishers was formed in Glasgow in the year 1201. These men lived in a row of houses fronting the river which was called the *Fisher's gate*, till the bridge was built when it was called *Bridgegate*. Salt for curing the Society's fish having been sold in the vicinity of the Fisher's gate, gave name to the *Saltmarket*.)

Walter, chaplain to the king, was elected bishop towards the close of 1207, and was consecrated by licence of the Pope, at Glasgow, on the 2nd November, 1208. He died in 1232. During the reign of the last three prelates, the Church of Glasgow steadily increased in wealth and power. It acquired the patronage of many churches round about; and fruitful lands were added to its already broad domains, and the most powerful nobles in the country trembled at the frown of the Church dignitaries. The proud families of Carrick and Lennox paid tribute to the Bishop of Glasgow, and the son of the Earl of Carrick, in token of repentance for injuries he had formerly inflicted on the Church, gave a church and some land to the parish of Straiton within the diocese.

The next bishop was William de Bondington, Archdeacon of Lothian, who was the descendent of a Roxburghshire family, and was consecrated at Glasgow, on the Sunday after the Nativity of the Virgin, 1233, by Andrew, Bishop of Moray. This prelate introduced the ritual of Sarum, composed by Bishop Osmund about 1076, into his diocese, which form of divine service continued till the Reformation. He also established the liberties and customs of Salisbury as the future constitution of the Cathedral of Glasgow. It is further said of this bishop that he made great additions to the building of the cathedral, to which very little had been done since the days of Joceline. Indeed, it is supposed by Mr. Honeyman, architect, and others that Bishop Bondington was the founder of the present cathedral, as very little of the former cathedral was retained when he began his building operations. He built the beautiful choir, which, the late Mr. James Pagan says, " is the most sacred part of the edifice, in which the principal altars were erected and high mass was performed, and is an exquisite specimen of the early English style. In length from the centre of the piers of the great tower to those which support its eastern gable, and separate it from the Lady Chapel, the choir is ninety-seven feet; the width is thirty; and the side aisles sixteen feet three inches each; the height of the main storey, triforium and clarestories, are the same as the nave—viz., thirty-one, thirteen and eighteen feet six inches respectively. The main arches of the choir are on each side, five in number, resting upon majestic columns, having rich and beautifully cut foliaged capitals all different in design, but harmonizing in their general appearance. On the vaulting are seen numerous coats of arms of the different bishops and prebends; amongst these, on the left of the high altar are the royal arms of Scotland, placed there in the time of James IV, who was himself a canon and member of the chapter."

This bishop also founded about 1246, the Blackfriars Monastery, the site of which is now occupied by the Blackfriars Parish Church. Bishop Bondington in his later years resided much in his native border land, and died at his house at Ancrum on 12th November, 1258, and was buried at Melrose Abbey, near the high altar.

Robert Wishart, Archdeacon of Lothian, was consecrated at Aberdeen in 1272, by the Bishops of Aberdeen, Moray, and Dunblane. This warlike prelate, who was a descendant of the ancient family of the Wisharts of Pitarrow of the shire of Kincardine, affords a singular example of inextinguishable patriotism under the tyranny of circumstances, while the rapidity with which he changed sides, and the ease with which he took oaths and violated them, give a strange insight into the morality of the times. At the competition for the throne between Bruce and Baliol, the bishop took the oath of fealty to Edward, but was the first to break it by instigating Baliol to ravage the English territories. The fate of Baliol being sealed, he hastened to swear homage to the English king; but scarcely had Edward reached the Continent, than he stimulated Wallace and Bruce to arms, and joined them clad in mail at the head of his retainers. Again fortune frowned on his country, and again he took the oath of fealty, only to break it ere a month had passed, by instigating a new rebellion. A fourth time he solemnly submitted, but only to march against the Prince of Wales, at that time acting in Galloway against Wallace and Bruce. Again he vowed and repeated his oath at St. Andrews, in presence of the assembled barons of both countries. But on the rise of Bruce he hastened to give him plenary absolution for the murder of Comyn, robed him at his coronation, and preached a holy crusade against the oppressors of his country. The very timber which Edward had given him to build the steeple at Glasgow, he converted into engines with which he stormed the Castle of Kirkintilloch. He shared in all the changes of his country, and spent his last years in furnishing Fordun with materials for his chronicle of the times. He died on the 26th November, 1316, and was interred in the Cathedral Church between the altars of St. Peter and St. Andrew.

Afterwards John Lindsay, a younger brother of the Lindsays of Crawford, was preferred to the See in 1322. There are two different accounts regarding the fate of this prelate. One that he died and was buried in the cathedral in 1335. The other account is a more tragic and romantic one, which is given on the authority of the *Registrum Episcopatus Glasguensis*, and which runs as follows:— "About the Feast of the Assumption, 1337, two ships coming from France to Scotland were encountered and taken after a stout resistance by John de Ros, the English admiral. On board were John de Lindsay, Bishop of Glasgow, and with him many noble ladies of Scotland, and men-at-arms, and much armour, and £30,000 of money, and the instruments of agreement and treaty between France and Scotland. The men-at-arms were all slain or drowned in the sea. The Lord-Bishop and part of these noble ladies, for very grief refused to eat or drink, and died before the fleet made the land. Their bodies are buried at Wystande in England."

The famous William Rae was the next Bishop of Glasgow, who appears to have reigned from 1337 till 1367. To this prelate is assigned the honour of having built the stone bridge over the Clyde, called the old Glasgow Bridge, and more recently the Stockwell Bridge, which is said to have been built in 1345 or 1350, and stood through storm and tide till the year 1850. Regarding this bridge Mr. Andrew MacGeorge says:—"The foundations of this old bridge had been laid in what was then the bed of the river, by Bishop Rae in the year 1350; and when the bridge was taken down in 1850, the remarkable fact became apparent that the original foundations had stood no less than five feet *above* the modern bed. It was also found that means had been taken from time to time to compensate the lowering process by artificially raising the portion of the channel immediately adjoining the piers, partly by compact masses of stone, and partly by strong ranges of piles. The old foundations had been laid on beams of oak, and it is interesting to know that when they were taken out after the lapse of 500 years, they were found to be as fresh as when first put in. This, however, is not so surprising when we know that the older Canoes found under the Trongate were comparatively fresh when found, although they had been made from oaks which must have been growing where Glasgow now is, at least 4,000 years ago."

According to M'Ure, it would appear that Bishop Rae was assisted in his good work of erecting the bridge by the Lady Lochow, who is said to have contributed the third arch at the north end. There were eight arches in all, and they continued entire till the year 1671, when the southmost arch fell, but was quickly replaced at the cost of the community.

Bishop Rae governed the See till his death on 27th January, 1367.

His successor was Walter Wardlaw, Archdeacon of Lothian, who held the office from 1368 to 1387. He was of the Wardlaws of Torry, in Fife, and was so much employed in embassies and negotiations with foreign powers that he was created a cardinal by Pope Urban VI in the year 1381. He was uncle to an even more famous prelate—viz., Bishop Henry Wardlaw, of St. Andrews, who held that office for the long period of thirty-six years. Bishop Walter's coat-of-arms is placed near the middle of the choir of our cathedral, on the right side of the high altar, and over it his name—*Walterus Cardinalus*—was inscribed in gilded Saxon letters.

After the death of Cardinal Wardlaw the Pope tried to intrude a friar minor named John Framisden into the See, and craved the assistance of Richard II for his settlement by force, but the attempt proved a failure; and the next Bishop was Matthew Glendinning, a Galloway man, of a notable family. He had formerly been a Prebendary or Canon of Glasgow. He was a man of parts, and was much employed in the public transactions that were in agitation between Scotland and England. During his reign the steeple of the cathedral, which had been built of wood from Lochlomond by one of his predecessors, was struck by lightning, and burned down. Glendinning collected materials for building it of stone, but the work was not commenced when he died in 1408.

The next Bishop was William Lauder, of the ancient family of the Lauders of Hatton-in-the-Merse, who was presented to the Bishopric by Pope Benedict XIII of his own authority, without the election of the Chapter; but his appointment was not disputed. It is believed that Lauder carried on and completed the building of the existing spire of the cathedral. He also built the beautiful crypt below the Chapter-house, and carried up a part of the west storey, but death prevented him finishing his design. In 1423-4 he was made Chancellor of the Kingdom, and at the same time he was honoured by being appointed Plenipotentiary from Scotland to negotiate with the Court of England for the relief and ransom of James I, who had been virtually a prisoner there for eighteen years. Bishop Lauder died on 14th June, 1425. His arms are carved a short way up on the outside of the western wall of the cathedral.

The successor to Lauder in the Bishopric of Glasgow was the notable John Cameron, of the family of Lochiel, and commonly called the "magnificent." He had formerly been Provost of Lincluden Abbey, near Dumfries, and Secretary of State, and occupied the See of Glasgow from 1426 to 1446. He was also promoted to the Chancellorship, which he held till 1440; and filled during his lifetime a good many other public offices. He resumed the building of the chapter-house of the cathedral. His arms are carved upon the central pillar which supports its groined roof, and they are also placed on the western wall outside, a little above those of Bishop Lauder. He is also credited with the completion of the Lady Chapel; and, as we will see further on, he built the Great Tower of the Bishop's Castle. Cameron was a man of great state and ambition. The See of Glasgow during his reign reached the height of its temporal prosperity. But it does not appear that he was greatly noted for sanctity of character. Old M'Ure says of him—"But for all the good things Bishop Cameron did, and which is strange, he is as little beholden to the charity of our historians as any man in his time." Buchanan and Spottiswoode, the historians, characterised him as a very worldly kind of man, and a great oppressor, especially of his vassals within the Bishopric. Moreover, both of these authors declare that he made a fearful and tragical exit at his country seat of Lochwood, five or six miles north-east of the city of Glasgow, on Christmas Eve, 1446. The legend regarding his death is thus given by Spottiswoode:—

"In the year 1446, the night before Christmas day, as he lay asleep in his house of Lochwood, some seven miles from the city of Glasgow, he seemed to hear a voice summoning him before the Tribunal of Christ, and give an account of his doings. Thereupon he awaked, and being greatly terrified, did call his servants to bring lights and sit by him. He himself took a book in his hand, and began to read; but the voice being again heard, struck all the servants with amazement. The same voice calling a third time, far louder and more fearfully, the Bishop, after a heavy groan, was found dead in the bed, his tongue hanging out of his mouth."

The worthy William Turnbull, to whom is ascribed the honour of founding our noble University, became Bishop in the year 1450. Bishop Turnbull belonged to the family of Turnbull of Minto, in Roxburghshire, and was formerly Archdeacon of Lothian and Keeper of the Privy Seal. During his occupation of the See he obtained from James II a charter erecting the town and patrimonies of the Bishopric into a regality; and after he did many acts highly beneficial to the age in which he lived, and worthy to be remembered by posterity, died at Rome, on the 3rd September, 1454.

He was succeeded by Andrew Muirhead, a Canon of the See, who belonged to a Lanarkshire family, and who was consecrated in 1455. He founded and endowed the St. Nicholas Hospital, one of the earliest of our charitable institutions, situated near the Bishop's Castle. He also repaired the north aisle of the Cathedral, and, according to M'Ure, "founded the clerical vicars, and built apartments for them to the north of the Cathedral in that place where there are only gardens now (1736), and are called the vicar alleys." Muirhead was much employed in the public service, having been a member of the Regency during the minority of James III; several times a commissioner to treat with England; and one of the ambassadors to negotiate the marriage of James with Margaret, "the maiden of Norway," in 1468. He died 20th November, 1473.

Robert Blackadder, Bishop of Aberdeen, was elevated to the See of St. Mungo in 1484. He belonged to the Blackadders of Berwickshire. He stood high in the estimation of his countrymen, for we are told that on the very day of the Battle of Sauchie, in which James III was slain, he repaired to the Castle of Edinburgh, and secured and took an inventory of the jewels, plate, and apparel, which belonged to the late king at the time of his decease, although it would appear this duty had been loosely performed, as part of the treasures were stolen. Shortly after this, Whitelaw, sub-dean of Glasgow, was made secretary to the young king, James IV. Blackadder was also honoured by being appointed commissioner, along with the Earl of Bothwell and Andrew Forman, Apostolical Prothonotary, to arrange the preliminaries of the marriage of James IV to the Princess Margaret, daughter of Henry VII of England. The treaty for this marriage was finally signed in the Palace of Richmond on the 24th January, 1502. When the proposition was made before the English privy council, one of the lords present objected that "the Princess Margaret being next heir to her brother Henry, England might chance to become a province of Scotland." "No," replied king Henry, "the smaller will ever follow the larger kingdom." And so the wisdom of the king was commended, and the Lady Margaret granted to the king of Scotland.

It was during Blackadder's occupancy that the See of Glasgow was erected into an archbishopric. M'Ure says this was in 1473, but that is an error, for Blackadder did not succeed to the See till 1484; and it would appear that the real date was 1491. The See of St. Andrew's had been erected into an archbishopric about the same time; and it would appear that the two prelates were for some time engaged in a violent litigation before the pope, respecting their jurisdiction, the expense of which, it was declared, had been attended with "inestimable damage to the realm." The king, at the request of his parliament, interfered and threatened, if they did not withdraw their suit, their tenants would be interdicted from paying their rents!

Towards the close of his career, Archbishop Blackadder undertook a pilgrimage to the Holy Sepulchre, but being now far advanced in life, his strength proved insufficient for the fatigues of the journey and voyage, and he died on 28th July, 1508, when almost in sight of the Arabian shore.

James Bethune, or Beaton, was the second Archbishop of the See. He was of the house of Balfour in Fife, and was uncle to the famous Cardinal Beaton. After taking Holy Orders, he was made, in 1503, Provost of the Collegiate Church of Bothwell; and next year was chosen Abbot of Dunfermline. In 1505 he became Lord High Treasurer for Scotland, and about three years afterwards, was promoted to the Bishopric of Galloway. But before he had filled that office a year he was elevated to the Archbishopric of Glasgow, being appointed to the See on 9th November, 1508, and consecrated at Stirling on 15th April, 1509. He held other great benefices, such as the Abbacies of Arbroath and Kilwinning. Beaton enclosed his palace at Glasgow with a noble stone wall of ashlar work, with a bastian on the one angle, and a stately tower, with an embattled wall on the other—fronting the High Street—where were fixed, in different places, his coat of arms. He also increased the altars in the choir of the Cathedral, and did good work in building and repairing bridges within the regality. In 1515 he was made Chancellor of the Kingdom by the Regent Albany, and was translated to the See of St. Andrew's in 1523. Like most of the eminent clerics of those times, Archbishop Beaton took a prominent part in the party struggles of his day, and in the quarrel between the houses of Angus and Hamilton he espoused the cause of the latter. On the 29th April, 1520, a convention was held in Edinburgh to compose the differences of the two parties. The Hamiltons appeared in military guise, and Beaton, their chief counsellor, sat in his house at the bottom of Blackfriars Wynd (or lane) with armour under his robes, ready to join the forces of the Hamiltons in the event of a quarrel. Gavin Douglas was deputed by his nephew, the Earl of Angus, to remonstrate with the Archbishop against the hostile preparations of his party. In trying to gloss over the matter, Beaton struck his hand upon his breast, and swore by his conscience that he knew nought of it, and in doing so the mail under his gown rattled. Douglas replied with double meaning, "Methinks, my lord, your conscience clatters." In the conflict that ensued in the streets, the Hamiltons were worsted, and Beaton had to take refuge in the Blackfriars Church. Being found there by the Douglases, he had his rochet torn from his back, and would have been slain on the spot, but was saved through the interposition of the Bishop of Dunkeld. He had to retire into obscurity for a time, but was brought back into public life by the Duke of Albany, and promoted to the See of St. Andrew's as stated above. It is further said that the insurrection of the Earl of Lennox, in 1525, which ended in the triumph of the Douglases and the death of the Earl at Linlithgow Bridge, was stirred up by the Archbishop as a means of emancipating the king. After this unhappy event, the Douglases persecuted him with such keenness that to save his life he assumed the guise of a shepherd, and tended an actual flock upon Bagrian Knowe in Fife, until he made his peace with Angus by great gifts, both in money and in church lands. Beaton died in 1539.

His successor in the See of Glasgow was Gavin Dunbar, of Mochrum, in Wigtonshire, who was consecrated at Edinburgh on 5th February, 1525. He was educated at our University, and being a man of learning he became tutor to James V, holding at the same time the office of Prior of Whithorn. His qualifications soon attracted the notice of the Lords of the Regency, who elevated him to the Archbishopric, and in 1526 he was further promoted to the Chancellorship of the Kingdom. About the year 1544, he built the noble gate-house at the Arch-Episcopal Palace. Dunbar was a man of amiable and gentle manners, and was opposed to the violent and cruel measures that were being adopted for extirpating the doctrines of the early reformers. He was, however, somewhat bigoted and narrow-minded, and when a Bill was brought into Parliament in 1542, to allow the reading of the Bible in the common tongue, he protested against allowing "that the Holy Write be writ in our vulgar tongue." The Bill passed notwithstanding. He held the office of Archbishop for the long period of 23 years, and died on 30th April, 1547. He was buried in a stately tomb in the Cathedral, which was, however, entirely swept away by the over-heated zeal of the reformers in after years.

James Bethune or Beaton, nephew to the celebrated cardinal, and at that time Abbot of Arbroath, was preferred to the See, and consecrated at Rome in 1552. He now became one of the most important personages of the kingdom; he enjoyed the confidence of the Governor, the Earl of Arran; his niece, Mary Beaton, one of the "Four Maries," was the favourite of the young Queen Mary, then residing in France; and he was esteemed very highly by the Queen-Dowager, Mary of Lorraine, who was aspiring to the Regency. During the subsequent sway of the Queen-Regent, the Archbishop enjoyed her highest confidence. It was to him that she handed the celebrated letter addressed to her by John Knox, saying, with a careless air, "Please you, my lord, to read a pasquil." In 1557, when the marriage of the youthful Mary to the Dauphin of France was about to take place, James Beaton stood the first of the Parliamentary Commissioners appointed to be present at the ceremony. After his return in 1558 he acted as Privy Councillor to the Queen Regent, till she was unable any longer to contend with the advancing tide of the Reformation. In November, 1559, his former friend, the Earl of Arran, who had now become a leading Reformer, came with a powerful retinue to Glasgow, and cleared the cathedral of all the images, placing a garrison at the same time in the Archbishop's Palace. Beaton soon after recovered his Palace by means of a few French soldiers: but he speedily found that neither he nor his religion could maintain a permanent footing in the country.

In June, 1560, the Queen-Regent expired, almost at the very moment when her authority became extinct. Her French troops sailed next month for their native country; and in the same ship was the Archbishop of Glasgow, along with all the plate and records of the Cathedral, which he said he would never return till the Catholic faith would again be triumphant in Scotland. Some of these articles were of great value. There was a gold image of Christ, and silver images of the twelve apostles. There were also two chartularies, one of which had been written in the reign of Robert III, and was called the *Red Book of Glasgow*. All these objects were deposited in the Scots College at Paris, where the MSS. continued to be of use to Scottish antiquarians up to the period of the French Revolution, when it is believed they were destroyed or dispersed. Beaton was received by Queen Mary at Paris with the distinction due to the trusted councillor to her late mother. On her departure next year to assume the reins of government in Scotland, she left him in charge of her affairs in France. He spent the rest of his life as ambassador from the Scottish Court to the French King. During this period Mary addressed him frequently in her own hand, and a letter in which she details to him the circumstances of her husband's death is a well known historical document.

In 1587 James VI restored Beaton his title and estates as Archbishop of Glasgow, a proceeding quite anomalous, as the Presbyterian religion was now established in Scotland. The Archbishop died on 24th April, 1603, in the 86th year of his age. He had been ambassador to three generations of the Scottish Royal family, and had seen in France a succession of six kings. He had also the satisfaction of seeing his sovereign accede to the English throne. James learned the intelligence of his death while on his journey to London, and immediately appointed the historian, Spottiswoode, as his successor in the Cathedral Chair of Glasgow. Spottiswoode speaks of him as "a man honourably disposed, faithful to the Queen while she lived, and to the King, her son. A lover of his country, and liberal according to his means to all his countrymen." He died in possession of a fortune of £80,000, all of which he left to the Scots College, for the benefit of poor scholars in Scotland—a gift so munificent that he was afterwards considered as the second founder of the institution, the first being the Bishop of Moray in 1325.

Archbishop Beaton was the last of the long line of Roman Catholic prelates of the See of Glasgow, and from the brief sketches given above, it will be seen that many of them were men of great influence and power not only in the city, but in the kingdom. Mr. Cosmo Innes, in closing his valuable preface to the *Registrum Episcopatus Glasguensis* beautifully remarks :—" It is impossible for a student of ecclesiastical antiquities not to look back with fond regret to the lordly and ruined church which we have traced from its cradle to its grave, not stopping to question its doctrines, and throwing into a friendly shade its errors of practice. And yet, if we consider it more deeply, we may be satisfied that the gorgeous fabric fell not till it had completed its work, and was no longer useful. Institutions, like mortal bodies, die and are reproduced. Nations pass away, and the worthy live again in their colonies. Our own proud and free England may be destined to sink, and to leave only a memory, and those offshoots of her vigorous youth which have spread civilization over half the world. In this view it was not unworthy of that splendid hierarchy, which arose out of the humble family of St. Kentigern, to have given life and vigour to such a city as Glasgow, and a school of learning like her University."

CHAPTER III.

THE BISHOP'S CASTLE AND MANOR HOUSES.

"Many have told of the monks of old,
 What a saintly race they were;
But 'tis more true that a merrier crew
 You could not find elsewhere:
For they sang and they laughed,
 And the rich wine quaffed,
And they lived on the daintiest cheer."—*Old Song*.

THE large and stately edifice called the Bishop's Castle, stood on a prominent site a little to the west of the cathedral, and after lying in a ruinous condition for many years it was entirely demolished and its ruins removed in 1789-90, when the present Royal Infirmary was erected. Of its earliest history there does not appear to be any record. It is mentioned in an old charter as early as 1290. At first a mere fortress or place of strength, its extension and improvement was the work of successive prelates, and this work was done according to their varied tastes and the circumstances of the times. It is said to have been occupied for the space of three days by Edward I of England in 1301. The "great tower" and some other parts of the structure were built by the "magnificent" prelate, John Cameron, of the Lochiel family, between 1430 and 1450. A smaller tower was built by Archbishop Beaton a short time before the battle of Flodden in 1513, and he also surrounded the castle with a protecting wall. A very handsome gateway was erected by Archbishop Dunbar, the last but one of the Roman Catholic prelates who died in 1547; and this was in all likelihood, the last kindly hand lent to the extension and embellishment of the ecclesiastical palace of Glasgow. The Protestant prelates partially repaired and occasionally resided in the castle; but the insecure character of their own tenure, and the disjointed times in which they lived, confined their attention merely to keeping the place habitable. Morer, who wrote his short account of Scotland about 1689, says that "at the upper end of the great street stands the Archbishop's palace, formerly, without doubt, a very magnificent structure, but now in ruins." In 1690, however, when Captain Slezer drew his picture of Glasgow, the building was evidently quite entire externally; for all its turrets are sharply defined, and Bishop Dunbar's handsome gateway occupies a prominent position in the foreground.

Within this castle the bishops, in the palmy days of the See, kept a splendid court, and entertaining as they did, princes and other visitors of rank, their expenditure must have been considerable. Behind the castle were the bishop's stables, and immediately to the north of these was what was called the Stable Green Port, so named because of its proximity to the episcopal mews. Attached to the castle were beautiful gardens and spacious courts; and we are told that it was in the "inner flower garden" that the Archbishop in 1553, received the Provost and Council of the city, when they waited upon him for the purpose of his nominating the Bailies for the year. But after the Reformation the fortunes of the castle began to decline. Yet although the building was becoming ruinous, and the Archbishops were poor, they still exercised a limited hospitality, but it was little they could afford to do in that way. We give two interesting glimpses of the castle; one in its palmiest days, when Cameron the "magnificent" occupied it; the other in the post-Reformation days.

Regarding the former of these periods we are told that, " the proudest days of the Episcopal Palace were probably those when Bishop Cameron was its occupant. While providing for the renovation and enlargement of his own peculiar residence, he at the same time compelled the thirty-one members of his chapter to build suitable houses for themselves in its immediate neighbourhood (viz., in the Rottenrow and its vicinity), and thus did much to add to the size and appearance of the town. The ancient castle was then surrounded with many new, and for the period, handsome erections, and itself adorned with sundry imposing additions." It is also recorded that "Cameron worthily earned the title of the 'magnificent prelate,' and that the great resort of dignified ecclesiastics, and of noblemen of the first consideration rendered the court of this spiritual prince not much second to that of royalty itself. He was fond of celebrating the great Festivals of the Church; and on these occasions he entered the choir of the cathedral through the nave, by the great western door, preceded by many high officials, one of whom bore his silver crozier or pastoral staff, and the others carried costly maces and other emblems. These were followed by the members of the chapter, and the procession moved on amidst the ringing of bells, the pealing of the great organ, and the vocal swell of the choristers, who were gorgeously arrayed in vestments of high price; the *Te Deum* was then sung, and high mass celebrated." (*Macgregor's History of Glasgow.*)

Regarding the condition of the Bishop's Castle towards the middle of the seventeenth century Sir William Brereton says, "going into the hall of the castle, which is a poor and mean place, the Archbishop's daughter a handsome and well bred proper gentlewoman, entertained me with much civil respect, and would not suffer me to depart until I had drunk Scotch ale, which was the best I had tasted in Scotland." This, says Mr. Macgeorge, was in 1634. The Archbishop was Patrick Lindsay, a descendant of an old branch of the Earl of Crawford, a quiet gentlemanly man by all accounts. In 1638, when matters came to a crisis he was deposed and excommunicated with the other bishops by the General Assembly, when he left the castle and withdrew into England, where he died in poverty. But it is pleasant to know that his handsome and hospitable daughter was well married.

Before the Reformation, the meetings of the Town Council appear to have been held in the Castle, but after the flight of Beaton they were removed to the Old Tolbooth at the Cross. Under date, 28th September, 1576, there is an entry in the Burgh Accounts of a payment "for bringing down of the Counsal hous burds furth of the Castell," and another for the bringing of "furmes, coilles, and peittis, fra the Castell."

The Bishop's Castle was twice besieged. In the course of the troubles during the minority of Mary Queen of Scots, the Earl of Lennox placed a garrison in it, which was assailed by the troops of the Regent Arran, who battered the walls with engines, which were then regarded as of immense power—viz., brass guns, carrying balls from ten to twelve pounds weight. For nine days the garrison made a heroic defence, but on the tenth day it surrendered, on condition of being allowed to retire unharmed and unmolested. To the foul disgrace of Arran, however, the brave defenders were almost all butchered so soon as they opened the Castle gates. It also sustained a brief siege in 1570, while it was held in the name of the infant king, James VI. In the spring of that year, the Regent Murray had been shot at Linlithgow—an event which instantly called the Hamilton party to arms, with the avowed object of restoring Queen Mary to the throne. After marching to Edinburgh to liberate the Duke of Chatelherault, their chief, and many other friends to their cause, who had been there kept in confinement, the Hamiltons laid siege to the Castle of Glasgow. It is said the governor was then absent, and that the garrison consisted of only 24 men, who, however, successfully defended their post, until the besiegers were obliged to retire on the approach of an English army, by which Queen Elizabeth, under the disguise of pretended friendship towards the young king, sought to bring mischief and ruin upon the Scottish nation.

Sometime after 1576 the building fell into disrepair. It was partially restored in 1611 by Archbishop Spottiswoode, who made it his residence. Ray, writing in 1681, speaks of it as a "goodly building," and still in good preservation. We have already seen what Morer and Slezer said about it in 1689 and 1690, and we learn further that after their day it was occasionally used as a prison. So late, comparatively, as 1715, the Castle was still so entire as to be hastily fitted up as a place of confinement for about 300 of the Highlanders who were engaged in the first Jacobite Rebellion. But after this period it would seem that no one cared for it, and it underwent a process of silent but rapid demolition. Many of its stones, timbers, and "sklates" were carried off and used in the erection of dwelling-houses in the town, and it is said that there are buildings still extant which were raised from stones taken or stolen from its dismantled walls. Some of the ornamental stones of Bishop Dunbar's famous gateway were recently presented by Ex-Bailie Millar, the proprietor of a tenement into which they had been built, to Sir William Dunbar, the lineal descendant of the Bishop's family, for the purpose of being built into his new mansion in Wigtonshire; and there is, we understand, an oak panel in the possession of the Archæological Society of Glasgow.

There is a tradition that the Bishops of Glasgow had, not very far from the Castle, a rural manor in a locality which was then a part of the old Bishop's Forest, but is now almost in the heart of Glasgow, and which is traversed by Bishop Street, Anderston. But positive confirmation of this tradition has not been obtained. An elderly woman who had all her life resided in Bishop Street, informed Mr. Macgeorge recently that when she was a child she was told by a person, then a very old woman, that the Bishop's house was situated in the midst of gardens on the west side of the street: and she described a narrow lane existing in her day, and running northwards from the Main Street of Anderston, on the east of Bishop Street as what had been the Bishop's entry to the house. It was called the Bishop's Walk. The name of the present street, and the name of the corn mills on the west side of it—Bishop's Garden Mills—give countenance to this tradition.

It is certain, however, adds Mr. Macgeorge, that the Bishops had, from very early times, a manor at Partick. Mention is made of it as early as the twelfth century in a charter by King David (1136), giving lands in "Perdeyc" to the Church of Kentigern in Glasgow. In 1277, the grant by Maurice, Lord of Luss, of wood for the repair of the church is dated at Partick, where he was, no doubt, on a visit to the Bishop; and a notarial instrument executed in 1362 bears to be dated "apud manerium dicti domini Glasguensis Episcopi de Perthik."

There was another castle at Partick which stood in a ruinous condition till within a comparatively recent date, near to the confluence of the Clyde and the Kelvin, which was sometimes called the "Bishop's Castle," and Chalmers, in his elaborate work, *Caledonia*, states that Archbishop Spottiswoode, who greatly repaired our Cathedral and the

Archiepiscopal Palace, "also built in 1611, a castle at Partick, to serve as a country seat for the Archbishops." And again the same author mentions Partick Castle as built by the Bishops "on an elevated site on the west bank of the Kelvin, nearly three miles westward of the Cathedral Church of Glasgow," and he adds that it was used by the Bishops as a rural habitation, and that when in ruins it was called the Bishop's Castle. This statement, however, has been ascertained to be erroneous. From authentic papers it has been discovered that Partick Castle was indeed built in the year ascribed to it by Chalmers, but it was erected as a dwelling-place for himself by Mr. George Hutcheson, one of the founders of the well known "Hutcheson's Hospital." It is not improbable, however, that Mr. Hutcheson built his mansion on the site of the Bishop's residence, and may indeed have used some of the old stones for his new house.

Besides these residences the Bishops possessed, from the beginning of the fourteenth century, another mansion at Lochwood, about six miles eastward from Glasgow, in the parish of Old Monkland. Here Cameron the "magnificent" died on Christmas Eve, 1446. The Castle was, in March 1572-3, committed to Robert Boyd of Badinheath, and by this keeper was demolished. The estate of Lochwood now belongs to the family of the Bairds of Gartsherrie.

Another rural residence of the Bishops of Glasgow, at a very early period, was situated in the Barony of Ancrum. Of this manor and barony they were the earliest possessors on record, and the lands are mentioned as belonging to the See as early as the year 1116. Here the Bishops often resided, and from here they dated many of their charters. Its remains now form part of the present mansion of the Scotts of Ancrum.

The Bishops of Glasgow had still another residence— "Castel Tarras" or "Castel Staris," a locality now known as Carstairs, where Bishop Wyschard—of whom it is said, "no Scotsman defended more strenuously the honour and independence of his country against the encroachments of the King of England than himself did"—built a castle. He was called to account by Edward I for building this castle without his (the king's) permission, but was afterwards allowed to complete it (*Macgeorge*).

CHAPTER IV.

THE UNIVERSITY AND SOME NOTABLE PROFESSORS.

"Teach me, like thee, in various nature wise,
To fall with dignity, with temper rise;
Form'd by thy converse, happily to steer
From grave to gay, from lively to severe:
Correct with spirit, eloquent with ease,
Intent to reason, or polite to please."
—*Pope*.

ALTHOUGH we may not, perhaps, claim for the University of Glasgow that distinguished position, as regards the superior excellence of its educational influence, or the eminence of its professors and students, occupied by those of Oxford and Cambridge, and although in some of these respects it may be considered as a little less notable than that of Edinburgh, yet, considering that its seat was in a Scottish provincial city, deeply engrossed in the pursuit of trade and commerce, in which literature, the fine arts, and mental cultivation, may be supposed to have been of secondary consideration, the record of our University is a most brilliant one, and one which the citizens may regard with pride and congratulation. We have all along had amongst us teachers of the very highest qualifications, whose fame has extended over the civilized world; and a large number of our students have risen to high eminence, and exerted a powerful influence in every department of human affairs. In this, and the following chapter, we can only hope to refer to a very few of these men; and to be in keeping with the character of this Work, our references will be of an incidental and anecdotal description.

The College of Glasgow was founded by Bishop Turnbull in 1450-1. A bull was procured through King James II from Pope Nicholas V constituting a University, to continue in all time to come in the City of Glasgow, "it being ane notable place, with gude air, and plenty of provisions for human life." The bull is dated at Rome, 7th January, 1450. By the care of the Bishop and his Chapter, a body of Statutes was prepared, and a University established the following year. King James bestowed considerable revenues and endowments upon the new institution. The first building, called the schools, was a house which had belonged to the parson of Luss, and was afterwards called the "Auld Pedagogy." It was situated in the Rottenrow, and is supposed by Professor Innes to have been in existence and used as a Chapter-house before the papal foundation. It included a dwelling-place for students of arts, which was named *Collegium*, in which they had chambers and a common hall. This old building remained till the middle of the present century. The first rector of the new College was David Cadzow, who was re-elected in 1452. During the first two years, upwards of a hundred members were incorporated, most of them secular, or regular clergy, canons, rectors, abbots, priors, and monks. The whole incorporated members, students, as well as doctors and masters, were divided into four parts, called the *Quatuor Nationes*, according to the place of their nativity.

A meeting of the whole was annually called the day after St. Crispin's day; and being divided into four nations, each nation by itself chose a procurator and intrant, and the intrants, meeting by themselves, made choice of a rector and a deputation of each nation, who were assistants and assessors to the rector. The students themselves now elect their Lord Rector, except when the "Nations" are equally divided, when the Lord-Chancellor gives the casting vote.

The "nations" are constituted as follows :—(1) The *Natio Glottiano* consists of all matriculated students born within the County of Lanark. (2) The *Natio Transforthiana*, of those born within the counties of Orkney and Shetland, Caithness, Sutherland, Ross, Cromarty, Inverness, Nairn, Moray, Banff, Aberdeen, Perth, Forfar, Kincardine, Clackmannan, Fife, Kinross, Argyll, Stirling, and Dumbarton. (3) The *Natio Rothesiana* consists of all students born within the counties of Bute, Renfrew, and Ayr. (4) The *Natio Loudoniana* consists of students not included in any of the other nations.

In the year 1459, only eights years after its foundation, James, Lord Hamilton, bequeathed to Mr. Duncan Burch (or Bunch), Principal-Regent of the College of Arts, and his successors, for the use of the College, a tenement, with the pertinents lying on the north side of the church and convent of the Dominicans, together with four acres of land in the Dovehill, contiguous to the Molindinar Burn, "on condition that the regents and students every day after dinner and supper, should stand up and pray for the souls of him, Lord James, of Euphemia, his spouse, Countess of Douglas and Lady of Bothwell, of his ancestors and successors, and of all from whom he had received any benefit, for which he had not made a proper return; and that if a chapel or oratory should be built in the College, the regents and students should also there assemble, and on their bended knees sing an *ave* to the Virgin, with a collect and remembrance to himself and his wife." These four acres of land became part of the College Garden; and from this time the College continued to receive grants of land and property, and to add to their accommodation.

In 1475 another tenement, with lands adjoining the College, was bequeathed by Sir Thomas Arthurlie. These lands were about two acres in extent, and stretched from the Molindinar Burn to the High Street, and on them the professors' houses appear to have been afterwards built. About 1563, Queen Mary became the benefactress of the College, by granting the "manse and kirkroom of the Friars' preachers, with thirteen acres of land in the Dovehill, and certain rents from tenements in the city and elsewhere." And in 1577, her son, James VI, made further grants which more completely endowed the University. The king established twelve persons—viz., a principal, three professors of philosophy, four bursars (students), and one provisor (who supplied the table with provisions), the principal's servant, a janitor and cook.

A goodly number of other benefactors from time to time gave contributions to the Institution, and in course of time, the College authorities commenced the erection of that famous old University in High Street, which, till recently, was the great seat of learning in the West of Scotland. The building was begun in 1632 and completed in 1656, with the exception of that portion in which were the professors' residences, which were not erected till afterwards. It would appear that many of the students resided within the walls of the College, and were placed under very strict discipline. The gates were shut at nine in winter and ten in summer, and woe betide the luckless youth who stayed out beyond these hours. The governors of the College appear to have assumed legal functions to themselves, independent of the magistrates of the Burgh, and fines and imprisonment for various offences were quite common. One student was fined for cutting the gown of another; one was dealt with for challenging a fellow-student to fight a duel; another was publicly reprimanded for being "found drinking in an ale-house, with some town's people at eleven o'clock at night." On another occasion, a student named John Satcher, was confined in the College steeple for sending an insolent letter to the Principal. But in this case his fellow-students came to his rescue, broke open the prison door and set him at liberty. Satcher then "threw off his gown and withdrew himself from the College till next morning, when he was seized and put into his former place of confinement"; and he was only released when he made humble confession of his guilt and promised amendment.

To show the extent to which the University Court asserted their legal prerogative, it may be stated that in the year 1670, they actually tried a student named Robert Bartoune on the charge of murder. The Rector, Sir William Fleming, of Farme, presided, and the Procurator Fiscal of the University, one "John Cummyng, wryter, in Glasgow," along with "Andrew Wright, cordoner, in Glasgow, neirest of kine to umquhill Jonnet Wright"—the murdered woman—gave in the charge or indictment. They demanded a penalty of death. A jury was empannelled, and the case went to trial. But this was carrying the jurisdiction of the College authorities to an extreme, and fears began to be entertained as to the legality of their proceedings, and the jury demanded security for their own safety, in the event of their bringing in a verdict of guilty. After some demur the guarantee was given. But after all, the jury seem to have had doubts on the subject, for a verdict of "not guilty" was returned.

That the University of Glasgow bore a high reputation in olden, as well as in modern times, has been amply testified on all hands. James Melville, the historian, in his diary says, "I daresay there was no place in Europe comparable to Glasgow for guid letters during these yeirs, for a plentiful and guid chepe mercat of all kynds of langages, artes, and sciences."

There have been many men of remarkable talent and force of character connected with the University of Glasgow from first to last, either in the capacity of rectors, principals, professors, or students, and an entire volume of most interesting story and racy anecdote might be written concerning them. But our space will only admit of a few random selections.

Amongst the earlier of these "men of mark," may be mentioned the REV. ZACHARY BOYD, who was Rector of the University during the years 1634-5 and '45. Zachary was born in Carrick, Ayrshire, in 1585. He was descended from the Boyds of Pinkell in that district, and was cousin to Andrew Boyd, Bishop of Argyll, and to Rev. Robert Boyd of Trochrig, another eminent divine of the 17th century, and a native of Glasgow. Zachary Boyd received his elementary education in Kilmarnock, after which he went to the University of Glasgow. He finished his education at the College of Samur in France, under his relative, Robert Boyd. In 1621 he returned to his native country. He relates the following anecdote in one of his sermons, which we give as showing his strong opposition to the papacy, and at the same time his bold, outspoken manner. "In the time of the French persecution," he says, "I came by sea to Flanders, and as I was sailing from Flanders to Scotland, a fearful tempest arose which made our mariners reele to and fro, and stagger like drunken men. In the meantime there was a Scots Papist who lay near mee, while the ship gave a great shake: I observed the man, and after the Lord had sent a calm, I said to him, 'Sir, now ye see the weaknesse of your religion; as long as yee are in prosperitie yee cry to this sainct and that sainct; in our great danger I heard yee cry often, Lord! Lord! but not a word yee spake of our Lady.'" In 1623 Boyd was appointed minister of the Barony Parish, for which the crypts beneath the Cathedral Church then served as a place of worship—a scene well fitted, by its sepulchral gloom, to add to the impressiveness of his Calvinistic eloquence.

As another illustration of his fearlessness as a pulpit orator, we may remind our readers that, when on one occasion he preached before the great Protector, Oliver Cromwell, on one of his two visits to Glasgow, he did not mince his words, The incident is thus related by Baillie:—
"Cromwell, with the whole body of his army, comes peace-

ably to Glasgow. The magistrates and ministers all fled away; I got to the Isle of Cumray with my Lady Montgomery, but left all my family and goods to Cromwell's courtesy, which, indeed, was great, for he took such measures with the soldiers that they did less displeasure at Glasgow than if they had been at London, *though Mr. Zachary Boyd railed on them all to their very face in the High Church.*" This was on the 13th of October, 1650, and it has been found, from a manuscript note upon the preacher's own Bible, that the chapter he expounded on the occasion was Dan. viii. In this is detailed the vision of the ram with two horns, which is at first powerful, but at length overcome and trampled on by a he-goat; being an allegory of the destruction of Medea and Persia by Alexander of Macedon. It is evident Mr. Zachary endeavoured to extend the parable to existing circumstances, and of course made out Cromwell to be the *he-goat.*

Besides being a fearless and eloquent preacher, Mr. Boyd was a voluminous author, and his writings display, even more fully, his quaint, vigorous, and original habit of mind, His language was often more vigorous than elegant. He wrote a metrical version of the Psalms, and tried hard to get it adopted by the Presbyteries and Assembly, but in this he was disappointed, as on 23rd November, 1649, Rous's version, revised and improved, was sanctioned by the Commission, with authority of the General Assembly, and any other discharged from being used in the churches, or in their families. He also wrote two volumes of poetry, under the title of *Zion's Flowers, or Christian Poems for Spiritual Edification.* The following extract from these *Flowers of Zion* is a specimen of his rough, coarse, unconscious humour, although he generally wrote in a finer strain:—

JONAH IN THE WHALE'S BELLY.

"Here apprehended, I in prison ly;
What goods will ransom my captivity?
What house is this, where's neither coal nor candle,
Where I nothing but guts of fishes handle?
I and my table are both here within,
Where day neere dawned, where sunne did never shine;
The like of this on earth man never saw,
A living man within a monster's maw—

Buried under mountains which are high and steep,
Plunged under waters hundreth fathoms deep.
Not so was Noah in his house of tree,
For through a window he the light did see;
Hee sailed above the highest waves—a wonder,
I and my boat are all the waters under;
He in his ark might goe and also come,
But I sit still in such a straitened roome
As is most uncouth, head and feet together,
Among such grease as would a thousand smother.
I find no way now for my shrinking hence,
But here to lye and die for mine offence.
Eight prisoners were in Noah's hulk together,
Comfortable they were, each one to other;
In all the earth like unto mee is none,
Far from all living, I heere lye alone,
Where I, entombed in melancholy, sink
Choakt, suffocat, with excremental stink;
This grieves mee most, that *I for grievous sinne*,
Incarcer'd lye within this floating inn."

Mr. Boyd was twice married: first to Elizabeth Fleming, of whom no memorial is preserved; and secondly to Margaret Mure, third daughter of William Mure of Glanderston (near Neilston, Renfrewshire). By neither of his wives had he any offspring. The second wife, surviving him, married for her second husband the celebrated Durham, author of the *Commentary on the Revelation*, to whom, it would appear, she had betrayed some partiality, even in her first husband's lifetime. There is a traditional anecdote, that, when Mr. Zachary was dictating his last will, his wife made one modest request—viz., that he would bequeath something to Mr. Durham. He answered, sarcastically, "Na, na, Margaret, I'll lea' him what I canna keep frae him; I'll lea' him thy bonnie sel'." He divided his estate, which amounted to £4,527, between his relict and the College of Glasgow. About £20,000 Scots was realized by the College, besides his library and manuscript compositions. We understand the latter are in course of preparation for the press. Mr. Boyd died in the spring of 1653. He had just completed an extensive MS. work, entitled, *The Notable places of Scripture Expounded*, at the end of which he adds, in a tremulous and indistinct hand-writing, "Heere the author was near his end, and was able to do no more, March 3rd, 1653." The famous

Donald Cargill was appointed his successor as minister of Barony.

ROBERT BAILLIE, one of the most eminent and moderate of all the Scottish Presbyterian clergy during the time of the Civil War, was not only a pupil, but also a regent and professor of the College of Glasgow, and was besides a native of the city, having been born in the Saltmercat in the year 1599. His father, Thomas Baillie, a Glasgow citizen, was descended from the Baillies of Lamington; his mother, Helen Gibson, was of the family of Gibson of Durie, in Fife, both of which families were distinguished Presbyterians. Baillie was very intimate with the Eglinton family, and was for some time tutor to the Earl's son, and was appointed by the Earl to the parish of Kilwinning, he being then an Episcopalian, and had imbibed from Principal Cameron, of Glasgow, the doctrine of passive resistance. He appears, however, to have been brought over to opposite views between 1630 and 1636. In the latter year, being desired by Archbishop Law to preach at Edinburgh in favour of the Canon and Service Books, he positively refused, writing, however, a respectful apology to his lordship. Endeared to the resisting party by this conduct, he was chosen to represent the Presbytery of Irvine in the General Assembly held at Glasgow in 1638, by which the royal power was braved in the name of the whole nation and Episcopacy formally dissolved. In the ensuing year, when it was found necessary to vindicate the proceedings of the Glasgow Assembly with the sword, Baillie entered heartily into the views of his countrymen, and took the field. In one of his letters, he says, "I furnished to half a dozen good fellows muskets and pikes, and to my boy a broadsword. I carried myself, as the fashion was, a sword, and a couple of Dutch pistols at my saddle; but I promise, for the offence of no man, except a robber in the way; for it was our part alone to pray and preach for the encouragement of our countrymen, which I did to my power most cheerfully." Again, he writes, "For myself, I never found my mind in better temper than it was all the time since I came from home, till my head was again homeward; for I was as a man who had taken my leave from the world, and was resolved to die in that service without return." These incidents will give the reader an idea of his mild, yet brave, character. He was a man of great learning, as well as piety, being well versed in no fewer than thirteen languages. In 1642 he was appointed joint-professor of divinity at Glasgow, along with Mr. David Dickson, an equally distinguished, but less moderate, divine. Baillie, besides his *Letters* and *Journals*, and a variety of controversial pamphlets, was the author of a learned work, entitled *Opus Historicum et Chronologicum*, which was published in folio, at Amsterdam. He died in July, 1662, in the sixty-third year of his age. When he was in declining health, he was visited by the new made archbishop (Andrew Fairfowl), to whom he thus freely expressed himself—"Mr. Andrew," said he, "I will not now call you my lord. King Charles would have made me one of these lords; but I do not find in the New Testament that Christ has any lords in his house." He left a large family; one of his daughters becoming the wife of Walkinshaw of Barrowfield, was, by a strange chance, the ancestress of Miss Clementina Walkinshaw, well known from her connection with the history of Prince Charles Stuart; and also grandmother to the celebrated Henry Home, better known under the judicial designation of Lord Kames.

Of equal ability, and with even greater force of character than Baillie, was DAVID DICKSON, his colleague in the professorship of divinity in the college. Dickson was also a native of Glasgow, having been born in the Trongate in 1583. His father, John Dick or Dickson, was a merchant in the city. The latter was possessed of considerable wealth, and the proprietor of the lands of Kirk o' Muir, in the parish of St. Ninians, in Stirlingshire. He and his wife, both persons of eminent piety, had been several years married without children, when they entered into a solemn vow, that, if the Lord would give them a son, they would devote him to the service of His church. A day was appointed, and their Christian townsmen were requested to join with them in fasting and prayer. But when their son was born the vow was so far forgot, that he was educated for mercantile pursuits, in which he was eminently unsuccessful, and the cause of much pecuniary loss to his parents. This circumstance added to a severe illness of their son, led them to remember their vow, and Mr. David was then "put to his studyes, and what eminent service he did in his generation is knowen." Soon after taking the degree of M.A., Mr. Dickson was appointed one of the regents or professors of philosophy in the University of Glasgow. In this situation he remained for several years, when, in 1618, he was ordained minister of Irvine. In that year the General Assembly had agreed to the five ceremonies now known as the Perth Articles, and a close examination convinced Dickson that they were unscriptural. Soon after, when a severe illness brought him near death, he openly declared against them; and Archbishop Law of Glasgow summoned him before the Court of High Commission. He appeared, but declined the jurisdiction of the Court, and sentence of deprivation and confinement was passed upon him. His friends prevailed upon the Archbishop to restore him, on condition that he withdrew his declinature; a condition with which he would not comply. Soon after, Law yielded so far as to allow him to return to his parish, if he would come to his castle and withdraw the paper from the hall table without seeing him; terms which Mr. Dickson spurned, as being "but juggling in such a weighty matter." At length he was permitted in July, 1623, to return unconditionally.

When the General Assembly of 1638 was convoked, David Dickson, Robert Baillie, and William Russell minister of Kilbirnie, were appointed to represent the Presbytery of Irvine, "to propone, reason, vote, and conclude, according to the Word of God, and confession approved by sundry General Assemblies." He went out in the short campaign of 1639, as chaplain of the regiment of which the Earl of Loudoun was colonel, and which consisted of 1,200 men. He became Moderator of the General Assembly that same year, and in the following year he was appointed professor of Divinity in the University of Glasgow, to which office a competent lodging and a salary of £800 Scots (£66, 13s. 4d. sterling), was attached. While he held this office he preached every Sunday forenoon in the High Church. His religious zeal in the presbyterian cause was so great, that when three noted royalists were executed in Glasgow—viz., Sir William Rollock, Sir Philip Nisbet, and Alexander Ogilvy, Dickson was much elated, and as the gibbet did its work he is reported to have exclaimed, "the wark gangs bonnily on."

Mr. Dickson was made Professor of Divinity in the University of Edinburgh in 1650, where he dictated to his students in Latin what has since been published in English under the title of *Truth's Victory over Error*. The greater number of the ministers in the west, south, and east of Scotland, were educated under him. He continued in his professorship in Edinburgh till the Restoration in 1660, when he was ejected for refusing to take the oath of supremacy. He died in January, 1663. On his death-bed, his life-long friend, Mr. John Livingstone, visited him and asked him how he found himself; his answer was: "I have taken all my good deeds and all my bad deeds, and cast them through each other in a heap before the Lord and fled from both, and betaken myself to the Lord Jesus Christ, and in Him I have sweet peace!"

Mr. Dickson was a voluminous author in Theology and Divinity. He wrote Commentaries on the Psalms, on the Gospel of Matthew, on the Epistles; a *Treatise on the Promises;* also a work entitled *Therapeutica Sacra*, and *Truths Victory over Error* already referred to. This last work was translated into English by the eccentric George Sinclair, and published as his own in 1684; but Sinclair's trick was soon and easily detected. One of Mr. Dickson's students had copied his professor's dictates, and when he read the translation he inserted in the running title, the following couplet:—

"No errors in this book I see,
But G. S. where D. D. should be."

Of David Dickson, Wodrow the historian remarks: "If ever a Scots biography and the lives of our eminent ministers and Christians be published, he will shine there as a star of the first magnitude." Fleming in his work on the *Fulfilling of the Scriptures*, says of Dickson's pulpit ministrations: "that for a considerable time few Sabbaths did pass without some evidently converted, or some convincing proof of the power of God accompanying his Word." His works were long popular in Scotland, and in many homes of the better class of working people, some volume of Dickson's Theological Treatises or Commentaries may even yet be seen.

Although nothing of very striking interest occurred in

the life of Robert Wodrow the celebrated ecclesiastical historian of Scotland in the beginning of the eighteenth century, yet it would be an unpardonable omission to leave him out of these sketches of old Glasgow worthies; for his writings have proved a perfect storehouse of valuable materials to students of Scottish history during the past century and a half. Wodrow was born in Glasgow in 1679, probably in the old college, High Street, for his father James Wodrow was professor of divinity in that college, and was a man of singular piety and learning. His mother was Margaret Hair, daughter of William Hair, proprietor of a small estate in the parish of Kilbarchan. In this parent he was equally fortunate. To all the piety of her husband she added a degree of strength of mind, not often associated with her sex. In 1691 Wodrow was entered a student in the University of his native city, and passed through the usual course of education there. He studied divinity under his father, and while engaged in this pursuit he was appointed librarian to the college. This office he held four years, and it was during this time that he acquired the greater part of that knowledge of the ecclesiastical and literary history of his country, which he applied to such good purpose in his after life. On completing his studies Mr. Wodrow went to reside with Sir John Maxwell of Nether Pollok, a distant relative of his family; and while here he offered himself for trial to the Presbytery of Paisley, and was licensed to preach the Gospel in March, 1703. On 28th October, following, he was ordained minister of the parish of Eastwood, and continued in that office during the remainder of his life; though frequently invited to accept charges in Glasgow, Stirling, and elsewhere. The quietness and ease of that small rural parish, as it then was, suited his studious habits admirably.

His great work, the *History of the Sufferings of the Church of Scotland from the Restoration to the Revolution*, was begun in 1707, although he had contemplated it from an early period of his life, and it was not completed and published till 1721-22. It was published in three large folio volumes, and on its appearance the author was attacked with the vilest scurrility and abuse by those whom his fidelity as a historian had offended. Anonymous and threatening letters were sent to him, and every description of indignity was thrown on both his person and his work. The faithful, liberal, and impartial character of the history nevertheless procured its author many and powerful friends. Copies of the work were presented to their Majesties, and the Prince and Princess of Wales, and were received with so much approval, that by a warrant dated 26th April, 1725, he was awarded from the Scottish Exchequer a grant of 100 guineas as a testimony to its merits.

Wodrow afterwards planned and executed the scheme of a complete history of the Church of Scotland, in a series of Biographical Memoirs of all the eminent men who appeared from the beginning of the Reformation down to the period at which he wrote. This work still lies in MS. in the library of the University of Glasgow, although a selection from the Memoirs was published in 1834, for the members of the Maitland Club. He also wrote six small but closely written volumes of traditionary and other memoranda regarding the lives and labours of remarkable ministers from 1705 to 1732. This curious and interesting *Analecta* as it is called, is preserved in the original MS. in the Advocates' Library in Edinburgh, where it is often consulted by students and others. Twenty-four volumes of his Correspondence are also preserved in the Advocates' Library. In 1842 the Earl of Glasgow presented the first two volumes of the *Analecta* to the members of the Maitland Club, of which the Earl was president, and in the same year a portion of his MSS. was purchased by order of the General Assembly, and now remains its property.

The "Wodrow Society" was established at Edinburgh in May, 1841, for the purpose of printing from the most authentic sources the best works of the original reformers, fathers, and early writers of the Kirk of Scotland.

Mr. Wodrow died on the 21st March, 1734, in the 55th year of his age, after a long and painful illness extending over a period of eight years. He had married in 1708, Margaret Warner, grand-daughter of William Guthrie of Fenwick, and daughter of the Rev. Patrick Warner of Ardeer, in Ayrshire, and minister of Irvine. He had a family of *sixteen* children, of whom four sons and five daughters survived their father. His eldest son succeeded him in the parish of Eastwood, but was compelled to retire from it by an infirm state of health.

The celebrated mathematician, DR. ROBERT SIMSON, though not a native of the city—having been born at Kirton-Hall, Ayrshire, on 14th October, 1687—may yet justly be claimed as a Glasgow citizen. He entered as a student in our University in 1701 at the early age of 14, and ten years afterwards he became professor of mathematics in his *alma mater*. For nearly half a century he occupied that important position, teaching mathematics to two separate classes at different hours for five days in the week during a continued session of seven months. His lectures were given with such perspicuity of method and language, and his demonstrations were so clear and successful, that among his scholars several rose to distinction as mathematicians; among whom may be mentioned the celebrated names of Colin M'Laurin, Dr. Matthew Stewart, professor of mathematics, Edinburgh; the two Rev. Drs. Williamson, one of whom succeeded Dr. Simson at Glasgow; the Rev. Dr. Traill, professor of mathematics, Aberdeen; Dr. James Moor, Greek professor at Glasgow; and Prof. Robinson, of Edinburgh, and many others of great merit.

Dr. Simson never was married; he devoted his life purely to scientific pursuits. His hours of study, of exercise and amusement, were all regulated with the most unerring precision. The very walks in the squares or gardens of the College were all measured by his steps; and he took his exercises by the hundred of paces, according to his time or inclination. His disposition was by no means gloomy; when in company of friends his conversation was animated, enriched with much anecdote, and by a degree of natural humour. "Every Saturday for years he sallied forth from his comfortable bachelor-ménage," says a writer in the *North British Daily Mail*, November, 1870, " in the University as the College clock struck one, and turned his face in the direction of Anderston. . . . One Saturday, while proceeding towards Anderston, counting his steps as he was wont, the Professor was accosted by a person who, we may suppose, was unacquainted with his singular peculiarity. At this moment, the worthy geometrician knew that he was just 573 paces from the College, towards the snug parlour which was anon to prove the rallying point of the Hen-Broth Amateurs; and when arrested in his career, kept repeating the mystic number at stated intervals, as the only species of mnemonics then known. 'I beg your pardon,' said the personage accosting the Professor, 'one word with you, if you please.' 'Most happy—573,' was the response. 'Nay,' rejoined the gentleman, 'merely *one* question!' 'Well,' added the Professor —'573!' 'You are really too polite,' interrupted the stranger, 'but from your acquaintance with the late Dr. B——, and for the purpose of deciding a bet, I have taken the liberty of inquiring whether I am right in saying that that individual left £500 to each of his nieces?' 'Precisely,' replied the Professor—'573.' 'And there were only four nieces, were there not?' rejoined the querist. 'Exactly,' said the Mathematician—'573.' The stranger, at the last repetition of the mystic sound, stared at the Professor, as if he were mad, and muttering sarcastically, '573!' made a hasty obeisance and passed on. The Professor, seeing the stranger's mistake, hastily advanced another step, and cried after him, 'No, sir, *four* to be sure—574!' The gentleman was still further convinced of the mathematician's madness, and hurried forward, while the Professor paced on leisurely towards the west, and at length, happy in not being baulked in his calculation, sat down delighted amid the circle of The Anderston Club."

Dr. Simson was exceedingly absent-minded. As a proof of this, Lord Brougham mentions that "one of the College porters, being dressed up for the purpose, came to ask charity, and in answer to the Professor's questions, gave an account of himself closely resembling his own history. When he found so great a resemblance, he cried out, 'What's your name?' and on the answer being given, 'Robert Simson,' he exclaimed, with great animation, 'Why it must be *myself*,' when he awoke from his trance."—(*Glasgow and its Clubs*, by Dr. Strang, pp. 18-21.)

FRANCIS HUTCHESON, a distinguished philosopher of last century, was the son of a presbyterian minister in the North of Ireland, where he was born in 1694. He studied for the Church at the University of Glasgow, but shortly after the completion of his theological course, he was induced to open a private academy in Dublin, which proved highly successful. In 1720 he published his *Inquiry into the Original of our Ideas of Beauty and Virtue*, which was the means of introducing him to many influential personages such as

Lord Granville, then Lord-Lieutenant of Ireland, Archbishop King, Primate Boulter, and others. This work was followed in 1728 by his *Essay on the Nature and Conduct of the Passions;* and in the year after, he was appointed Professor of Moral Philosophy in the University of Glasgow. Here he died in 1747. His largest and most important work, *A System of Moral Philosophy,* was published at Glasgow in 1755 by his son Francis Hutcheson, M.D., with a Preface on the life, writings, and character of the Author, by Dr. Leechman, Professor of Divinity in the same University. As a metaphysician Hutcheson may be considered the pioneer of the "Scotch School." From the period of his lectures, according to Dugald Stewart, may be dated the metaphysical philosophy of Scotland, and, indeed, the literary taste in general, which marked that country during the last century. But it is as a moral philosopher rather than as a metaphysician that he shines best. His system is, to a large extent, that of Shaftesbury, but it is more complete, coherent, and clearly illustrated. Hutcheson was a strong opponent of the doctrine that benevolence has a selfish origin, and termed that faculty by which moral distinctions are recognised, the *moral sense.*

ADAM SMITH, LL.D. and F.R.S.L. and E., author of *The Wealth of Nations,* and one of the brightest ornaments of the literature of Scotland, was a professor in the University of Glasgow for a period of thirteen years—viz., from 1751 to 1763. Elected in 1751 to the chair of Logic, he was in the following year transferred to that of Moral Philosophy, which he continued to occupy till the end of 1763, when he resigned to accompany the then young Duke of Buccleuch during his tour on the Continent. He used to consider the period of his residence in Glasgow as the happiest of his life. He resided, of course, within the walls of the old College in High Street. Smith was born in Kirkcaldy, on the 5th June, 1723, and entered the University of Glasgow in 1737. Chosen an exhibitor on Snell's Foundation, he was sent to Balliol College, Oxford, in 1740, whence he returned to Kirkcaldy in 1747. In the year 1748, he removed to Edinburgh, where he delivered lectures during three years on Rhetoric and Belles Lettres. These established his literary reputation, and secured his appointment in Glasgow as above.

He was the only child of Adam Smith, Comptroller of the Customs at Kirkcaldy and Margaret Douglas, daughter of Mr. Douglas, of Strathendry, near the village of Leslie in Fifeshire. His father having died some months before his birth, the duty of superintending his early education devolved entirely upon his mother. A singular accident happened to him when he was about three years of age. As he was amusing himself one day at the door of his uncle, Mr. Douglas's house at Strathendry, he was carried off by a party of gipsies. The vagrants, however, being pursued by Mr. Douglas were overtaken in Leslie Wood, and his uncle "was thus the happy instrument of preserving to the world a genius which was destined not only to extend the boundaries of science, but to enlighten and reform the commercial policy of Europe." The constitution of Dr. Smith during infancy was infirm and sickly, and required all the delicate care and attention of his surviving parent. Though she treated him with the utmost indulgence, this did not produce any unfavourable effect either on his disposition or temper, and he repaid her affectionate solicitude by every attention that filial gratitude could dictate during the long period of sixty years. He received the first rudiments of his education at the Grammar School of Kirkcaldy, which was then taught by Mr. David Miller, a teacher in his day of considerable reputation. He soon attracted notice by his passion for books, and the extraordinary powers of his memory. Even at this early period, too, he seems to have contracted those habits of speaking to himself, and of absence in company, for which through life he was so remarkable. Although not able from bodily weakness to take a great share in the sports and pastimes of youth, yet he was much beloved by his companions on account of his friendly and generous disposition. His favourite pursuits at our Glasgow University, as a student, were mathematics and natural philosophy. He also attended the lectures of Dr. Hutcheson on moral philosophy, and it is probable that they had a considerable effect in afterwards directing his attention to those branches of science in which he was to become so distinguished. At Oxford he devoted himself to the study of ancient and modern languages. He also studied the philosophy and logic of Aristotle, which still maintained their ascendancy in both the English universities. But he did not confine himself to that system, as the following incident shows:—The suspicions of his superiors having been excited as to the nature of his studies in private, the head of his college one day entered his apartment without notice, and unluckily found the young philosopher deep in the study of Hume's *Treatise of Human Nature*. The offender was, of course, severely reprimanded, and the objectionable work seized and carried off.

Having found that the clerical profession was not suited to his tastes, he returned to Kirkcaldy without any fixed plan of life, and resided there nearly two years with his mother. During his subsequent residence in Edinburgh, he formed the acquaintance of David Hume, which lasted till Hume's death in 1776. It was a friendship on both sides founded on the admiration of genius and love of simplicity. For although Hume was a man of sceptical opinions, there can be no doubt about his great genius, learning, and high moral character.

During his professorship in Glasgow, Dr. Smith delivered those lectures which were afterwards published under the titles of the *Theory of Moral Sentiments* and *An enquiry into the Nature and Source of The Wealth of Nations*. So that the students in our Glasgow College had the first benefit of these able and instructive works. Both of these works were of the highest excellence and importance, and, the latter especially, has ever since served as the foundation of most of our schemes and systems of commercial policy, and has been acknowledged by the leaders among all classes of men as the source of their parliamentary or commercial inspiration. His reputation as a professor was raised by these lectures very high, and a multitude of students from great distances resorted to the University merely on his account. Those branches of science which he taught became fashionable, and his opinions were the chief topics of discussion in clubs and literary societies. Even the small peculiarities in his pronunciation or manner of speaking were imitated.

Dr. Strang tells us that while in Glasgow, Dr. Smith was a member of the Anderston Club, along with the absent-minded Professor Simson, Dr. James Moore (father of the Hero of Corunna), Dr. Cullen, and Mr. Thomas Hamilton, the great promoters of medical science; Professor Ross, a very Cicero of Roman literature; and the brothers Foulis, the never-to-be-forgotten Elzivers of the Scottish Press. This celebrated Club met in the excellent hostelry of "ane God-fearing host," yclept John Sharpe, in the then weaving village of Anderston, situated in those days a full mile from the city of Glasgow, with green fields and produce gardens intervening. And here, over a savoury dish of *hen-broth*, and other more substantial edibles, washed down with the contents of a "goodly sized punch-bowl," these learned men, unbent from their abstruse studies, and engaged in the fun, frolic, and eccentricities of social fellowship. No special anecdotes have been recorded regarding Dr. Smith, but if not consciously witty or humorous, he would doubtless give occasion to a good deal of merriment by his absent-minded blunders and peculiarities.

In 1787 he was appointed Lord Rector of Glasgow University, and on that occasion he addressed a letter to the Principal, in which he pays the University a high compliment. "No preferment," he writes, "could have given me so much real satisfaction. No man can owe greater obligations to a society than I do to the University of Glasgow. They educated me; they sent me to Oxford. Soon after my return to Scotland, they elected me one of their own members; and afterwards preferred me to another office, to which the abilities and virtues of the never-to-be-forgotten Dr. Hutcheson had given a superior degree of illustration. The period of thirteen years which I spent as a member of that Society I remember as by far the most useful, and, therefore, as by far the happiest and most honourable period of my life; and now, after three and twenty years' absence, to be remembered in so very agreeable a manner by my old friends and protectors, gives me a heartfelt joy which I cannot easily express to you." Dr. Smith died in Edinburgh in July, 1790, at the age of 67, after a lingering and painful illness.

Dr. THOMAS REID, an eminent metaphysician and moral philosopher, who, in 1763, was chosen as the successor of Adam Smith as professor of moral philosophy in the University of Glasgow, and held that office for the period of eighteen years, may he regarded as one of those notable men who gave to our college its high character and great renown. Born at Strachan, in Kincardineshire, on 26th

April, 1710, he was educated for the ministry at the Grammar School of Kincardine O'Neil and the Marischal College, Aberdeen, and in 1737 was presented, greatly against the minds of the parishioners, to the Parish Church of New Machar, in Aberdeenshire. But by his unwearied attention to the duties of his office, the mildness and forbearance of his temper, and the active spirit of his humanity, he soon overcame all their prejudices, and gained their highest esteem and affection. On his departure from the parish, some of the old men are said to have remarked, "We fought *against* Dr. Reid when he came, and would have fought *for* him when he went away." At an early period of his life he evinced a great love for mathematical and physical studies, and gave much thought to the organs of sense and their operations on the external world, which formed the broad basis of his philosophy. In 1752 the professors of King's College, Aberdeen, elected Reid professor of philosophy. This office he held till he came to Glasgow in 1763. In the following year, 1764, he published his great work, *An Inquiry into the Human Mind upon the Principles of Common Sense*, which may be said to have proved the chief basis of the modern Scotch School of Philosophy, and his system was afterwards taken up and expounded by his friend and biographer, Dugald Stewart, in his *Philosophy of the Human Mind*. In 1785 he published his *Essays on the Intellectual Powers of Man*, and in 1788 those on the *Active Powers*. "These treatises," it has been said, "must always be looked upon as constituting the first complete and systematic work on the science of the human mind." For many years they were regarded as the standard works on mental philosophy in the universities and learned circles of Scotland. We cannot find that Dr. Reid was ever a member of that convivial coterie of learned men, the *Anderston Club*. The founder of that club was Dr. Robert Simson, the eminent mathematician, who died in 1768, five years after Reid came to our city, and the club appears to have come to an end when Dr. Simson died.

In 1781 Dr. Reid retired from the chair of moral philosophy, and devoted his remaining strength to the publication of his works on the mind. He appears to have spent the last years of his life in Glasgow. In the summer of 1796 he spent a few weeks in Edinburgh, and Dugald Stewart, his biographer, who was his almost constant companion, mentions that, with the exception of his memory, his mental faculties appeared almost unimpaired, while his physical powers were progressively sinking. On his return to Glasgow, apparently in his usual health and spirits, a violent disorder attacked him about the end of September, and after repeated strokes of palsy, he died on the 7th October following. His affectionate biographer, in summing up the character of this eminent and excellent man, says: "Its most prominent features were—intrepid and inflexible rectitude, a pure and devoted attachment to truth, and an entire command (acquired by the unwearied exertion of a long life) over all his passions." Dr. Reid was under the middle size, but had great muscular strength, and was addicted to exercise in the open air.

The following curious incident of his boyhood, communicated in a letter to a friend, written late in life, appears to have been recollected by him in connection with the commencement of some of his philosophical speculations:— "About the age of fourteen," he wrote, "I was almost every night unhappy in my sleep from frightful dreams, sometimes hanging over a dreadful precipice, and just ready to drop down; sometimes pursued for my life, and stopped by a wall, or by a sudden loss of all strength; sometimes ready to be devoured by a wild beast. How long I was plagued with such dreams I do not recollect. I believe it was for a year or two at least, and I think they had quite left me before I was sixteen. In those days I was much given to what Mr. Addison, in one of his *Spectators*, calls "castle building," and in my evening solitary walks my thoughts would hurry me into some active scene, where I generally acquitted myself much to my own satisfaction, and in these scenes of imagination I performed many a gallant exploit. At the same time, in my dreams I found myself the most arrant coward. Not only my courage but my strength failed me in every danger, and I often rose from my bed in the morning in such a panic that it took some time to get the better of it. I wished very much to get free of these uneasy dreams, which not only made me unhappy in sleep, but often left a disagreeable impression in my mind for some part of the following day. I thought it was worth trying whether it was possible to recollect that it was all a dream, and that I was in no real danger, and that every fright I had was a dream. After many fruitless attempts to recollect this when the danger appeared, I effected it at last, and have often, when I was sliding over a precipice into the abyss, recollected that it was all a dream, and boldly jumped down. The effect of this commonly was, that I immediately awoke. But I awoke calm and intrepid, which I thought a great acquisition. After this my dreams were never uneasy, and in a short time I dreamed not at all."

Our space forbids anything like a sketch, however short, of all the professors who have adorned—or otherwise—the University of Glasgow. From the selection we have already made, it will be seen that men of the highest talent and influence, whose fame extended far beyond our city, have been engaged in the training of our youth; and have given a standing and a name to our University that place it in the first rank of the educational institutions of the world. That there have been professors among us who were only men of mediocre ability; and some whose influence rather detracted from than added to the reputation of the University, goes without saying. But, on the whole, the record has been a noble one; and if the youth of Glasgow, and of Scotland at large, have not been thoroughly educated in the arts, sciences, philosophies, and literature of their times, it has not been for the want of competent teachers. Even in more modern days, the Professors of Glasgow College have mostly been men of superior ability, and, in some instances, equal to the most learned of their predecessors. We regret that we can only name a few of the more prominent of these. As, for example, Professor Thomas Thomson, one of the most eminent chemists and mineralogists of this country; the able and learned Professor Ramsay, who for a long series of years presided over the Humanity Classes with the highest credit to himself and benefit to his students, and whose erudite work on Roman Antiquities was for a long period a standard book both in College and Academy. The eloquent and accomplished Greek Professor, Dr. Lushington, the friend of Tennyson, and a man who was greatly beloved and esteemed by all who knew him, and who happily still lives in dignified retirement, and who recently had conferred upon him the honour of being chosen Lord Rector for the University which he served so long and so honourably. The famous Professor R. Buchanan ("Logic Bob," as he was affectionately but somewhat irreverently called), who taught the difficult art of reasoning to his hard-headed Scotch students, with great acceptance; and who was not more renowned as a logician than beloved as a friend by his pupils. The worthy Professor Fleming, of the Moral Philosophy Chair, who also served faithfully for many years, and whose "Vocabulary of Philosophy" is a most valuable and useful book. The able Professor Macquorn Rankine, who, for the period of seventeen years, presided over the classes of civil engineering and mechanics in a most satisfactory manner, and did good service to the city by his advocacy of the Loch Katrine Water Scheme, and who was the author of many valuable works connected with his own particular branch of knowledge. Sir William Thomson, who has earned a world-wide reputation as an electrician and natural philosopher. The noble Principal Caird, who is not surpassed for eloquence as a preacher by any other divine of the present generation; who has given a tone to the entire Scottish pulpit, which is of the greatest possible influence; and who is, moreover, the author of several rare, beautiful, and profound works on philosophy and other cognate subjects. The dashing and brilliant, yet massive and original Professor Edward Caird, who grapples ably and well with the deepest problems of philosophy, and who is yet in the zenith of his power, and who is acquiring for himself a name that will not speedily pass away. The polished, devoted, and estimable Professor John Pringle Nichol, whose astronomical researches and disquisitions gave an impetus to the starry science in Glasgow, which was of the greatest benefit not only to the students but to the entire community. His son, Professor John Nichol, who ably fills the Chair of English Literature in our University, and who has done, and is doing, good service to that hitherto greatly neglected subject, both in the College classes and amongst the general public. The genial and poetical Professor Veitch, presently professor of logic; the co-editor, with Mansel, of Sir William Hamilton's works; and a man of great culture and taste, as well as a keen lover of Scottish rural scenery and of Scottish poetry and romance. We close this sketch—somewhat lengthy, yet painfully incomplete—of the University and its professors, with one or two anecdotes related of Professor Ramsay. The custom with the professors of humanity in the old Glasgow College had been to call upon some individual student to stand up and translate part of the passage which happened to be the subject of study. Ramsay called on one occasion upon a great stalwart Highlandman, who knew more about ewes, and wethers, and stirks, and Gaelic than of Horace. He had evidently, however, tried to prepare his task, and in the broadest West country brogue read out the first lines of Ode xxx, B iii. So far, with the exception of pronouncing "impŏtens" "impŏtens," and "diruĕre" "diruĕre" (Professor Ramsay detested nothing so much as a false quantity) Donald got on indifferently well. The translation was another matter. The first line runs—*Exegi monumentum ære perennius*—"I have erected a monument more lasting than brass," which the unfortunate Donald, led astray by confounding "exegi" with "edi," translated, "I have *eaten* a monument *more harder* than brass." It was too much for Ramsay, who could only in his astonishment gasp out, "Then for heaven's sake man, sit down and digest it." Donald sat down, amid the convulsions of the class, and if he didn't swallow the monument, did his best to swallow the joke.

Another story equally good is also told. It was in the good old days, when the professors and students mixed more with each other than they do now, and certain of the latter who had gained prizes for essays were entertained to supper by their hospitable teacher. As it drew near to "toddy time," a discussion arose as to what kind of drink a writer should take to strengthen him for the throes of composition. After some talk, the professor turned to one of his young guests of rather jovial repute, and said :—

"And what drink do you take before writing your essay ?"

"Whisky, sir," was the frank reply.

"Aye, aye, James," was the quick retort, "and I have nae doot, *Esse takes the same case after it that it does before it.*"

An equally good story is told of one of Ramsay's predecessors in the same chair. A youth happening to come into the class-room after prayers one day, and neglecting in his confusion to shut the door, a student called out (they

spoke in Latin in those days)—*Claude ostium puer!*—
"Shut the door, boy!" The professor wittily rebuked
the officiousness of the speaker by parodying his words,—
Claude os tuum puer!—"Shut your mouth, boy!" (Strang's
Glasgow and its Clubs).

But the laugh was not always on the side of the professor, if the following anecdote be a veritable one. One of the professors, who was certainly not famed for courtesy, was on one occasion much irritated at the stolidity and incapacity of one of the students, an apparently raw youth from the rural districts. After questioning him on some matter, and receiving very unintelligent replies, the professor touched his forehead, and asked, 'Is there not something wanting here?" The student without a moment's hesitation replied, "There may be something wanting there, sir, but (touching his own forehead) I can assure you there's nothing wanting here," and this retort set the whole class in a roar at the expense of the professor, who took good care to let that youth alone afterwards.

CHAPTER V.

DISTINGUISHED STUDENTS OF GLASGOW UNIVERSITY.

" Joys ineffable they find,
Who seek the prouder pleasure of the mind ;
The soul, collected in those happy hours,
Then makes her efforts, then enjoys her powers ;
And in those seasons feels herself repaid,
For labours past and honours long delayed."
—*Crabbe*.

ONE of the earliest students of our University after its commencement by Bishop Turnbull was a man who rose to very high eminence in after years, and was a credit to his *Alma Mater*, as well as to the city of which he was a native. We refer to WILLIAM ELPHINSTON, who became Bishop of Aberdeen and founder of the university of that city. He was born in Glasgow in 1431. His father, William Elphinston, was a younger member of the noble family of Elphinston, who took up his residence in Glasgow during the reign of James I, and was the first of its citizens who became eminent and acquired a fortune as a general merchant. His mother was Margaret Douglas of the house of Mains in Dumbartonshire, which, at a later date, became allied to the Campbells of Blythswood. Indeed, it was Mr. Elphinston himself who acquired the estate of Blythswood along with that of Gorbals on the south side of the Clyde. Young Elphinston was educated first at the Grammar School, and then at the university of his native city. He took his degree of M.A. in 1457, and after studying divinity, he took holy orders, and was thereafter made rector of Kirkmichael, with a residence in the vicinity of the Cathedral. After holding that office for four years, he went over to France, where he applied himself to the study of the Civil and Canon Law, and was afterwards chosen professor of laws first at Paris, and then at Orleans. He attained a high reputation in France. After spending about nine years there, he returned to Glasgow, and became parson in the cathedral church there, and, at the same time, was made Rector of the University. But he was destined to higher honours still. He became Official of Lothian; an office which he discharged so much to the satisfaction of all concerned that James III sent for him to Parliament, and appointed him one of the lords of his Privy Council. It may be noticed here, as a curious fact, that at this period men of various degrees sat and deliberated and voted in Parliament without any other authority than being summoned by His Majesty as wise and good men, whose advice might be useful in the management of public affairs. About this time a difference arose between the French and Scottish Courts, and the latter being alarmed for the stability of the ancient alliance of the two countries, sent out an embassy for its preservation. This embassy consisted of Earl Buchan, Lord Chamberlain Livingston, Bishop of Dunkeld and Elphinston; and the last named so managed matters as to have the success of the embassy wholly attributed to him. As a reward for his services, he was made Archdeacon of Argyll in 1479, and shortly afterwards in 1482 Bishop of Ross, while in the following year he was promoted to the Bishopric of Aberdeen. In the following year, he, along with two or three other eminent men, was sent to the court of Richard III of England to settle all disputes between the two countries. In subsequent disputes with the Scotch nobles, Bishop Elphinston adhered stedfastly to his king, and James was so well pleased with his conduct, that he constituted him Lord High Chancellor of Scotland, the principal state office in the country. Of all our Scottish bishops, no one has been by our historians more highly commended than Elphinston He has been celebrated as a great statesman, a learned and pious churchman, and one who gained the reverence and love of all good men. He lived to a good old age, having died on his way to Edinburgh, to which he had been summoned at a time of great trouble in the Kingdom, on 25th October, 1514, in the 83rd year of his age. It is said that he was so grieved at the disastrous news of the battle of Flodden in 1513, that he was never seen to smile afterwards. The respect and veneration that he was held in will appear from what is related to have happened at the time of his burial by the historians who lived near his time :—On the day his corpse was brought forth to be interred, the pastoral staff, which was all of silver, and carried by Alexander Lauder, a priest, broke in two pieces, one part falling into the grave, where the corpse was to be laid, and a voice was heard to cry, *Tecum, Gulielme, Mitra sepelienda*—" With thee the mitre and glory thereof is buried."

Among other eminent students of our University in these olden times, we can only refer to the following :—

SIR WILLIAM ALEXANDER of Menstrie, an eminent nobleman, statesman, and poet of the reign of James VI and Charles I. The original rank of this personage was that of a small landlord or laird, but he was elevated, by dint of his various accomplishments, and through the favour of these two sovereigns, to the rank of Earl of Stirling. When only in his fifteenth year, he was smitten with the charms of some country beauty, " the cynosure of neighbouring eyes," and he wrote no fewer than a hundred sonnets as a ventilation to his feelings, but all his poetry was in vain, so far as the lady was concerned. She thought of matrimony, while he thought of love, and accordingly, on being solicited by a more aged suitor, in other respects eligible, she did not scruple to accept his hand. But he consoled himself by afterwards marrying the daughter and heiress of Sir William Erskine. His century of sonnets was published in London in 1604, under the title of *Aurora, containing the First*

Fancies of the Author's Youth, by W. Alexander of Menstrie." King James is said to have been a warm admirer of the poems of Alexander, to have honoured him with his conversation, and called him "my philosophical poet." In 1626 he was, by the favour of Charles I, made Secretary of State for Scotland, and in 1630 was raised to the peerage under the title of Viscount Stirling, and in 1633, at the coronation of Charles in Holyrood Chapel, he was promoted to the rank of an earl. In his latter years he was employed in revising the version of the Psalms prepared by King James, which duty was imposed upon him by the king himself. He died in 1640, leaving three sons and three daughters, whose posterity was supposed to have been completely extinct, till a claimant appeared in 1830, as descended from one of the younger branches of the family, and who assumed the titles of Stirling and Devon.

The celebrated GEORGE BUCHANAN, one of the most distinguished reformers, political and religious, of the sixteenth century, and the best Latin poet which modern Europe has produced, received a part of his early education in Glasgow University. He was born in the parish of Killearn, Stirlingshire, in February, 1506, "of a family," to use his own words, "more ancient than wealthy." His father inherited the farm of Moss, on the western bank of the water of Blane, where the house, though it has been several times rebuilt, still, in honour of the illustrious George, preserves its original shape and dimensions, with a considerable portion of the original materials. At the age of fifteen Buchanan was sent by his maternal uncle, James Heriot, to complete his education at Paris. Here he studied with great diligence for a period of two years, when, in consequence of his uncle's death, he was cast upon his own resources, exposed to all the miseries of poverty and bodily affliction. Returning to Scotland, he served as a private soldier in one campaign against the English. Shortly afterwards he studied logic in St. Andrew's University, and in 1524 returned to Paris, where he became a student in the Scots' College, and attained the degree of M.A. in 1528. He imbibed the doctrines of the Reformation, and on account of his great learning was made tutor to the youthful king, James VI, who, it is said, owed to his tutor all the erudition of which in later life he was so vain. Buchanan ruled the young prince with much severity and strict discipline, and many apocryphal stories are told of the manner in which he snubbed and rebuked him. The following may, however, be regarded as authentic. The Master of Erskine, who was the prince's playmate, had a tame sparrow, the possession of which was coveted by James, but was denied by its owner. James had recourse to violence in order to obtain the bird, and the one boy pulled and the other held till the poor sparrow was killed in the struggle. The Master of Erskine then burst into tears and made a great outcry over his loss. This brought the matter to the knowledge of Buchanan, who gave the king a box on the ear, and told him "that what he had done was like a true bird of the bloody nest out of which he had come."

A more pleasing anecdote is thus related:—One of the earliest propensities of the young king was an excessive attachment to favourites, and this weakness continued to retain its ascendency during every stage of his life. Buchanan used a ludicrous expedient to try and correct this fault in his pupil's character. He presented the king with two papers, which he requested him to sign, which James, after some slight inquiry, readily signed without even glancing over their contents. One of them was a formal transference of the regal authority for the term of fifteen days. Having quitted the royal presence, one of the courtiers accosted him with the usual salutation, but to this astonished nobleman he announced himself in the new character of a sovereign; and with that happy urbanity of manner for which he was so distinguished, he began to assume the high demeanour of royalty. He afterwards acted in the same manner towards the king himself, and when James expressed his amazement at such extraordinary conduct, Buchanan admonished him of his having resigned the crown. The king's surprise was not lessened by this reply, and he began to think that his tutor's mind had become deranged. Buchanan then produced the instrument by which he was formally invested, and with the authority of a tutor, proceeded to lecture his pupil on the absurdity of assenting to petitions in so rash a manner.

In the latter years of his life Buchanan wrote and published an elaborate history of Scotland in Latin. It was printed by Alexander Arbuthnot at Edinburgh, in 1582.

and there have been no fewer than seventeen editions of the work, some of these being translated into the Scotch and others into the English language. A few months before it was published, and when Mr. Buchanan was in his 76th year, and an invalid confined to the house, he was visited (in September, 1581) by Andrew Melville, James Melville, and his cousin, Thomas Buchanan. The following interesting account of this visit has been left by James Melville :—

"That September, in tyme of vacans, my uncle, Mr. Andro, Mr. Thomas Buchanan, and I, heiring yt Mr. George Buchanan was weak, and his historie under ye press, past ower to Edinbro annes errand to visit him and sie ye wark. When we cam to his chalmer, we fand him sitting in his charre teatching his young man that servit him in his chalmer to spell a, b, ab ; e, b, eb, &c. After salutation, Mr. Andro says, 'I sie, sir, ye are not ydle.' 'Better,' quoth he, 'than stelling sheep or sitting ydle, which is als ill.' Yrefter he shew us the Epistle dedicative to the king, the whilk when Mr. Andro had read, he told him that it was obscure in some places, and wanted certain wordis to perfyt the sentence. Sayes he, 'I may do na mair for thinking on another matter.' 'What is that?' says Mr. Andro. 'To die,' quoth he, 'but I leave that an' mony ma things to you to help.' We went from him to the printer's wark hous, whom we fand at the end of the 17 buik of his Chronicle, at a place qhuilk we thought verie hard for the tyme, qhuilk might be an occasion of steying the hail wark, anent the burial of Davie (David Rizzio). Therefore, steying the printer from proceeding, we cam to Mr. George again, and fand him bedfast by (contrary to) his custome, and asking him how he did, 'Even going the way of weilfare,' sayes he. Mr. Thomas, his cousin, shaws him of the hardness of that part of his story, yt the king wald be offendit with it, and it might stey all the wark. 'Tell me, man,' sayes he, 'if I have tald the truth.' 'Yes,' says Mr. Thomas, 'I think so.' 'I will byd his feide and all his kins, then,' quoth he, 'Pray, pray to God for me, and let Him direct all.' Sa be the printing of his Chronicle was endit, that maist learned, wyse, and godlie man endit this mortal lyff."

Mr. Buchanan died on Friday, the 28th September, 1582.

He died in much peace, expressing his full reliance on his Saviour. He was buried in the Greyfriars Churchyard, a great multitude attending his funeral. An obelisk has, by the gratitude of posterity, been reared to his memory in his native village, Killearn, and is in a state of good preservation.

Amongst the eminent men who, in more modern days, received their education in our University—and their name is legion—not one occupies a higher position than the late SIR WILLIAM HAMILTON, of Preston, Bart., of whom it has been said by a competent authority that he was "incomparably the most scholarly of all Scottish philosophers, and incomparably the most philosophic of all Scottish scholars." He was born in Glasgow on the 8th March, 1788, and was not only the son, but also the grandson of professors in our University, the former, Dr. William, and the latter, Dr. Thomas, having held in succession the chairs of anatomy and botany. It was at our University that Sir William was educated, and there he distinguished himself, especially in the philosophical classes, and laid the foundation of those intellectual habits and acquirements which afterwards obtained for him a European reputation; although it was in Balliol College, Oxford, that the superstructure was reared. Hamilton was trained for the law, and was admitted a member of the Scottish Bar in 1813. But the law—except Roman law—had no charms for him. The study of mental philosophy occupied him so exclusively that he had neither time nor inclination for the study of statutes and precedents. On the death of Dr. Thomas Brown, in 1820, by which the professorship of moral philosophy in the University of Edinburgh became vacant, he contested with John Wilson (Christopher North) for the vacant chair, but without success. He was, however, subsequently appointed professor of logic and metaphysics for that University. And this was his true sphere for which his tastes and talents best suited him. The same authority we have already quoted, says—"In the science of logic he towered, not only above all his Scottish predecessors and compeers, but above both Kant and Leibnitz; and he must probably take his place in all time coming next to Aristotle himself." As a professor, his metaphysical lectures excited a keen interest in philosophy among all his students, who were qualified for severe abstract thinking, while they guided the thinking of not a few into channels in which it long or always continued to flow; while his examinations of the students were of the most thorough, searching, and educative character. He was a voluminous contributor on philosophy to the *Edinburgh Review;* and, of his first contribution, M. Victor Cousin, the great French philosopher, said there were probably not fifty persons in the country who would be able to appreciate its value, or even to understand its meaning. For, when Sir William took the Chair of Logic and Metaphysics in Edinburgh, philosophy was at the lowest ebb in Britain. But through his efforts the Scottish intellect returned to those legitimate pursuits for which, in former times, it had shown such a peculiar aptitude, and upon which its best distinctions were founded. Sir William also edited the complete works of Thomas Reid, with notes and supplementary dissertations; and, before his death, he had all but completed an edition of the collected works of Dugald Stewart. His own lectures were carefully revised and edited by Professors Mansel and Veitch, and were published in four volumes in 1859. Sir William died in Edinburgh, on 6th May, 1856; and the following eulogium has been passed upon him by another Glasgow writer:—"His name will assuredly, hereafter, be reckoned among the greatest in the history of British philosophy—

> ' His grave is all too young as yet
> To have outgrown the sorrow that consigned
> Its charge to it.'

But the place of his birth and early education may be allowed at least a passing tribute to his memory; and if ever the time shall come when the philosophy of the conditioned shall occupy its fitting place as the handmaid and auxiliary of Christian truth, voyaging through the seas of thought with the laws of the human mind for its chart and the Word of God for its polestar, among the fathers and teachers of that philosophy, most consulted and most revered, will stand the name of Sir William Hamilton."

The famous JOHN WILSON himself, though a native of Paisley, and a professor and citizen of Edinburgh, was also a student of our University; where from his fourteenth to his seventeenth year he studied Greek and Logic under Professors Young and Jardine; and regarding these Professors it has been said—"Few literary minds could pass under the training of such teachers, and especially the last, without finding it constitute a most important epoch in their intellectual history. And it was to Jardine that Wilson's great rival in critical literature—Jeffrey—acknowledged those first mental impulses which he afterwards prosecuted so successfully."

It is rather a remarkable fact, and forms an indication of the high reputation of our University, that the eminent lawyer and littérateur, FRANCIS JEFFREY, though born and reared in Edinburgh, received his first College education not at the Edinburgh, but the Glasgow University. Born in the year 1773, he was sent to our College when in his fourteenth year. His first year was devoted to the study of Greek under Professor John Young, the second to Logic under Professor Jardine. Of this latter Professor Jeffrey said—"It is to him and his most judicious instructions that I owe my taste for letters, and any little literary distinction I may since have been enabled to attain." Such was his declaration when he had attained the very highest literary distinction; and the tears rolled down the cheeks of the good old professor when he found himself thus gratefully and unexpectedly requited. Jeffrey, during his third session, attended the course of Moral Philosophy under Professor Arthur, the successor of Reid, a man whose promise of high distinction was closed by an early death.

Another distinguished pupil of the University, and this time a native of the city, was JAMES SMITH of Jordanhill, whose father, Archibald Smith, was a merchant in Glasgow, and whose mother, Isabella Ewing, a remarkable woman, who died so recently as 1855 in her 101st year, was the friend and correspondent of Mrs. Grant of Laggan, and to whom many of the *Letters from the Mountains* were addressed. James Smith was born in August, 1782, and at the University he was the friend and contemporary of John Wilson, Dr. Alexander Blair, and John Richardson. In 1809 he married Mary Wilson, grand-daughter of Dr. Alex. Wilson, Professor of Astronomy in the University of Glasgow, whose reputation as an original thinker was in recent times revived, from the now very general

F

acquiescence in his speculations on the nature of the molar spots. Mr. Smith was "an ardent cultivator of geographical science and discovery, besides being an accomplished linguist, a theoretical and practical architect, a zealous student of family and historical antiquities, and a geologist." From 1839 to 1847 he resided successively at Madeira, Gibraltar, Lisbon, and Malta, and published interesting papers on the geology of each of these localities. His residence at Malta was the occasion and commencement of a remarkable series of researches connected with the writings of the earliest Christian writers, by which he is now best known, through his great work, "*The Voyage and Shipwreck of St. Paul*, with Dissertations on the Life and Writings of St. Luke, and the Ships and Navigation of the Ancients," published in 1848. Mr. Smith died at Jordanhill, on the 17th January, 1867.

Not less eminent though in a different walk, was James Smith's son, ARCHIBALD SMITH, LL.D., F.R.S., who, though a barrister-at-law and a fellow of Trinity College, Cambridge, yet devoted the greater portion of his lifetime to the study of iron ship construction; and his researches into compass deviations were regarded as specially valuable. He was a member of many learned societies, and was well known in most of the scientific circles throughout Europe. He was a native of Glasgow, having been born there in 1814, and received his first collegiate education in our University. In 1853 he was married to Susan Emma, youngest daughter of the late Vice-Chancellor Parker, and he died on the 26th December, 1872.

Prior to these notables in point of time, and perhaps in common popularity, was the famous TOBIAS SMOLLETT the novelist, author of *Roderick Random*, *Peregrine Pickle*, and other works of a similar kind, and who also continued the *History of England* begun by David Hume. Born in the old family house of Dalquhurn, near the modern village of Renton, in Dumbartonshire, in 1721, Tobias was sent at an early age to study at Glasgow College, with a view to some learned profession. There he was led, through his intimacy with some medical students, to embrace the profession of physic, which he studied along with anatomy, at the same time serving an apprenticeship in town to a surgeon named Gordon, whom he is supposed to have afterwards caricatured in *Roderick Random* under the title of *Potion*. He was rather a wild youth, addicted to satire and practical joking. One winter evening when the streets were covered with snow, he was engaged in a snowball fight with some boys of his own age, among whom was the apprentice of a surgeon, whom he is supposed to have delineated under the name of *Crab* in his famous novel. The master of this apprentice having entered his shop while the youth was in the heat of the engagement, rebuked him very severely, for having quitted the shop. The boy excused himself by saying that, while engaged in making up a prescription, a fellow had hit him with a snowball, and he had gone in pursuit of the delinquent. " A mighty probable story truly," said the master in an ironical tone; " I wonder how long I should stand here before it would enter into any mortal's head to throw a snowball at me?" Just as he pronounced these words, Smollett, who had heard them at the door, gave him a most unexpected answer by throwing a snowball, which hit him a severe blow on the face and extricated his companion.

But the early years of Smollett were devoted to better pursuits than these. While still studying medicine at College, he composed a tragedy on the death of James I of Scotland, entitled the *Regicide*, and which, though not fitted for the stage, displayed considerable ability. At the age of 18, he had the misfortune to lose his grandfather, who died without making any provision for him or any of his father's family, and the young man shortly afterwards went to London to push his fortune, where, after a vain attempt to get into practice as a physician, he assumed the character of an author. Previous to this, however, he had made a voyage to Carthagena as a surgeon's mate, in a ship of the line under Admiral Vernon. He left the ship at Jamaica, where he resided for some time, during which residence he formed an attachment to a Miss Lascelles, an elegant and accomplished young lady who had the expectation of a fortune of £3,000, and he afterwards married her, though she was disappointed of her fortune through a lawsuit.

His career as an author was of a chequered description. He was a most voluminous writer, and for his works he procured large sums of money, but from his satirical disposition, he was continually getting himself into trouble, and latterly he laboured under a constant state of ill-humour, the result of morbid feelings and a distempered bodily system. He travelled on the Continent for two years, but this failed to restore his health. On his return he revisited Scotland, spending some time in Glasgow, and also at Bonhill. Once more, however, he was recommended to try a change of air, and he set out for Italy in 1770, taking up his abode in a cottage near Leghorn, where he published in 1771, the *Adventures of Humphrey Clinker*, in which his own character as it appeared in later life under the pressure of bodily disease, is delineated in the person of Matthew Bramble. During the summer of 1774, he declined very rapidly, and at length on the 21st October, death put an end to his sufferings. His widow—the *Narcissa of Roderick Random*—was left poor in a foreign land. Had her husband only lived a few years longer he would have succeeded his cousin of Bonhill as heir of entail in the possession of an estate of £1,000 a year, besides other private means, all of which descended to his sister Mrs. Telfer. But the widow was assisted by Mr. Smollett, her husband's cousin before his death; and among others, by Mr. Graham of Gartmore, who with his other intimate friend Mr. Bontine, was trustee to the ill-fated novelist. On the 3rd March, 1784, a benefit was procured for her in the Theatre Royal, Edinburgh, on which occasion, the play of *Venice Preserved* was acted, with a prologue written by Mr. Graham. The money, amounting to £366, with private donations, was remitted to Italy, and this was all that Scotland ever sacrificed for the sake of one of the most illustrious of her sons (*Eminent Scotsmen*).

To enumerate all the eminent men who have been trained in our ancient and honourable University would require a whole volume; and so, with the foregoing brief sketches as samples, we must conclude this chapter, except to state that the sons of a large number of our Scottish nobility, till a comparatively recent date were educated here. These young noblemen were generally attended by their own servants, and they were not always famed for good behaviour, but were on the contrary among the wildest and most unruly of all. Could the ancient tenements in the High Street tell of all the scenes of fun, frolic, riot, and disorder, that have taken place in their presence amongst these scions of nobility and their compeers, they could unfold many a strange and startling tale. But with our statelier building in Gilmorehill, and with a more advanced and perfected system of education, we must confess that the social status of our students has declined. Our sprigs of nobility have deserted our learned halls and fled to the milder regions of Oxford and Cambridge, there to carry on their pranks, and too often neglect their studies. Yet we verily believe that the mental and moral calibre of those who now frequent our seat of learning has in no wise diminished since the days of old, and after all, as Burns says—

"The rank is but the guinea stamp,
The man's the gowd for a' that."

CHAPTER VI.

SKETCHES OF NOTABLE POETS AND LITERARY MEN OF GLASGOW.

" The outward shows of sky and earth,
Of hill and valley he has view'd ;
And impulses of deeper birth
Have come to him in solitude.

" In common things that round us lie
Some random truths he can impart,
—The harvest of a quiet eye
That broods and sleeps on his own heart."
—A POET'S EPITAPH—*Wordsworth.*

IN spite of its keen trading instincts, its somewhat rough and boisterous manners, and its unromantic and unsavoury physical conditions, our good city has had considerable leanings towards the finer arts, and has produced a few good poets, a great many minor cultivators of the muse, and not a few men of high culture, and general literary, and classical attainments. It has been, moreover, a generous patron of poetry, literature, and art, and has ever been quick to recognize the work of true genius wherever found. Many of those who have in after-life shone as bright stars in the intellectual and imaginative spheres, have had their light kindled or fanned into a flame, amidst the smoke and din and bustle of Glasgow. A large volume could be written full of interesting and instructive narrative relating to the poets and literary men of the city; but our space will only permit us to glean a few representative sketches, as samples of the whole galaxy.

It is interesting to know that one of the earliest literary men of Glasgow was the excellent Bishop Jocelinc, who towards the close of the 12th century wrote and published a work on the *Life and Miracles of St. Kentigern*, with the proceeds of which he laid the foundation of our noble Cathedral. His successors in the sacred office were not as a rule famous for authorship; their duties generally being of a more active, and even political and military character. Yet not a few of them were men of learning and culture, amongst whom may be ranked Bishop Gavin Dunbar, who became tutor to James V; and Spottiswoode the great historian, and others. Then in connection with our University, we find that even in early times it bore a high reputation for learning and culture, as was amply testified by the Reformer James Melville, and other high authorities. Amongst the early professors and rectors of our college, we have Zachary Boyd, who was both a poet and prose writer of no mean order, and although his writings would scarcely be called elegant in these modern days, yet considering the times in which he lived, they were remarkable productions. The literary works of Baillie, Dickson, Wodrow, are still to be found in our public libraries, and although they are now only consulted by antiquarians, historians, and students, yet in their day they had a wide circulation and exerted a powerful influence. In more modern days among the professors of Glasgow University, as will be seen from the sketches we have already presented to our readers, were some of the most eminent writers of their day, and their disquisitions in science, philosophy, theology, and other weighty subjects, held a high place in the literary world both at home and abroad.

But it will be more in keeping with the character of this book, and more generally interesting, if, in this chapter, we deal with a more varied and popular school of literature. The most eminent name in this connection is, undoubtedly, that of Thomas Campbell, "the poet of hope"; but there were a few prior to his day who are worthy of honourable mention. Among these may be ranked

Mrs. Grant of Laggan,

who was born in Glasgow on 21st February, 1755. Her father, Duncan M'Vicar, was an officer in the British army; her mother was a descendant of the ancient family of Stewart of Invernahyle, in Argyllshire. Shortly after the birth of their daughter, the father accompanied his regiment to America, and was afterwards joined by his wife and child. The girl was chiefly educated by her mother, and the home teaching of Scotland was transplanted to the back settlements of New York State. From the sergeant of a Scottish regiment she learned the art of penmanship, and this worthy man presented her with the poem of *Wallace*, by Blind Harry. He also taught her to understand the meaning of that quaint and difficult work. From this source she mainly derived that enthusiastic love of her native country which was a prominent feature in her character. Another notable book fell into her hands at this period—Milton's *Paradise Lost*—which she studied with eagerness and delight. Her father did not succeed in America, and returned to Scotland with his family in 1768. A few years after he was appointed barrack-master at Fort Augustus. Here Miss M'Vicar formed an acquaintance with the military chaplain, Rev. James Grant, an accomplished scholar, and of amiable manners, to whom she was married, and some years after this event her husband was appointed in 1779 to the parish of Laggan, in Inverness-shire. On becoming the wife of a parish minister, Mrs. Grant set herself to become useful among the people of the parish, and to enable her to do so, she studied and mastered the Gaelic language. No idea of authorship had then entered her mind. But a literary life was to be her *weird*, and stern necessity was to be the instrument of its accomplishment. After four successive deaths in her family, her husband died, and she was left a helpless widow, with eight children dependent upon her exertions, while the manse, so long her happy home, had to be vacated. After unsuccessfully attempting to maintain herself and family by taking charge of a farm, she removed to Stirling in 1803, and at the suggestion of her friends, she tried the experiment of authorship. She had written many verses, which had been greatly admired, in MS., and these were collected into a volume and published. About 3,000 subscribers were secured, and the volume was well received. With the proceeds of this venture she discharged the debts she had contracted at Laggan; and, encouraged by success, she published her famous *Letters from the Mountains* in 1806. These letters had been written in the manse at Laggan to her friends, and were so full of descriptions of Highland scenery, character and legends, expressed in the happiest style, that they were thoroughly appreciated, and went through many editions. Their publication also procured her the friendship of many eminent persons. The only other works which she subsequently published were *Memoirs of an American Lady* and *Essays on the Superstitions of the Highlanders of Scotland;* and it is enough to say that they did not detract from the reputation she had already won. Her productions are thus characterized by Sir Walter Scott—"Her literary works, although composed amidst misfortune and privation, are written at once with simplicity and force, and uniformly bear the stamp of a virtuous and courageous mind, recommending to the reader that patience and fortitude which the writer herself practised in such an eminent degree. Her writings, so popular in her own country, derive their success from the happy manner in which they breathe a spirit at once of patriotism, and of that candour which renders patriotism unselfish and liberal. We have no hesitation in attesting our belief that Mrs. Grant's writings have produced a strong and salutary effect upon her countrymen, who not only found recorded in them much of national history and antiquities, which would otherwise have been forgotten, but found them combined with the soundest and the best lessons of virtue and morality."

In 1810 Mrs. Grant removed to Edinburgh, where she resided during the rest of her life. But still her domestic calamities pursued her, and all her children died successively, except her youngest son, who survived her. She was aided during her later years by a pension from the literary fund, first of £50, but afterwards of £100 per annum. The application made on her behalf in 1825 was subscribed by Sir Walter Scott, Francis Jeffrey, Mackenzie (the Man of Feeling), Sir William Arbuthnot, Sir Robert Liston, and Principal Baird, and was cordially granted by

George IV. Mrs. Grant was long an invalid. Seven years before she obtained her pension, she had a fall in descending a stair, from the effects of which she was confined almost wholly to her house during the rest of her life. But still she was resigned, and even happy; and her frequent study of the Bible, as well as her conversation, betokened the sure foundation upon which her comfort was established. Thus she lived, honoured and beloved, till the 84th year of her age, when a cold, that increased into influenza, ended her days on 7th November, 1838. Her chief talent lay in conversation, in which she was unrivalled, and hence the high fame she acquired among the literary circles of her day. " That voice has passed away, of which her works are but an echo, and thus the works themselves are now rated beneath their merits. Still, however, the *Letters from the Mountains* will continue to attest the high talent of their writer, and will be perused with pleasure and profit." *

MICHAEL SCOTT.

A somewhat remarkable Glasgow man of letters was Michael Scott, the author of that racy and brilliant series of articles originally contributed to *Blackwood's Magazine* under the name of *Tom Cringle*, and afterwards published in two volumes, entitled *Tom Cringle's Log*. This talented writer was born in Glasgow on 30th October, 1789. He received his education first at the High School, and afterwards at the University of his native city. As he was destined for business, his stay at the College was a brief one; and, in October, 1806, he sailed for Jamaica, and was there employed in the management of several estates till 1810, when he joined a mercantile house in Kingston, Jamaica. In these situations he acquired an intimate knowledge of West India character and scenery, which he afterwards so powerfully delineated. He returned to Scotland in 1817, and was married in the following year, after which he went back to Jamaica; but after remaining there till 1822, he finally bade adieu to the West Indies, and returned to his native country. He subsequently wrote

* We have been partly indebted for this and several other sketches in this work to Blackie's *Biographical Dictionary of Eminent Scotsmen*.

and published his celebrated work, which, in graphic style, detailed "the voyage of a strange life through calm and hurricane, through battle and tempest," as they successively occurred to his fancy. The *Quarterly Review* characterized the papers as the most brilliant series of magazine articles of the time; while Coleridge, in his *Table Talk*, proclaimed them "most excellent." The public were of the same opinion, and the question was asked on all hands, "Who is the author of *Tom Cringle's Log?*" But no one could answer, not even Blackwood himself, so well had the author preserved his incognito; and that eminent publisher descended to his grave without knowing assuredly by whom the most popular series in his far-famed Magazine had been written. Afterwards the chapters were published as an entire work in two volumes; and so highly was it prized, that it was generally read on the Continent; while, in Germany, it has been repeatedly translated. After Michael Scott had thus led a life almost as mythical as that of his wondrous namesake, the necromancer of the thirteenth century, he died in Glasgow on the 7th November, 1835; and it was only through that sad event that the full fact of his authorship was ascertained by the son of Mr. Blackwood. Mr. Scott was also the author of that well known work, *The Cruise of the Midge*, and many other miscellaneous contributions.

It would be unpardonable in a review of the literary characters of Glasgow, however brief and summary, to overlook the claims of

DOUGAL GRAHAM,

the "Skellat" bellman of our good city. It is not known exactly whether he was a native-born Glaswegian, but it is certain he lived here from his early youth. He left Glasgow to follow the contending armies during the Rebellion of '45, not however as a warrior, but as a pedlar or packman, and on his return he wrote and published a long and interesting metrical history of that movement. The book had an immense popularity among the common people. So racy indeed was the work, that Sir Walter Scott even entertained the idea of printing a correct copy of the original edition, with the view of presenting it to the Maitland Club, as he thought "it really contained some traits and circumstances of manners worth preserving." In addition to this, Dougal was the author of a large number of "chap books," containing stories illustrating Scottish life and character, which were largely circulated all over the country by himself and other pedlars. Among these may be mentioned "Geordie Buchanan," "Paddy from Cork," "John Cheap the Chapman," "Jocky and Maggie's Courtship," "John Falkirk the Merry Piper," "The Creelman's Courtship," &c., &c. Two other well known productions of our chapman poet were "John Highlandman's Remarks on Glasgow" and "Turnamspike Man," Dougal Graham was elected Bellman of the city about the year 1770, out of a host of competitors. The candidates were put to a practical test of their skill by the magistrates, and when Dougal's turn came round, he seized the bell and giving it a loud and sonorous ring, he called out with stentorian voice—

"Caller herring at the Broomielaw,
Three a penny—three a penny."

And then calling his ready wit and power of versification into play, he added with a grin—

"Indeed my friends
But it's a' a bleflum,
For the herrin's no catched
An' the boat's no come."

This display of humour seems to have captivated our civic rulers, and Dougal received the much coveted post. For nine or ten years after that, he instructed and amused the lieges by alternate announcements and jocular extemporized verses, until he heard his own last summons on the 20th July, 1779.

REV. JAMES GRAHAME

author of *The Sabbath*, a poem of great excellence, was born in Glasgow, on the 22nd April, 1765. He was the son of Mr. Thomas Grahame, a writer in the city, a gentleman who stood at the head of the legal profession there, and held in high esteem for his many amiable qualities. His mother was a woman of uncommon understanding, and left a deep and beneficial impress upon the mind of her son. He was educated at the Grammar School and University of Glasgow. At this time his father possessed a beautiful villa on the then romantic banks of the Cart, near Glasgow, to which the family removed during the summer months; and it is pleasing to remark the delight with which Grahame, in after years, looked back upon the youthful days spent there. In the *Birds of Scotland* we have the following pleasing lines, which show that these days were still green in his memory—

> " I love thee pretty bird ! for 'twas thy nest
> Which first, unhelped by older eyes, I found ;
> The very spot I think I now behold !
> Forth from my low-roofed home I wandered blythe,
> Down to thy side sweet Cart, where 'cross the stream
> A range of stones, below a shallow ford,
> Stood in the place of the now spanning arch ;
> Up from that ford a little bank there was,
> With alder copse and willow overgrown,
> Now worn away by mining winter floods ;
> There at a bramble root, sunk in the grass,
> The hidden prize of withered field straws formed,
> Well lined with many a coil of hair and moss,
> And in it laid five red-veined spheres, I found."

Grahame greatly distinguished himself both at school and college, and he was also noted for the activity of his habits, and the gaiety of his disposition. His character, however, seems to have changed, and his constitution to have received a shock from a blow he received on the back of his head, which ever afterwards entailed upon him occasional attacks of headache and stupor ; and there seems little doubt that this blow was ultimately the cause of his death. He was designed by his father for the law, and he commenced to study under his cousin, Mr. Laurence Hill, W.S. After finishing his apprenticeship, he was admitted a member of the Society of Writers to the Signet in 1791. But he had no taste for the profession, and after the death of his father towards the close of that year, he resumed his original desire of entering the Church. But he continued at his profession for several years after that ; varying the dry details of his work with poetical compositions, which he contributed to the *Kelso Mail* and other publications, and they were afterwards published in a volume under the title of the *Rural Calendar.*

In the year 1801 he published a dramatic poem, entitled *Mary Queen of Scotland;* but his talents were by no means dramatic, and this poem never became popular. In 1802 Mr. Grahame was married to Miss Grahame, eldest daughter of Richard Grahame, Esq., Annan, a woman of masculine understanding and elegant accomplishments. She at first discouraged her husband's poetical propensities from the idea that they interfered with his professional duties; but on discovering that he was the author of *The Sabbath,* she no longer attempted to oppose the bias of his mind. *The Sabbath* was published anonymously; the poet even concealed its existence from his relations. The mode which he took to communicate it to his wife presents a pleasing picture of his diffident disposition. "On its publication he brought the book home with him, and left it on the parlour table. Returning soon after he found Mrs. Grahame engaged in its perusal; but without venturing to ask her opinion he continued to walk up and down the room in breathless anxiety, till she burst out in the warmest eulogium on the performance; adding—'Ah, James, if you could but produce a poem like this.' The acknowledgment of the authorship and the pleasure of making the disclosure under such circumstances may be easily imagined."

About the year 1806 Grahame published a well written pamphlet, entitled *Thoughts on Trial by Jury,* and shortly afterwards a poem in blank verse, entitled *The Birds of Scotland.* In 1808 he wrote the *British Georgics,* also in blank verse. At length, yielding to his long cherished wish, he entered holy orders as a clergyman of the Church of England, and after some difficulty, was ordained on 28th May, 1809. But he did not long survive the realization of his desire. He obtained the curacy of Shefton, in Gloucestershire, in July, 1809, and held that office till the March following, when he was called to Scotland on family affairs. Here he became candidate for St. George's Episcopal Church, Edinburgh, but without success. In August, 1810, he was appointed interim curate to the chapelry of St. Margaret, Durham, where his eloquence quickly collected a crowded congregation; and after having officiated there for a few months, he obtained the curacy of Sedgefield, in the same diocese. But being afflicted with oppressive asthma and violent headaches, he was induced to try the effect of a change to his native air; and he, along with his wife, proceeded to Glasgow, where he died two days after, on 14th Sept., 1811, at Whitehill, the residence of his eldest brother, Mr. Robert Grahame, of Whitehill, a well known merchant citizen of Glasgow. It is said of James Grahame that "there is no author, excepting Burns, whom an intelligent Scotsman residing abroad would read with more delight." In addition to the above works, Grahame wrote—*Sabbath Walks*, and *Biblical Pictures*, both in blank verse like the others.

Incidents in the Life of Thomas Campbell.

This poet, so justly entitled "the bard of hope," was born in the High Street of Glasgow, on 27th July, 1777. He was the son of Alexander Campbell, merchant, and one of a family of eleven. His father was an intimate friend of Thomas Reid, author of an *Inquiry into the Human Mind*, while his mother appears to have been a lover of literature, and a woman of strong sense and refined taste. At the early age of ten young Campbell gave evidence of poetic talent, and in his twelfth year he composed his *Poem on Description*, which gained for him a prize in the Logic class four years afterwards. He entered our University in 1791, and was even then a ripe scholar in Latin and Greek. He was famed among his fellow-students, not only for his poetical ability and learning, but also for his wit and humour. It is said of him that, being a slender, delicate lad, he was fond of a place near the College hall fire in the cold winter mornings, before the professor made his appearance; but as he often found the fireside crowded by other students, amongst whom some Irish youths were conspicuous, he used to resort to a trick to draw them away. This consisted in his writing some original witty effusion on the wall, at a distance from the fireplace, and their curiosity soon led his fellow-students away from their place at the fire in order to peruse his latest squib. On one occasion it was reported that he had written something derogatory of the Irish character, and the Irish students rushed in a body over to see it, and vowing vengeance upon the author of the libel. But their anger turned to merriment when they read the following couplet:—

"Vos, Hiberni Collocatis
 Summum bonum in—potatoes!"

It will thus be seen that in his youth Campbell was of a gay and lively disposition, but the tone of his after life was greatly changed by a remarkable incident. Like many other young men of studious habits, his whole soul was engrossed with the literature of Greece and Rome—with Brutus and Cassius and ideas of liberty. But while with others this was a mere passing fancy, with Campbell these sentiments were, by an event which happened at that time, indelibly stamped upon his mind and heart, and became a life-long passion. It was in the height of the French revolution, which movement affected even the minds of "canny" Scotsmen among others, leading them into dangerous and semi-treasonable courses of action. Some of these men— viz., Muir, Palmer, Gerald, and others—were tried at the High Court of Justiciary in Edinburgh, and young Campbell became possessed with a great desire to witness and hear these trials. He got five shillings from his mother, set out on foot to Edinburgh, and directed his way to Parliament House, where the trial of Gerald was going on; and this man was at the moment addressing the jury in an eloquent and passionate manner:—"Gentlemen of the jury," he said, in his closing appeal, "now that I have to take leave of you for ever, let me remind you that mercy is no small part of the duty of jurymen; that the man who shuts his heart on the claims of the unfortunate, on him the gates of mercy will be shut, and for him the Saviour of the world shall have died in vain." Campbell was deeply impressed with these words and the deep silence of the multitude of listeners, and he gave vent to his emotion by exclaiming, "By heavens, sir, that is a great man." "Ay, sir," replied the man beside him, apparently a decent tradesman, "he is not only a great man himself, but he makes every other man great who listens to him." Campbell returned to Glasgow, a sadder if not a wiser man, and, to the astonishment of his companions, his jokes and flashes of merriment were now laid aside. He was ever after to be the poet of liberty. The *Pleasures of Hope* was written when he was little over twenty years of age. During its composition he was a teacher of Latin and Greek in Edinburgh. "In this vocation," he says himself, "I made a comfortable livelihood as long as I was industrious; but the *Pleasures of Hope* came over me. I took long walks about Arthur's Seat, conning over my own (as I thought them) magnificent lines; and as my *Pleasures of Hope* got on, my pupils fell off." A lady thus describes the personal appearance of the poet at this period. "Mr. Campbell's appearance bespoke instant favour; his countenance was beautiful, and as the expression of his face varied with his various feelings, it became quite a study for a painter to catch the fleeting graces as they rapidly succeeded each other. The pensive air which hung so gracefully over his youthful features, gave a melancholy interest to his manner which was extremely touching. But when he indulged in any lively sallies of humour, he was exceedingly amusing; every now and then, however, he seemed to check himself, as if the effort to be gay was too much for his sadder thoughts, which evidently prevailed."

The appearance of his great poem took the public mind by storm. The learned Dr. Gregory, stepping into the shop of Mr. Mundell, the publisher, saw the volume fresh from the press, lying upon the counter. "Ah! what have we here?" he said, taking it up—"the *Pleasures of Hope*." He looked between the uncut leaves, and was so struck with the beauty of a single passage that he could not desist until he had read half the work. This *is* poetry," he enthusiastically exclaimed; and added "Where is the author to be found? I will call upon him immediately." The promise of the professor was quickly fulfilled, and from that period he became one of Campbell's warmest friends and admirers.

After the publication of his poem, Campbell travelled upon the Continent and witnessed some of the horrors of war at Ratisbon, which made a deep impression upon his sensitive mind. Returning home by London, the fame of his poem was a passport to him to the best society in the metropolis. After a short stay there, he directed his course homeward. "Returning to Edinburgh by sea," he writes in his memoranda of 1801, "a lady passenger by the same ship who had read my poems, but was personally unacquainted with me, told me to my utter astonishment that I had been arrested in London for high treason, and committed to the Tower, and expected to be executed. I was equally unconscious of having either deserved or incurred such a sentence." He however found, on reaching Edinburgh that it was no joke. The report had spread there also, and greatly alarmed his mother. He had messed with French officers at Ratisbon during an armistice, and, in that period of rumour and suspicion, this simple fact had been amplified into a plot concerted between himself, Moreau, and the Irish at Hamburg, to land a French army in Ireland. He waited upon Mr. Clerk, the sheriff of Edinburgh to refute the report and testify his loyalty; but here, to his astonishment, he found that the sheriff believed in his guilt and had a warrant out for his apprehension. This was intolerable and Campbell could not help exclaiming "Do I live to hear a sensible man like you talking about a boy like me conspiring against the British Empire?" He offered himself for strict examination before being sent to prison, and the inquisition was held amidst an array of clerks ready to take down his answers. A box of his letters and papers which had been seized at Leith was brought forward, and carefully examined. But the contents put all suspicion to the rout. Nothing could be found more treasonable than *Ye Mariners of England*, which was already prepared for the press, with a few other poems of distinguished merit. The whole inquest ended in a hearty laugh and a bottle of wine.

Shortly after this he composed *Lochiel's Warning* and the *Battle of Hohenlinden*. It is said that that striking line in the former poem,

"Coming events cast their shadows before,"

cost him a whole week of study and anxiety; but it was worthy all the pains.

Telford, the celebrated engineer, asked in a letter to a friend, "Have you seen his *Lochiel?* He will surpass everything ancient and modern—your Pindars, your Drydens, and your Grays." A similar feeling, but in a more poetical fashion was expressed of its merits by Mrs. Dugald Stewart, wife of the distinguished philosopher. When the poet read it to her in MS. she listened in deep silence and when it was finished, she gravely rose, laid her hand upon his head and said, "This will bear another wreath of laurel yet," after which she retired to her seat without uttering another word. "This," said Campbell, "made a stronger impression on my mind than if she had spoken in a strain of the loftiest panegyric. It was one of the principal incidents of my life that gave me confidence in my own powers." This poem being also read in MS. to Sir Walter Scott, he requested a perusal of it himself, and then repeated the whole from memory—a striking instance of the great minstrel's power of recollection.

A humorous anecdote relating to the well known poem on *Hohenlinden* may be told here as illustrating the jovial wit of the literary men of the last generation when met together in social fellowship. One evening a *symposium* of the poets and *litterateurs* of Modern Athens was held at the lodgings of one of their number in one of those tall tenements in the High Street or Lawnmarket, where the stairs were numerous and the lights few. The company embraced Campbell, *Christopher North*, the Ettrick Shepherd, and other notabilities, and when the long *sederunt* was over and the parties were about to return to their respective homes, the burly "Kit" had the misfortune to slip a foot and fall down the stair. Campbell, who was in front, hearing the noise and commotion, cried out, "Who's there? What's the matter?" The inimitable professor, though somewhat bruised by his fall, could not resist the opportunity of cracking his joke, and he roared in reply—

"'Tis I, Sir, rolling rapidly;"

and a loud burst of laughter followed the *bon mot* at the expense of our poet.

On the 10th September, 1803, the poet was married to Miss Matilda Sinclair, who had been the object of his youthful admiration nine years before. She was the daughter of his mother's cousin, a gentleman who had been a wealthy merchant and provost in Greenock, and was now a trader in London. The poet's whole fortune at this time did not exceed £50, and, to add to his cares, the support of his aged mother devolved upon him. But he was strong in hope, and besides the production of his poems he worked on the staff of the *Star* newspaper for four guineas a week. His incessant labour and anxiety told upon his health, and he was on the point of breaking down, when, through the influence of an unknown but influential friend, he was awarded a pension of £200 per annum from his majesty's bounty. He was then living at Sydenham.

Our space forbids further details of Campbell's interesting life. He was three times successively elected Lord Rector of Glasgow University—his *Alma Mater*—viz., in 1826-7-8. He had two sons born to him by his beloved wife. One of these, the eldest became a lunatic and was confined to an asylum. The other died in infancy. In 1826, his affectionate wife, Matilda, died, and he found himself alone in the world. He was editor of the *New Monthly Magazine* and it had prospered greatly under his supervision, but it passed out of his hands by an unlucky incident. A paper was inserted by mistake in its pages without having been subjected to his editorial examination, and, as the article was offensive in the highest degree, Campbell in 1830 abandoned the magazine and a salary of £600 a year which he derived from it.

In connection with Campbell's election as Lord Rector of our University, the following story is told of him in a recent number of *Temple Bar:*—"When he reached the College Green on his way to deliver his address the snow lay on the ground, and he found the youths pelting each other with snowballs. That he was just going to deliver a solemn address to the same youths never for a moment crossed his mind. The feelings of his youth came upon him, the spirit of past years animated him. He rushed into the *mêlée* and joined in the frolic in his fiftieth year, as if he had been but fifteen. Then, when the moment for delivering the address was come, the students being summoned, and he proceeding in the van, they entered the hall together. There could not be a better picture of the temperament and character of the man than such an incident—so impulsive and lively at a moment when gravity was on every other adult visage."

He had all along taken a deep interest in the cause of Poland, and the fall of Warsaw with the subsequent miseries with which the devoted country was afterwards visited, sank deep into his soul. Still he struggled nobly, and spoke, and wrote, both in prose and poetry on her behalf. And his labours were not in vain. He awoke a deep sympathy in her favour wherever his influence extended, and succeeded by means of the Polish Committee in London in relieving thousands of the expatriated refugees. Thomas Campbell died at Boulogne, on the 15th June, 1844, in the 67th year of his age; solaced by all the consolations of the Word of God, and attended to in his last moments by his niece and by his faithful physician and biographer, Dr. Beattie, who had crossed over from London to soothe the departing hours of his affectionate patient.

> " This spirit shall return to him
> That gave its heavenly spark ;
> Yet think not, sun, it shall be dim,
> When thou thyself art dark !
> No, it shall live again, and shine
> In bliss unknown to beams of thine,
> By him recalled to breath,
> Who captive led captivity,
> Who robbed the grave of victory.
> And took the sting from death !"

A somewhat notable literary character belonging to our good city in the past generation was

ROBERT MACNISH, LL.D.,

the author of *The Anatomy of Drunkenness*, *The Philosophy of Sleep*, and a considerable number of essays and tales contributed to *Blackwood*, *Fraser*, and other magazines. He was born at Glasgow on 15th February, 1802. His father and grandfather were both eminent surgeons of this city, and he himself was trained for the same calling at the High School and University. At an early age he became deeply attached to literature, and at 17 he ventured to send his first literary effort to a periodical then published in Glasgow, and conducted by a divinity student. To his great joy the contribution was accepted, and he was thus encouraged to cultivate his talent for composition with renewed ardour. He furnished poetical pieces as well as prose tales and essays, some of them possessing merit of no mean order. He had, indeed, some difficulty in convincing the editor that they were his own productions. Like most other Glasgow periodicals, this one soon died a premature death. At the age of 18 he received his degree of *Magister Chirurgiæ*, and soon after proceeded to Caithness as an assistant to Dr. Henderson, of Clyth. The wild scenery of that county made a deep impression upon a mind already tinged with a love of the mysterious and sublime, and gave a tone to his subsequent literary productions. During his stay there he contributed some articles to the *Inverness Courier*. His health giving way he returned to Glasgow, visiting on his way home the grand, gloomy, and rugged scenery of Glencoe, which left an impression on his mind that was never effaced. After recruiting his health in some measure, he went to Paris for the purpose of completing his medical studies, and here, among other things, he heard a course of lectures by Gall, the eminent phrenologist. Gall, on one occasion, while treating of the organ of comparison, pointed out Macnish as an instance of its remarkable development. After a stay of about six months in Paris, he returned to Glasgow in 1825, when he received his diploma from the Faculty of Physicians and Surgeons. *The Anatomy of Drunkenness* was presented as his inaugural essay, and was received with much commendation. It was afterwards published by the late Mr. M'Phun. It passed through many editions, and was highly praised by the first critics of the day, and was subsequently greatly enlarged. He at this time began to contribute to *Blackwood's Magazine*. His first story was entitled "Metempsychosis," which evinced some of the weird and mystical characteristics of his mind, and created quite a sensation. He continued for several years a regular contributor to *Blackwood* under the *nom de plume* of "Modern Pythagorean." Among his other contributions there successively appeared—"The Man with the Nose," "The Man with the Mouth," "The Barber of Gottingen," "Colonel O'Shaughnessy," "The Man Mountain," and a variety of others. Some of these quaint, humorous, and sometimes grotesque stories were afterwards published in *Tales from Blackwood*. He dashed off "The Barber of Gottingen" in one night after returning from an evening party. The idea occurred to him on his way home; he sat up all night, and did not stop till he brought it to a conclusion. He was immediately after attacked with a fever which brought him to the brink of the grave. All his stories bear the mark of original genius. His connection with *Blackwood* soon brought him into contact with Professor Wilson, "Delta" (D. M. Moir), De Quincey, Aird, Hogg, and other famous literary men connected with "Old Ebony," and he occasionally joined their carousals at

Ambrose's, and now and then figured in the "Noctes Ambrosianæ." He became particularly intimate with Moir, towards whom he cherished to the last the warmest friendship.

His grandfather having died, he went into partnership with his father, and relaxing somewhat his literary efforts, he devoted himself to his profession with much success. But subsequently he resumed his literary work, and contributed several tales and poems to the *Forget Me Not* and *Friendship's Offering*. Of these we may mention "The Vision of Robert the Bruce" and "The Covenanters," both displaying great versatility and power. "The Covenanters" was dramatised, and performed at the English Opera House, London, where it had a long and successful run. He also wrote his great work, *The Philosophy of Sleep*, which was published by Mr. M'Phun in 1830. It is a most remarkable work, full of acute, subtle reasoning, and strange, mysterious illustration. His glowing fancy and eloquent diction lent a charm to subjects generally uninviting, and dull, dry details were invested with life and interest by the touch of his genius. To *Fraser's Magazine* he contributed one of his best stories—"Singular Passage in my own Life," and a clever burlesque, which he called "The Philosophy of Burking." He also sent to *Fraser* a great variety of humorous poems, many of them extremely good. Of his other fugitive pieces may be mentioned—"The Victims of Sensibility," "Terence O'Flagherty," "The Red Man," "Death and the Fisherman," and "The Psychological Curiosity." In 1834 he published his "Book of Aphorisms," and in the same and following year he travelled through a part of Scotland and over a considerable portion of the Continent of Europe. His health, however, gave way some time afterwards, and he was cut off with typhoid fever, after a short illness, on the 16th January, 1837, greatly regretted by all who knew him.

In person Mr. Macnish was about 5 feet 8 inches high, and although rather slightly formed, he possessed extraordinary muscular strength and activity. He excelled in gymnastics and pugilism. His head was uncommonly large, and not remarkably symmetrical. His brow was high and expansive, his complexion dark, and his large expressive eye indicated shrewdness and benevolence. His temper was naturally violent, but he kept it under strict control. In general society he was silent and reserved; with commonplace men he seldom shone; hence it was a surprise to many that he should display so much talent in his writings. But among congenial friends he was full of life, frolic, and playfulness, and in humorous description he was without a rival. He had great command of countenance, and the mock gravity and earnestness with which he detailed some ludicrous occurrence, bringing in one laughable illustration after another, were irresistible. His remains were interred in the burial ground of St. Andrew's Episcopal Church, Glasgow.

TWO REMARKABLE DREAMS.

The following illustrations, taken from *The Philosophy of Sleep*, will give a slight idea of the character of that work, and may be otherwise interesting:—"I lately dreamed," he says, "that I walked upon the banks of the Great Canal in the neighbourhood of Glasgow. On the side opposite to that on which I was, and within a few feet of the water, stood the splendid portico of the Royal Exchange. A gentleman, whom I knew, was standing upon one of the steps, and we spoke to each other. I then lifted a large stone, and poised it in my hand, when he said that he was sure I could not throw it to a certain spot which he pointed out. I made the attempt, and fell short of the mark. At this moment a well known friend came up whom I knew to excel in *putting* the stone; but strange to say, he had lost both his legs, and walked upon wooden substitutes. This struck me as exceedingly curious, for my impression was that he had only lost one leg, and had but a single wooden one. At my desire he took up the stone, and without difficulty threw it beyond the point indicated. The absurdity of this dream," he continues, "is exceedingly glaring, and yet, on strictly analysing it, I find it to be wholly composed of ideas which passed through my mind on the previous day assuming a new and ridiculous arrangement. For instance, I had on the above day taken a walk to the canal with a friend. On returning I pointed out to him a spot where a new road was forming, and where, a few days before, one of the workmen had been overwhelmed by a quantity of rubbish falling upon him, which fairly chopped off one of his legs, and so much damaged the other that it was feared amputation would be necessary. Near this very spot there is a park in which, about a month previously, I practised throwing the stone. On passing the Exchange on my way home I expressed regret at the lowness of its situation, and remarked what a fine effect the portico would have were it placed upon more elevated ground." By applying these facts to his dream in a very interesting manner, the writer comes to the conclusion that if it were possible to analyse all dreams, they would invariably be found to stand in relation to the waking state as the above specimen.

The following story of a dream is a more remarkable one, and though it does not relate to Glasgow, may be given as a further illustration of Mr. Macnish's work:—About the year 1731, a Mr. D., of K——, in the county of Cumberland, came to Edinburgh to attend the classes, and resided with his uncle and aunt, Major and Mrs. Griffiths, during the winter. When spring arrived, Mr. D. and three or four young gentlemen from England made parties to all the neighbouring places about Edinburgh. Coming home one evening, Mr. D. said, "We have made a party to go a-fishing to Inchkeith to-morrow, if the morning is fine, and have bespoke our boat: we shall be off at six." No objection being made, they separated for the night. Mrs. Griffiths had not been long asleep, till she screamed out in the most violent and agitated manner, "The boat is sinking; save, oh, save them!" The Major awaked her, and said, "Were you uneasy about the fishing party?" "Oh, no," said she, "I had not once thought of it." She then composed herself, and soon fell asleep again; in about an hour she cried in a dreadful fright, "I see the boat is going down." The Major again awoke her, and she said, "It has been owing to the other dream I had; for I feel no uneasiness about it." After some conversation, they both fell sound asleep, but no rest could be obtained for her; in the most extreme agony, she again screamed, "They are gone; the boat is sunk!" When the Major awaked her, she said, "Now I cannot rest; Mr. D. must not go, for I feel, should he go, I would be miserable till his return; the thought of it would almost kill me." She instantly arose, threw on her wrapping-gown, went to his bedside, and with great difficulty she got his promise for her sake to remain at home. . . .

The morning came in most beautifully, and continued so till three o'clock, when a violent storm arose, and in an instant the boat, and all that were in it, went to the bottom, and were never heard of.

It is somewhat disappointing to find the author saying that the remarkable coincidence here given, between the dream and the succeeding calamity, "like all other instances of the kind, must be referred to chance." It is evident that Mr. Macnish was no great believer in the supernatural.

It has been customary to associate the name of that excellent poet and *litterateur*,

WILLIAM MOTHERWELL,

with the neighbouring town of Paisley; but, in point of fact, he was a native of Glasgow, having been born there on the 13th October, 1797. His father was an ironmonger in the city. He was, however, educated partly in Edinburgh and partly in Paisley. In the former, he had for a school companion Jeanie Morrison, a beautiful young girl, who sat on the same form with him, and was at once the object of his first love, and the inspirer of one of the tenderest love songs of our Scottish muse. At the age of 15, young Motherwell was placed as a clerk in the office of the Sheriff-Clerk in Paisley, and at the early age of 21 he became Sheriff-Clerk Depute in that town. During the Radical commotions of 1818, he was furiously attacked by a mob, who were incensed against him for discharging his official duties, and he made a narrow escape of being thrown over the bridge into the river Cart. Up to this time he had "dreamed his dream of liberty," like many another ardent youth; but this incident cooled his Liberalism and he became a Conservative.

He was early devoted to literature, and wrote many poems and prose contributions for various magazines. He edited in 1819 the *Harp of Renfrewshire*, containing biographical notices of the poets of that county, from the sixteenth to the nineteenth century, and eight years afterwards he published in Glasgow a more important work entitled, *Minstrelsy: Ancient and Modern*. He was also editor of two Paisley newspapers, the *Paisley Magazine* and the *Paisley Advertiser*. Subsequently he succeeded Mr. James M'Queen in the editorship of the *Glasgow Courier*, an excellent journal in its day. This office he held from 1830 till his death in November, 1835. In addition to his onerous and often thankless duties as an editor of a Tory paper in a strongly Radical city, he contributed to a short-lived Glasgow magazine called *The Day*, edited by our late talented City Chamberlain, Dr. Strang, besides doing a great deal of other literary work. He was joined with Hogg, the Ettrick Shepherd, in preparing an edition of Burns' Works; he engaged in collecting a number of Norse Legends; and composed a large number of his longest and best poems. He was employed in collecting materials for a life of Tannahill, when he was suddenly cut off by a fit of apoplexy at the early age of 38. He was buried in the Glasgow Necropolis, and the large numbers of persons of all classes of political opinion, who attended his funeral, gave evidence of the affectionate esteem with which he was regarded. The taste, enthusiasm, and social qualities of Motherwell rendered him very popular among his townsmen and friends. As an antiquary, he was shrewd, indefatigable, and truthful. As a poet, he was happiest in pathetic or sentimental lyrics, though his own inclinations led him to prefer the chivalrous and martial style of the old minstrels. Among his larger productions may be mentioned the *Battle-flag of Sigurd*, and the *Sword-chant of Thorstein Raudi;* while his songs, *My heid is like to rend, Willie*, the *Midnight Wind*, and above all, *Jeanie Morrison*, will live as long as our language exists. Had he lived longer and devoted less of his time to the harassing work of journalism, he would doubtless have raised his name to the highest rank of Scottish poets.

JOHN STRANG, LL.D.,

City Chamberlain, author of the celebrated *Glasgow and its Clubs*, and of several other excellent works, was a Glasgow man in every sense of the word. He was born there in the year 1795. His father, John Strang, of Dowanhill, was a merchant of our city; and his mother, Miss M'Gilp, was the daughter of a substantial Glasgow trader. At the age of 14 his father died, and young Strang succeeded to his business of a wine merchant; but he had no taste for it, and it dwindled away in his hands. He was more interested in the acquisition of languages, of which he became a proficient in the French, German, and Italian. He visited France and Italy in 1817, and from that time, for many years, he took a trip to the Continent almost every summer. He translated tales and poems from the German and other foreign works, and was also a regular contributor on art and literature to the *Scots Times* (a Glasgow paper), the *Scotsman*, and other journals. Under the *nom de plume* of "Geoffrey Crayon, Jr.," he published a small volume entitled, *A Glance at the Exhibition of the Works of Living Artists, under the Patronage of the Glasgow Dilettanti Society*, which was greatly admired at the time for the acuteness and soundness of its art criticisms at a period when art was not so much appreciated in our city as it is now. Mr. Strang was also an artist himself, and would have excelled had he devoted his attention more to its practical study. As an indication of his love for his native city, it may be stated that the subjects of his brush were the quaint buildings of the old town, which were gradually being demolished by the improving habits of the age. In 1831 Dr. Strang suggested the plan of transforming the unsightly and useless hill called the Fir Park into a city of the dead, after the style of the "Père la Chaise" of Paris, in a small volume entitled, *Necropolis Glasguensis*, and his suggestion was successfully carried into execution in the formation of our noble Necropolis. At the close of his life his parting wish was expressed to one of his friends in the following words:—"I should like my bones to be laid in the Glasgow Necropolis, in the establishment of which, it is well known, I took so active and so zealous a part. If the Merchants' House would grant me and my wife a small last resting place, as a recognition of my labours connected with the cemetery, you will, of course, accept it; if not, you must purchase one." It is needless to say that this pathetic request was cordially granted. As we have already seen, Dr. Strang started the publication of *The Day*. This was in 1832, and *The Day* was an eight-page daily newspaper. It was the first daily newspaper published in Glasgow, but it was rather more of a literary than a news-paper. It lasted only six months. In 1834 Dr. Strang was appointed City Chamberlain, and held that important office for the long period of thirty years. His annual volumes on the *Vital Statistics of Glasgow* were perfect models of their kind, full of the most valuable information of all matters relating to the people of the city and their multifarious interests. But the most interesting of all Dr. Strang's literary productions was *Glasgow and its Clubs*, published in 1855. A more racy, quaint, and delightful series of descriptive sketches was surely never written of any city than that. The *genus* Glasgow citizen is there drawn to the life. The period covered by these sketches—from 1750 down to 1832—was perhaps the most interesting in the history of our city, and the glimpses given of the manners and habits of our citizens during that period are of the most graphic and enthralling character. The rough, boisterous humour, the jovial sociality, the keen trading instincts, the exuberant animal spirits, the ardent loyalty and the devotedness to the interests of their city of the merchants, lawyers, and professors, are in this volume presented in the most complete manner by one of the shrewdest, kindliest, and most genial of observers; and all through, the work abounds in richly illustrative anecdote and antiquarian notes. The style of writing is excellent throughout, and evinces not only the literary artist, but the accomplished scholar. No book is, even yet, more popular with our Glasgow readers, and old, battered copies of *Glasgow and its Clubs* no sooner appear in our second-hand book shops than they are bought up with avidity. Three editions of it have been published. In 1842 Dr. Strang married the daughter of Dr. William Anderson, an eminent physician of Glasgow; and soon afterwards the honorary degree of LL.D. was conferred upon him by our University. In the summer of 1863, in consequence of failing health, he revisited France and Italy, and contributed a series of letters to the *Glasgow Herald* giving interesting sketches of the scenes of his travel. It was thought that the efforts thus put forth aggravated his disease, and he returned home only to die. In the autumn of that year he received from his admiring and attached fellow-citizens a princely testimonial in the shape of £4,600, but he did not live long to enjoy the munificent gift. He died on the 8th December, 1863, in the 69th year of his age.

WILLIAM GLEN,

author of that beautiful, plaintive Jacobite song, "Oh! wae's me for Prince Charlie," was a native of Glasgow, having been born there in the year 1786. His father was an eminent merchant of the city, and William himself began his business life as a manufacturer. But he was better at weaving metres than weaving muslins, and the result was that while he was looked upon as a passable poet, he had the misfortune of tasting the "bitterness of adversity," like so many more of the "jingling brotherhood." In addition to his popular Jacobite song—and its popularity has not yet diminished—Mr. Glen wrote a patriotic song entitled "The Battle of Vittoria," which was long a favourite. But he was also the author of a large number of other poetical effusions written for special occasions, the interest in which has now faded away. He was a member of the famous "Anderston Social Club," and his presence at the weekly meetings of that fraternity threw a halo of happiness around the heads which wagged chorus to his patriotic songs. The following anecdote is related in connection with the song, "Wae's me for Prince Charlie:"—During a visit of Her Majesty to the North, this song received a mark of royal favour which would have sweetened, had he been alive, poor Glen's bitter cup of life. While at Taymouth Castle, the Marquis of Breadalbane had engaged Mr. Wilson, the celebrated vocalist, to sing before Her Majesty. A list of the songs Mr. Wilson was in the habit of singing was submitted to the Queen that she might signify her choice. She immediately fixed upon the following:—"Lochaber no More," "The Flowers of the Forest," "The Lass o' Gowrie," "John Anderson, my Jo," "Cam' ye by Athole," and "The Laird o' Cockpen." Mr. Glen's song was not in Mr. Wilson's list, but Her Majesty herself asked if he could sing "Wae's me for Prince Charlie," which fortunately he was able to do. Mr. Glen died in 1824. A daughter of his lived to a good old age, and died only a few years ago. For many years she resided in or near the "Clachan of Aberfoyle," and was entrusted by the City of Glasgow Parochial Board with the care of a goodly number of their orphan children under the excellent boarding-out system; and this duty Miss Glen discharged to the entire satisfaction of the Board.

JOHN DONALD CARRICK,

a somewhat famous poet in his day, was born in Glasgow in April, 1787. In his early years he was engaged for some time in the office of an architect, and he appears also to have been for a short period clerk in a counting house. But he was of a restless disposition, and so, in the year 1807, without stating his intention to any one, he left the city, and set out on foot for the great metropolis with only a few shillings in his pocket. Weary and worn he reached the town of Liverpool. On entering the town he met a party of soldiers beating up for recruits for the Peninsular war. He held a council with himself for some time, debating whether he would follow the drum or the route to London. Glory and gain strove for the mastery with such equal claims that, unable to decide the knotty point, he had recourse to a rustic form of divination ; and casting up in the air his trusty cudgel, he resolved to be guided by the direction in which it should fall. As it fell towards the road to London, he conceived the will of the gods to be that he should pursue his journey, with the hope—fully as well founded as that of Whittington—that he might yet be Lord Mayor of that famous city. He arrived in the metropolis with half-a-crown in his pocket. After many vicissitudes in search of employment, a decent tradesman from the Land of Cakes, pricking up his ear at the Doric, took compassion on the friendless lad, and engaged him in his service. He was afterwards engaged in an extensive house in the Staffordshire pottery line of business. He remained altogether about four years in the capital, when he returned to Glasgow in 1811, where he started business in Hutcheson Street for the sale of stoneware, china, &c., and continued in this business for nearly fourteen years. Latterly he turned his attention to literature. In 1825 he published a *Life of Sir William Wallace*, which was written for Constable's Miscellany, and was well received by the public. It has continued a favourite ever since. He was also engaged as sub-editor of the *Scots Times*, and contributed largely to an amusing series of local squibs which appeared in that paper. He was also a contributor to Dr. Strang's paper, *The Day*.

In a clever little work, entitled "Whistle-Binkie," published in 1832 by Mr. David Robertson, and which was a collection of songs and other poetical pieces, chiefly humorous, there appeared several by Mr. Carrick, rich in that peculiar vein of humour in which he excelled. Among these were "The Scottish Tea Party" and "Mister Peter Paterson," which the author used to sing himself to the great delight of his audience. In 1833, he was appointed manager of the *Perth Advertiser*, but only remained eleven months in the Fair City, when he threw up his situation in disgust. On the recommendation of his friend, William Motherwell, he was then appointed conductor of the *Kilmarnock Journal*. But here, too, his evil star was still in the ascendant His powers of keen wit and satire were too much for some of the thin-skinned people of "Auld Killie," and they withdrew their subscriptions from the paper. He was forced to retire from the editorial chair, and return to his native city. Here he contributed some excellent papers to the *Scottish Monthly Magazine* and various other periodicals. Several of his stories afterwards appeared in that famous book of wit and humour, "The Laird of Logan," which was published by David Robertson, and of which Carrick was the projector, editor, and principal contributor. But alas! in a few years more, poor Carrick was in his grave. He died of a painful disease on 17th August, 1837, and was buried in the High Church burying-ground, followed to the grave by many friends, in whose social circle he left a blank not to be easily filled up.

Of this amiable and unfortunate individual it has been said, "that whilst his genius and talents were not of the highest stamp, yet in his own peculiar walk of composition, as a delineator of the humorous phases of human life and manners, in its most minute details, and a skilful analyser of character, in combination with an overflowing humour and comic richness of expression, relieved and exalted by the frequent flashes of a delicate irony, and a pungent sarcasm—few writers have surpassed, and not many have equalled him."

Another Glasgow poet, but of higher genius and more enduring fame,

DUGALD MOORE,

was born in the Stockwell, in August, 1805. His father, a private soldier, died while his son was a mere child, and so great was the poverty of the widow, that Dugald's only education was that which she imparted to him. The seed sown by that worthy woman fell however into good ground, and bare rich fruit. After engaging for a short time in the coarse and not very elevating occupation of a tobacco spinner, young Moore found a situation with Messrs. James Lumsden & Sons, publishers, Queen Street. He early evinced a taste for poetical composition, and in this he was encouraged by his employer, Provost Lumsden. Through this means he was enabled to publish, in 1829, *The African, a Tale, and other poems*, which was received with much favour. Shortly afterwards he published *Scenes from the Flood, the Tenth Plague, and other Poems*. In 1831, he published *The Bridal Night, and other Poems*, a larger and more pretentious work than the others. From the profits derived from these works, Dugald, who had his aged mother to support, opened a bookseller's shop at 96 Queen Street, which became a favourite resort of literary men in the city. While prosecuting this honourable business, he continued to devote his attention to literature, and published in 1833 his famous work, *The Bard of the North*, a series of poetical tales descriptive of Highland scenery and character, which obtained much popularity. This was followed in 1835 by the *Hour of Retribution, and other Poems;* and in 1839, the *Devoted One, and other Poems*. All these works, though written within the compass of a few years, were distinguished by great excellence, and a lofty fancy, energy of feeling, and remarkable powers of versification. But like many other sons of the muse, Mr. Moore's career, so full of intensity of emotion, and of brain energy, was cut short at an early age. He died unmarried, after a brief illness, on the 2nd January, 1841, in the 36th year of his age, leaving his widowed mother in possession of a comfortable competency. He was buried in the *Necropolis*, and over his grave a massive monument surmounted by his bust was erected by his personal friends to perpetuate his memory.

Another literary man of whom our good city has reason to be proud was

JOHN GIBSON LOCKHART,

son-in-law and biographer of Sir Walter Scott. He was born in Glasgow in 1793. His father, Rev. Dr. John

Lockhart, was for nearly fifty years minister of Blackfriars Church, a worthy man, celebrated for his piety and worth, but also notable for two rather different qualities—wit and extreme absence of mind, about which many laughable stories have been told. Young Lockhart was educated at Glasgow and Oxford Universities. He was trained for the bar, but lacked one essential element of success—he was no speaker. When he rose to make a speech, his first sentence was only a plunge into the mud, while all that followed was but a struggle to get out of it. When a trial was going on in which he was supposed to be interested, instead of taking notes of the evidence, he would busy himself in sketching caricatures of the proceedings, the drollery of which would have convulsed both judge and jury with laughter. He made a happy allusion to this infirmity at a dinner given to him in Edinburgh when he was leaving to assume the charge of the *Quarterly Review*. He attempted to address the meeting, and broke down as usual, but covered his retreat with—" Gentlemen, you know that if I could speak we would not have been here."

Unsuited for the law he devoted himself to literature, and here he found his true vocation. He was a regular contributor to *Blackwood's Magazine*. He wrote, about the year 1817, a series of eloquent, vigorous, and truthful sketches on the distinguished Scotsmen of the period. These sketches were entitled *Peter's Letters to his Kinsfolk*, and were received with the highest commendation from all classes, although, from the keenness of their criticisms, they also provoked a good deal of angry comment. In May, 1818, he formed the acquaintanceship of Sir Walter Scott, through which he was introduced to Sir Walter's eldest daughter, Sophia, to whom he was married in April, 1820. The young couple took up their abode at the little cottage of Chiefswood, near Abbotsford, which became their summer residence. Here the great Wizard often retired, glad of a release from the worry of visitors and sightseers, who crowded to view him and the scenes he had immortalized.

In addition to his numerous contributions to *Blackwood*, Mr. Lockhart began to write and publish separate works with a fertility that seemed to have been inspired by that of his father-in-law. Among these were *Valerius*, one of the most classical tales of ancient Rome that has ever been written in the English language. Then followed a most interesting Scotch story entitled *Adam Blair;* *Reginald Dalton*, a three-volume novel containing reminiscences of student life at Oxford; and *Matthew Wald*, another novel, which fully sustained the high literary ability of the author. After a short interval, Lockhart came out in the new character of a poet by his *Ancient Spanish Ballads*, and in this field he was no less successful than in that of prose. He next turned his attention to biography, and produced an able *Life of Robert Burns* and a *Life of Napoleon Bonaparte*. But his greatest success in this department was his *Life of Sir Walter Scott*, which we have no hesitation in saying is one of the very best and most delightful biographies in the language. In 1825 Mr. Lockhart was appointed editor of the *Quarterly Review*, the great champion of Toryism in England, which office he filled for the long period of 28 years—viz., from 1826 to 1853. He conducted this magazine with consummate ability; but his trenchant criticisms, keen powers of satire, and pungent wit frequently brought him into trouble with authors whose works he reviewed. One of these quarrels became so serious that it resulted in bloodshed, and this doubtless tended to embitter the later years of our author. In 1853 he resigned the editorship of the *Quarterly* with his health seriously impaired, and he spent the following winter in Italy. But the maladies under which he suffered, although assuaged for a time, came back with redoubled violence on his return, and he died at Abbotsford—which had now become the seat of his son-in-law, Mr. Hope Scott—on the 25th November, 1854.

It may be interesting to notice that it was to Mr. Lockhart's son, "Master Hugh Littlejohn" that the celebrated "Tales of a Grandfather" were addressed. The lad was then in the sixth year of his age. He died in 1831. Mrs. Lockhart herself died in 1837. His other and only remaining son Walter Scott Lockhart Scott died in 1853.

We append one of the shorter of Mr. Lockhart's *Spanish Ballads:*—

MINGUILLO

"Since for kissing thee, Minguillo,
My mother scolds me all the day,
Let me have it quickly, darling!
Give me back the Kiss, I pray.

" If we have done aught amiss,
Let's undo it while we may,
Quickly give me back the Kiss,
That she may have naught to say.

" Do! She keeps so great a pother,
Chides so sharply, looks so grave;
Do, my love, to please my mother,
Give me back the Kiss I gave."

" Out upon you, false Minguillo!
One you give, but two you take;"
" Give me back the two, my darling!
Give them, for my mother's sake."

Another pleasing and able author of this period was ALEXANDER WHITELAW, who was born in Glasgow about the year 1798, and died there in 1846. He was assistant to Dr. Robert Watt in the preparation of the *Bibliotheca Britannica*, and wrote a number of the lives in Chambers' *Biographical Dictionary of Eminent Scotsmen*. He edited the *Casquet of Literary Gems* and the *Republic of Letters*—two admirable works, containing selections from the works of the best authors. The *Book of Scottish Song*—the most complete collection of Scottish songs yet published; and the *Book of Scottish Ballads*, which included the collections of Scott, Motherwell, Jamieson, and Peter Buchan. He was the author of St. Kentigern, a tale of the City of St. Mungo, and of many other poems and prose sketches. Good taste and a sincere devotion to literature are apparent in his work; and he was among the first to recognize and to proclaim the genius of Wordsworth. His "Tale of the Old Gorbals" in the *Casquet* is one of the most charming stories relating to old Glasgow, of the sixteenth century, we have ever read, and we only regret that our space will not admit of transferring it to our pages.

GEORGE OUTRAM, was born in Glasgow on 25th March, 1805, and died there in 1856. He was a worthy successor of the famous Samuel Hunter, in the editorship of the

Glasgow Herald, of which also Outram was one of the proprietors. He was called to the bar in 1827, but devoted his time and talents to his editorial and literary work. He wrote a number of humorous and satirical verses, of which a collection was published by Blackwood, and more recently under the editorial supervision of the late Mr. Stoddart. One of the most racy and popular of these is entitled—*The Annuity*, an exquisite piece of caustic humour.

One of the most popular and beloved of Glasgow literary men of modern times was the celebrated "Rambler,"

Hugh Macdonald,

who was born in Rumford Street, Bridgeton, on 4th April, 1817. His parents were in humble circumstances, and were unable to give their son a very liberal education. He was apprenticed to the block-printing trade in the works of Messrs. Henry Monteith & Co., at Barrowfield, at an early age. But the education which he did not derive from books, he acquired in his young days from nature. He was familiar with every hill and dale from Mearns Moor to Campsie Glen, and had explored the whole course of the Clyde from Stonebyres Linn to Bowling Braes. The whole of Clydesdale was dear to "the Rambler." One of his favourite haunts was the "guid auld toon" of Rutherglen, with the Cathkin Braes in its vicinity. From this town he obtained both of his wives, and the fine scenery of the " Braes " would possess an enhanced charm to his poetic eyes, from the fact that in his rambles there he would have the sweet society of first one and then another of these fair maidens in the happy courting days.

Macdonald was frugal and industrious in his habits, and having saved a little money at his trade, he embarked it in a grocery and provision shop in Bridgeton. But this was a line for which he was entirely unsuited. His nature was too open and generous to conduct a huckstering business with profit to himself. Not only did he deal fairly and honestly with his customers, but he gave credit to all who asked it. The result may easily be guessed. He was compelled to relinquish the trade, after having lost all his earnings in bad debts. He returned to the block-printing, and found employment at Colinslie, near Paisley. He continued to reside in

Bridgeton, however, and walked to and from his work, a distance in all of sixteen miles every day. Not only in fair weather and bright sunshine, but amid pelting storms of wind and rain did our author trudge on foot from Bridgeton to Paisley and back, and regularly completed his ten or twelve hours of arduous physical exertion every day. It was about this time, too, that his literary life may be said to have begun. His first effusions were poetical, and appeared in the *Chartist Circular*, a periodical of Ultra-Radical views. A nobler field was soon opened for him in the columns of the *Glasgow Citizen*, edited by that true poet and friend of poets, James Hedderwick. In the *Citizen*, he, in a series of letters, defended the character of Robert Burns from an attack made upon it by that literary free-lance, George Gilfillan, of Dundee. Macdonald appears to have come out of the controversy with flying colours. He became a regular contributor to the *Citizen*, and some of his sweetest poems appeared in its "poets' corner." About this time he obtained an interview with the famous John Wilson—Christopher North—of which he has left an interesting account. In 1849, Macdonald obtained a permanent situation as sub-editor of the *Citizen*, and became a voluminous contributor both in prose and verse to its pages. Among others may be mentioned his famous "Rambles round Glasgow," under the *nom-de-plume* of "Caleb," which have long been exceedingly popular with his fellow-citizens, and have run through several editions in volume form. In the *Citizen* also he commenced his equally interesting "Days at the Coast," but these were completed in the columns of the *Glasgow Times*, as he had by that time severed his connection with the *Citizen*, and joined the staff of the *Glasgow Sentinel*, owned and edited by Mr. Buchanan, father of the celebrated poet of the present day, Robert Buchanan. These two works are full of fine poetical descriptions of scenery, along with interesting topographical and antiquarian information. They have become handbooks to successive generations of Glasgow pleasure seekers, and have also given rise to a Modern Glasgow Club of the better sort, "The Ramblers," who tread the footsteps of the "gentle Caleb" with devoted zeal and affectionate remembrance. Macdonald was an intense lover of the Clyde with all its beauties, and never wearied of singing its praises. In a poem to the Clyde, he says :—

"O'er all the streams that Scotia pours
  Deep murmuring to the sea,
With warmest love my heart still turns,
  Fair, winding Clyde to thee !
Through scenes where brightest beauty smiles,
  Thy placid waters glide,
Linked to a thousand mem'ries sweet,
  My own, my native Clyde !

. . . .

"Dear stream, long may thy hills be green,
  Thy woods in beauty wave,
Thy daughters still be chaste and fair,
  Thy sons be true and brave !
And oh ! when from this weary heart,
  Has ebbed life's purple tide.
May it be mine, 'mongst those I've loved,
  To rest on thy green side."

In June, 1858, when the *Morning Journal* was started by Mr. Robert Somers, that gentleman succeeded in engaging Mr. Macdonald for the literary department of the paper, and in this connection he continued till it was brought to a melancholy and abrupt termination by death on 16th March, 1860. Before transferring his services to the new daily, the " Rambler " was entertained to a public dinner in the Royal Hotel, George Square, which was presided over by Mr. James Hedderwick, and attended by a number of mercantile, literary, and artistic friends. In January, 1860, Macdonald commenced in the *Morning Journal* a series of papers entitled " Footsteps of the Year," which were to be continued on through all the months of that year. But alas ! they came to a premature end with the second month of the year. Early in March he had made a pilgrimage to Castlemilk to see the snowdrops, for, like summer at the " Castle o' Montgomerie," there they are first unfolded, and there they " langest tarry," and he returned, took to his bed, and before his last illness was generally known, he expired in the 43rd year of his age, leaving a widow and family of one son and four daughters in comparative poverty. He left a policy of insurance on his life for £100, but that was insufficient to support and educate his family. In these circumstances his numerous friends and admirers came to their aid, and generously raised a testimonial of £900 on their behalf.

"Hugh Macdonald was possessed of all the characteristics of a true poet. His love of nature in all its moods, his intense love of flowers and birds, his tenderness of feeling and sympathy for humanity, his manly independence of spirit, his warm social qualities, and his fine literary instincts all combine in forming a character resembling in a remarkable degree that of his great countryman and forerunner, Robert Burns, of whom he was an ardent admirer, and at whose torch his own lamp was to a large extent kindled, though he had a genius and talent peculiarly his own. Many of his poems will linger in the memories and hearts of his countrymen as long as true Scottish song preserves its deserved popularity."

We have already alluded to his marriages. A pathetic interest attaches to both. His first wife was named Agnes and his second Alison. The former died within a year after their marriage, and was buried in the Southern Necropolis with a new-born babe in her bosom. The lady who became his second wife was bridesmaid at his first marriage, and it was the dying wish of his first spouse that if he married again he should wed her dearest friend. He entertained the warmest affection for this excellent woman, although he retained to the last a deep and lasting love for the wife of his youth. Whenever Burns's pathetic song of "My Nannie's awa'" was sung in Hugh's presence he shed silent tears, as he had a green remembrance of his own beloved Agnes.

Another illustration of his kindly heart will have a deep interest for our Glasgow readers. In the course of his ramblings through the country he had made the acquaintance of James Aitken, the Scottish tragedian and elocutionist, father of the highly esteemed Miss Maggie Aitken (now Mrs. Buntine), who has long been a favourite with Glasgow audiences as an actress and reader. Mr. Aitken was once a great actor in his way. In such characters as *Wandering Steenie*, in "The Rose of Ettrick Vale," he has never been surpassed. Latterly, however, he fell into poverty, and died at Paisley. The famous actor was kindly aided to the last by the generous interposition of the Bridgeton block printer, who buried his unfortunate friend at his own expense when but a working man. Miss Aitken cherished a warm regard for Mr. Macdonald ever afterwards, and repaid his kindness by speaking Mr. Hedderwick's beautiful prologue and acting with the Press Amateurs for the benefit of his widow.

SIR ARCHIBALD ALISON, BART.,

though not native-born, may well be claimed as a citizen of Glasgow, for he occupied the onerous and responsible office of Sheriff of Lanarkshire for the long period of thirty years. He was born at Kenley, in Shropshire, on 29th December, 1792, his father being then curate there. But the father removed with his family to Edinburgh in 1800, where he had charge of the Episcopal Church in Cowgate. Mr. Alison was famed in literary circles for his " Essays on the nature and principles of taste." Young Archibald went to the University of Edinburgh in 1805, and was at first intended for civil engineering and then for the banking business. But in 1808 he produced an " Essay on Population," and then he turned his attention to law, and studied for the Scottish bar. He visited Paris in 1814 when it was occupied by the allied troops, and the imposing spectacles there witnessed by him, seem to have suggested to his mind the great idea of writing a History of Europe. But the first pages of that famous work were not written till 1st January, 1829. In the interval he had made good progress in his profession. He was called to the bar in December, 1814, and within three years he was earning an income of £500 to £600 a year. He was made an advocate-depute in 1823, with good hopes of becoming Solicitor-General and ultimately Lord Advocate. But through some wire-pulling or favouritism he was disappointed in these hopes, and in 1830 he was even obliged to resign his advocate-deputeship, and all prospects of promotion in that direction. He turned his attention to literature to eke out his income at the bar. He wrote a work on Criminal Law, for the first edition of which he received from Blackwood 200 guineas. He also contributed political articles to *Blackwood's Magazine* during 1831, and in April 1835 the first two volumes of his History was published by Blackwood, who gave him 250 guineas for the first thousand copies. In December, 1834, Mr. Rose Robinson, Sheriff of Lanarkshire died, and Mr. Alison applied for the vacant office, and was appointed by Sir Robert Peel in February, 1835, at a salary of £1,400 a year.

Sheriff Alison took up his residence at Possil House, which he occupied during the whole of his after life. But his office at that time was on the second floor of a humble tenement in Stockwell; a wholesale whisky store being on the ground floor, and a barber's shop on the first. Within six months of his appointment he was called upon to suppress, at the head of a troop of horse, a formidable riot at Airdrie. In 1837, there was a great commercial panic in Glasgow and neighbourhood, complicated with an extensive strike among the cotton spinners and coal miners. About 80,000 destitute persons were let loose upon the community, and to cope with these, there was a police force of only 280 men. On 22nd July of that year, one of the "new hands" employed by the masters was shot dead on the streets. The masters offered a reward of £500 for the apprehension of the murderers, and three days afterwards two informers met Sheriff Alison by appointment in a vault under the Old College, and disclosed to him a plot for the murder of all the "new hands," and the masters one by one. Having ascertained the meeting place of the conspirators, the Sheriff at nine o'clock on a Saturday night, armed only with a walking stick, and accompanied by Mr. Salmond, fiscal, Captain Miller, and a number of policemen, proceeded to the "Black Boy Close," a vile den in Gallowgate, near the Cross. The room where the meeting was being held entered by a trap-door in the floor, through which Captain Miller passed, followed by the sheriff, the fiscal, and one sheriff officer. To prevent the light being extinguished Sheriff Alison took his post below the solitary gas jet. Then the Superintendent of Police called out each one of the panic-stricken conspirators by name, and handed them one by one over to the police. Not a blow required to be struck, so firmly and deliberately did the officials go about their work. On the Monday following the cotton spinners met on the Green and resolved to go in on their master's terms; and on Tuesday the factories were in full swing and peace was completely restored. The would-be assassins got seven years' transportation. Sheriff Alison was also actively employed in quelling the "Bread Riots" of 1848.

He also performed the dangerous and difficult task of conveying the two malefactors, Denis Doolan and his companion—who had been condemned for murdering their "ganger," or foreman, at Bishopbriggs, where they had been engaged in the formation of the Edinburgh and Glasgow Railway—from the Glasgow Jail to the place of execution, on the spot where the murder took place, and returning to the city with their dead bodies. A great deal of excitement was created by this execution, and so afraid were the authorities that a riot would take place, that 1,800 troops and two field guns were massed at the place of execution during the previous night. But the Sheriff discharged his duty with his usual nerve and coolness, while, it is said, the magistrates of Glasgow remained safely within the shelter of the courtyard of the jail!

But Sheriff Alison was privileged to perform more pleasant duties than these. He had the honour of being specially appointed to escort the Queen through the streets of Glasgow during her first visit to the city, in 1849, and to point out to Her Majesty all the notable sights that were to be seen, including the College Buildings, the Cathedral, &c. And perhaps no one was better qualified for the task than he. In 1845 he was elected Lord Rector of the Marischal College, Aberdeen, and in 1851 he was chosen to the same high office for the University of Glasgow. In 1853 he received his baronetcy, which he wore with much grace and dignity. During these years his elaborate *History* had been appearing in volumes, and its fame spread not only over his native country, but on the Continent, and even at a much greater distance. It was translated into French, German, Hindostani, and Arabic, and his reputation as a solid, if not a brilliant, historian was surely established. He, moreover, wrote many essays on "Population," "Currency," &c., and his autobiography was published after his death. He died at Possil House on 23rd May, 1867, and was buried in Dean Cemetery, Edinburgh, beside Cockburn, Jeffrey, and other eminent men of the learned metropolis. His wife— who was a granddaughter of William Tytler, the literary champion of Mary, Queen of Scots—survived him, but died in Edinburgh on 5th October, 1874. His son, Sir Archibald, has distinguished himself as a soldier in the Crimea, India, and Egypt. On his return from the last-named field of action a few years ago, he was presented with a valuable sword by his fellow-citizens in the City Hall.

Although the name of

HENRY GLASSFORD BELL

is not so famous even in the realm of literature as that of his predecessor in the Sheriffdom, yet it is generally admitted that he was the finer genius of the two, and possessed mental and social qualities that more endeared him to his fellow-citizens. He was born in Glasgow on 5th November, 1803, and was the son of a Scottish advocate, who held for some time the post of town clerk of Greenock. Henry followed his father's profession, and was admitted to the Scottish Bar in 1832. His literary taste appeared early in life. He was still in his *teens* when he started a penny paper in Edinburgh with the pedantic title of *Lapsus Linguæ*, He subsequently made a more ambitious literary venture in 1828 —viz., the *Edinburgh Literary Journal, a Weekly Register of Criticism and Belles Lettres*, in which he had the support of such eminent men as John Wilson, James Hogg, and Thomas Aird. But this venture did not succeed, and ultimately, his *Register* was merged in *Tait's Edinburgh Weekly Chronicle*. He afterwards wrote a *Life of Mary, Queen of Scots*, in two volumes, in which he valiantly defended the beautiful queen from the aspersions that had been cast upon her character. In 1831, he published his first volume of poems, entitled *Summer and Winter Hours*, which contained many excellent pieces, amongst which was his ever popular poem of "Mary, Queen of Scots," which is even yet a familiar subject of reading or recitation at social gatherings. In 1866, he published a second volume of poetry entitled *Romances and Minor Poems;* while, in 1865, he wrote a biography of Shakespeare which was prefixed to an edition of that great writer's works, issued under Sheriff Bell's care.

In his younger Edinburgh days, Mr. Bell enjoyed the friendship of many of our best literary characters, and could relate many racy stories of his intercourse with them. He could tell how he had handed the kettle to Joanna Baillie to make her tea, had danced with Letitia Landon, and had walked round the Calton Hill in the moonlight with Mrs. Hemans. He was on intimate terms with Professor Wilson, who immortalized him in the *Noctes* by the name of "Tallboys." Like Wilson, he was a member of the "Six Foot Club," a great chess player, and an enthusiastic angler.

Another of his literary reminiscences was that while a young man, he was present at that ever memorable banquet in connection with the Bannatyne Club, held on the 23rd February, 1826, when Sir Walter Scott publicly pled guilty to the authorship of the Waverley Novels.

In 1838, Mr. Bell was appointed Sheriff-Substitute for Lanarkshire in Glasgow, and on the death of Sheriff Alison in 1867, he was promoted to the office of Sheriff-Principal. He was greatly esteemed in this city. Though not regarded as an erudite, technical lawyer, yet he was richly endowed with a sound judgment and a strong sense of justice and rectitude. He was also an eloquent speaker, and no one was more sought after at public dinners and other gatherings than the genial sheriff. He was courteous, dignified, and gentlemanly in the old fashioned sense of the term, but in the social circle he was full of *bonhommie* and humour. Towards the end of his life, he suffered severely from cancer in the right hand, latterly necessitating its amputation. An attempt was made to obtain for him a temporary release from business while still holding his legal office, but to the lasting discredit of the Right Honourable Robert Lowe (now Lord Sherbrooke), who was then Home Secretary, the reasonable request was refused, and he was asked to send in his resignation. But death stepped in and kindly saved the tender-hearted noble sheriff from hearing of this brutal message. He died on the 7th January, 1874, and was buried in the nave of our grand old cathedral.

Had space permitted we had purposed giving sketches and reminiscences of several of our best known poets and literary men of the present day, and who are happily still among us: but this is now out of the question, and we must content ourselves with the briefest possible references to only a few of these. Foremost among them is the esteemed proprietor and editor of the *Citizen*, JAMES HEDDERWICK, LL.D., who is not only a poet of superior talent, but has also been for a long series of years the patron and friend of struggling genius in our city. Dr. Hedderwick was born in Glasgow in 1814. His father was latterly queen's printer in the city, and put his son to work in his establishment at an early age. He, however, was afterwards educated in London at the University, where he highly distinguished himself. When he was in his 23rd year he became sub-editor of the *Scotsman*. He returned to Glasgow in 1842, and started the *Citizen*, and this journal—which in its early days was *the* literary newspaper of Glasgow, and is still represented in that character by the *Weekly Citizen*—he has conducted with marked ability ever since, though of late years he has partially retired to his " Villa by the Sea " at Helensburgh, where he has devoted his leisure time to the cultivation of the muse. He has published several volumes of excellent verse, one of them so far back as 1844. In 1859 he published his "Lays of Middle Age and other poems," which established his name as a poet of fine taste and melodious beauty. A few years ago he published his " Villa by the Sea, and other poems," containing the mellowed fruits of his riper years, and amply sustaining his reputation. A good many years ago he started a literary magazine, entitled *Hedderwick's Miscellany*, and was assisted by some of the finest young spirits in the West of Scotland. But somehow or other, Glasgow has never been able to sustain for any length of time a purely literary magazine of its own, and the *Miscellany* had only a brief existence. Our city, however, owes much to Dr. Hedderwick for the healthy, manly, impartial tone of the *Citizen*, and the labour expended on that journal by our author can never be computed. As already stated, too, he has done much good in the way of gathering round him, and bringing into notice a goodly number of our most talented young men, and giving them their first start in their bright career of literary achievement and fame.

Perhaps one of his most brilliant pupils is the popular novelist, WILLIAM BLACK, whom we are proud to own as one of our native-born men of genius. He began his literary career in the office of the *Citizen*, and many of his earliest productions appeared in its pages. We remember hearing that Mr. Black at one time resided in humble lodgings in the classic village of Strathbungo. He had a taste for art as well as literature in his young days, and studied at the Glasgow School of Arts. At the age of 23, he removed to London, and shortly afterwards joined the staff of the *Morning Star*, when he was sent as special correspondent to the seat of the Franco-German War. On his return he wrote his first novel, " In Silk Attire," and soon after became editor of the *London Review*. Having subsequently occupied the position of assistant editor of the *Daily News* for about four years, he in 1875 relinquished journalism and devoted himself to fiction. Since then he has written considerably over twenty novels. They are all brilliant productions, abounding in beautiful and artistic sketches of scenery — chiefly Highland — and in most graphic and thrilling plot and narrative, intensely interesting, but far removed from the vulgar sensationalism of some modern novelists. No present day author is more widely read than William Black, and his readers belong to the finer and higher class of mind. There is a freshness, a vigour, and a refinement about his stories that are exquisitely pleasing; they are almost equal to a personal tour to the romantic Highland districts, which he so graphically depicts. Among his best known works are "A Daughter of Heth," "Macleod of Dare," "A Princess of Thule," "Sunrise," and "White Heather." But a remarkable quaint, curious, and most interesting story is that of "Judith Shakespeare," the scene of which is laid at Stratford-on-Avon, and the principal character in which is the wayward capricious daughter of the "Immortal Will." Mr. Black has also cultivated the poetic Muse, and has published a volume entitled "Rhymes by a Deerstalker," in which his ardent love of his native land, and especially of the Highlands, is abundantly manifested.

Among Dr. Hedderwick's talented young *protegés* may be mentioned WILLIAM FREELAND, who, though not a native of Glasgow, may yet be counted as one of our own poetic sons, inasmuch as he came amongst us at an early age, and has been with us almost ever since. He was born in Kirkintilloch in 1828, and was engaged in his young days in one of the finer branches of calico printing. Removing to Glasgow he made up the deficiencies of his early education by attending classes in the Athenæum, being an assiduous student there and at the public libraries of the city. He joined the staff of the *Citizen* in 1858 as sub-editor of the old *Weekly Citizen;* and while in that office he formed the acquaintance of that fine poet spirit, David Gray, of "The Luggie," a townsman of his own and also one of Dr. Hedderwick's young men. Their friendship was singularly deep and tender, and only ended when the grave closed over the precious dust of the sweet young singer in the "Auld Aisle." In 1866 Mr. Freeland joined the staff of the *Glasgow Herald*, on which paper, with the exception of a brief interval, he has ever since been engaged. He is at present editor of the *Glasgow Evening Times*. In 1872 he published a novel in three volumes on the subject of the Glasgow "Radical Rising" of 1820, which became very popular. But in the meantime he had been a constant and valued contributor of poetry to the magazines, and some years ago the Princess Beatrice paid him the high compliment of placing upon the title page of her beautiful *Birthday Book* the last stanza of his poem, "Reaping," which she had culled from a collection of poems by various authors. In May, 1882, Messrs. James Maclehose & Sons published a selection of his poems which, containing the matured productions of his genius, has met with a most favourable reception. This work is entitled "A Birthday Song and other Poems." It is a work of rare and sterling merit. Mr. Freeland is a member of the "Glasgow Ballad Club," and has contributed a number of racy and clever pieces to a volume recently published by that fraternity of song and poesy. All his work is characterized by vigour and deep moral earnestness, while his imagery is exquisite, and the language musical and refined.

Since the days of the redoubtable Samuel Hunter the editorial chair of the *Glasgow Herald* has almost invariably been filled by men who have made their mark in the world of literature. As a man of a rich, poetic, and withal humorous vein, George Outram, as we have seen, was possessed of genuine merit as a writer. In the gentle and genial James Pagan we had a historian and antiquarian of a high order. In Professor Jack we had a first class scholar and man of science and erudition. And in these later days JAMES H. STODDART, LL.D., has proved himself a worthy successor of these able and talented men of letters. Dr. Stoddart was born in the old fashioned Dumfriesshire village of Sanquhar in the year 1832, and commenced his literary career on the staff of the *Scotsman* in his 18th year. He came to Glasgow nearly thirty years ago, and connected himself with the *Herald*, of which he ultimately became editor in 1875, only resigning that office last year (1887). In addition to his onerous and multifarious duties as editor, he has found time to make many contributions to general literature. Many things, poetic and otherwise, from his pen have appeared in magazines, and in 1879 he published anonymously *The Village Life*, a rare and interesting volume of poetical sketches of quaint and original characters to be found in old Scottish villages of a past generation. It is believed that some of the subjects were found by the author in his own native village. The book received wide popularity, and its authorship becoming known, it gave him an undoubted place among our modern Scottish poets. It contains many passages remarkable for power of thought and depth of feeling. It reminds the reader of Crabbe's *Borough*, and his sketches of "The Beadle," "The Doctor," "The Old Boatman," "The Schoolmaster," "The Blacksmith," are excellent portraits of a class of worthies that are now almost extinct.

Dr. Stoddart is a thorough Scotsman of the sturdy, rugged, old fashioned type. His very appearance recalls the men of a former generation. Though in the prime of life, he might from his shaggy grey hair be taken for a compeer of the Ettrick Shepherd; while his rosy cheeks and keen, sharp eyes betoken a health and vigour that must have come with him from the moorlands of Dumfriesshire. He is somewhat retiring in his habits, but before resigning his editorial duties —hastened we believe by a sad domestic bereavement and failing health—he was frequently called upon to speak on behalf of literature at our civic feasts and other social gatherings. At the great centenary banquet of the *Herald* a few years ago, he presided over the large and brilliant assemblage of guests in an able and graceful manner. Shortly before his retiral from active life, he published another volume of poetry entitled *The Seven Sagas of Prehistoric Man*, but although it fully sustains his reputation as a poet of no mean order, it has not, we fear—from the abstruse and ancient character of its subject—been received with the like popularity with which his previous volume was greeted.

(It was hoped that from his seclusion and retirement, Dr. Stoddart might yet be heard of in the sphere of poetic literature, but alas! since the above lines were penned, his career has been cut short by death—to the grief and surprise of his many friends and admirers. Dr. Stoddart died at his residence, near Campsie, on 11th April, 1888, in the 56th year of his age).

Like the editor of the *Citizen*, Dr. Stoddart has trained a few rising young men who may yet be heard of in the world of literature, among whom we may mention Mr. George Deans, a fine poetic spirit, who has contributed many sweet and musical verses to various magazines, but who has not yet, so far as we know, ventured upon publication on his own account. There is also at present on the staff of the *Herald*, although he only recently transferred his services from the *Citizen*, a gentleman who has given a good deal of attention to historical research. We refer to Mr. George Macgregor, who, in 1882, published a goodly sized *History of Glasgow*, in which he has condensed into a compendious and handy form all the leading facts relating to our good city from its earliest to its latest times. He has also edited the works of Dougal Graham, the quaint author of the *History of the Rebellion of 1745*, and numerous "Chap Books," which were hawked about the country during the latter half of last century, and were exceedingly popular. Mr. Macgregor has also compiled an edition of the *gruesome* history of Burke and Hare, the notorious Edinburgh murderers; which may be interesting from a historical point of view, but cannot be very pleasant reading to the refined intelligence.

And what shall we more say regarding the innumerable minor poets and literary men of our smoky city? Time would fail us to tell of the late SHERIFF BARCLAY, of Perth, who was a Glasgow born man, and who, besides being a hard working lawyer, was also the author of several learned legal works, and of a pleasing gossipy book, entitled *Rambling Reminiscences of Old Glasgow*, in which he recounts with much zest the scenes and incidents of his boyish days. Of JOHN STUART BLACKIE, the Edinburgh professor of Greek, and the author of many exquisite poems and sketches, and of far more racy, humorous, and interesting speeches, containing a great deal of wisdom and common sense, with a fair sprinkling of arrant nonsense, but all breathing a brave, patriotic spirit. Of MR. SHERIFF SPENS, the author of *Darroll, and other Poems*—a really fine book; with several law works of much interest and practical value. Of HENRY JOHNSTONE, the active secretary of that useful institution—the Western Infirmary—who, amidst his multifarious duties, has found time to write one or two excellent novels, and to contribute many fine poems to some of our leading magazines. Of ALEXANDER LAMONT, the "Rector of Deepdale," who has also written a number of poems and moral sketches to the *Quiver, Good Words,* and other journals, all of high literary merit, and breathing a deeply poetic and religious spirit. Of honest JAMES NICHOLSON, the worthy author of *Father Fernie,* a popular work on botany; *Kilwuddie,* and several other volumes of truly excellent verse, mostly in the Scotch vernacular. Of DAVID WINGATE, the well known miner-poet, whose literary merits have been handsomely recognized and rewarded by the grant of a pension from the Civil Pension List, and who has published several volumes of verse, as well as interesting Scotch stories and sketches. Of TOM MACEWAN, who, besides being a superior and popular artist, is also the author of a goodly number of poems and ballads, written in a tender, touching, and beautiful style. Of Dr. WILLIAM T. MACAUSLANE, a fertile writer of fine religious poems and hymns, which have been much appreciated. Of A. G. MURDOCH, one of our working men who are a credit to their order, and who has produced some able, vigorous works in prose and verse, which are greatly sought after by the general reader. Of ROBERT BIRD, the author of *Law Lyrics,* and many other poems, brimful of humour, and characterized by much ability. Of GEORGE DONALD, author of a chaste, well written volume of poems, mostly of a serious and pathetic nature, and of numerous poetical contributions to the periodical and newspaper press of the day. His father was an able contributor of nursery rhymes to the "Whistlebinkie" collection of a former generation. Of the genial architect and magistrate, the late JAMES SALMON, who published a fine pastoral under the name of "Gowodean," and also composed innumerable impromptu verses, which he delivered at social gatherings, where he was a popular and welcome guest. Of ALEXANDER MACDONALD, town clerk of Govan, author of a racy story entitled "Love, Law, and Theology," and of several other able productions. Of H. BUCHANAN M'PHAIL, now an aged veteran; but who, in his early years, fought stoutly by means of pamphlets and lectures in behalf of the moral and social improvement of woman; and who was besides a poet of merit, and the friend of such other talented but unfortunate sons of the muse in Glasgow, as William Millar, author of "Wee Willie Winkie," and other nursery rhymes, and James M'Farlan, a man of real poetic genius, who, but for his dissipation, might have taken a high position among our local men of letters. Of the late ROBERT GEMMELL, who, though not a native of Glasgow, may be claimed as an adopted son, inasmuch as he lived amongst us for fully thirty years, working manfully at the desk from morn till eve, yet by diligent use of his spare hours, was able to produce several volumes of real merit in prose and verse, among which may be mentioned *Montague: a Drama*, *The Deserter*, and *The Village Beauty*. Of the late JAMES P. CRAWFORD, the author of the "Drunkard's Raggit Wean," and many other valuable temperance songs. But we must draw this chapter on our literary men to a close, not for want of material, but for want of space. We could have told of as many more men belonging to this dull prosaic trading city, who have to no mean purpose, contributed to the literature of our country and generation, and who have redeemed our city from the reproach of vulgarity which has been unjustly cast upon it.

CHAPTER VII.

COACHING AND THE POST OFFICE IN OLDEN TIMES.

"What news? what news? your tidings tell,
  Tell me, you must, and shall—
Say why bareheaded you are come,
  Or why you come at all?"
— *Cowper.*

THE speed, accuracy, and care with which the business of the Post Office is now conducted, present a strong and remarkable contrast to the careless and haphazard manner in which it was carried on in the "good old days" of a hundred years ago; and a few incidents relating to postal matters in those former days, may be interesting to our readers. Our gossipy historian "Senex" relates that on one occasion about the close of last century, he found the Fort William mail bag lying on the public road, a little way beyond Dumbarton, and he had to perform the office of post boy for several miles; and when he delivered the bag at the next post village, the postmaster never even said, "Thank you, sir," but with a *humph*, carelessly tossed the bag into a corner. This may be taken as a fair sample of the indifference with which postal matters were treated in those primitive days.

Before the Union of Scotland and England in 1707, the mail between Edinburgh and Glasgow was conveyed by a foot runner; but on 7th November, 1709, application was made to the United Parliament for a *riding* post between the cities, which application was successful; but the mail, in reality, had no proper protection, for, down to "Senex's" time, the rider with the mail was a mere boy, and his horse a sorry hack. About the year 1730, and for many years after, the Glasgow Post Office was located at No. 51 Princes Street, City, (then called Gibson's Wynd), and consisted of three small apartments. The delivery "bole" or wicket window was a hole broken through the wall of the close, which close was a common thoroughfare entry to King Street. The rent of the premises was some £6 or £8 a year. The salaries of the postmaster and clerks were of a similarly humble order; but these were supplemented by perquisites for extra services rendered to the wealthier merchants of the city in the special despatch of letters. About this period (latter half of last century) Glasgow was becoming a city of considerable importance; her merchants carrying on not only an extensive country trade, but also a foreign commerce of pretty large extent. The usual mode of despatching letters by the Post Office to the small provincial towns through running boys, whose regular delivery of letters could not be depended on, was felt by the Glasgow merchants as a great drawback to their business; it therefore came to be a practice with our wealthier merchants to send their letters *express* by special messengers of their own; but as this was a rather expensive method of transmitting their correspondence, they contrived the means of obtaining the assistance of the postmaster in sending off their *express* despatches under the cloak of the Post Office seal. A private party, who had occasion to despatch an express to any part of the country, applied to the Post Office for what was called *a despatch express*. The postmaster or some of his clerks were always so obliging as to accommodate gentlemen in this respect, and enclosed the letters in a cover, sealed with the Post Office seal; upon which the express boy proceeded on his way, and at all the stages he came to, he obtained horses by the authority of the Post Office. This practice became very common, and was found to be very convenient to our great tobacco merchants, many of whom had country houses at some considerable distance from the city. It was encouraged by the postmaster, who no doubt received "a consideration" for his services. But in course of time the system was put a stop to in a rather authoritative manner.

In the year 1774 the collector of pontage on the New Bridge (now Glasgow Bridge) stopped and detained a horse carrying the mail or packet from Paisley to Glasgow until he paid one penny of pontage for crossing the said bridge. Upon this being made known to Mr. Jackson, the Postmaster, he was grievously offended, and complained to the Hon. Arthur Connel, then Lord Provost of Glasgow, for redress, who, upon hearing parties, severely reprimanded the collector for his misbehaviour, and ordered the money to be returned. But in the following year—viz., on 1st December, 1775—David Cross, keeper of the Paisley Loan turnpike (situated at the junction of Bridge Street with Norfolk Street and Nelson Street), and William Ure, collector of pontage on the New Bridge, having laid their heads together, did stop and detain a horse carrying a packet or despatch, alleged to be an express from the Post Office of Glasgow, till the rider paid the turnpike and pontage duties imposed by law. In like manner, on the 14th of said month, Andrew Brown, keeper of the toll-bar at the south end of the village of Gorbals, did stop and detain a horse carrying the mail, or packet, or despatch, with an express said to be upon the public service from the Post Office of Glasgow. Mr. Jackson was in a mighty passion that these paltry toll gatherers should presume to stop the expresses of His Majesty George III, and therefore, in January, 1776, he brought an action before the Sheriff of Lanarkshire, concluding not only for repayment of the sums alleged to have been illegally abstracted from the post rider, but also to make payment to the pursuer of the sum of £20 in name of damages and expenses. The tollmen, in their answers, maintained that the said expresses were not sent *bona fide* upon Government business, but were despatches forwarded by Mr. Jackson to particular country gentlemen whom he wished to accommodate, and upon their private affairs only. The Sheriff, upon advising the condescendence, &c., ordained Mr. Jackson "specially to set forth whether the persons who were stopped were carrying the public mail or packet, which is regularly sent off at stated times, in the common course of the Post Office employment, or a packet despatched by special express from the Post Office; and whether such packet was a Government or public packet upon His Majesty's service, or a private packet sent off at the instance of a private person in regard to private affairs." This interlocutor seemed to have given Mr. Jackson great offence, for he gave in a reply saying—" That his duty as His Majesty's postmaster made it impossible for him to condescend in terms of the interlocutor, upon account of the impropriety of laying open and discovering *the objects of His Majesty's service.*" At this time there happened to be a prospect of a vacant seat on the Bench in the Court of Session, and Mr. Jackson added the following singular *argumentum ad hominem* for the consideration of the Sheriff:—"If one of the now expected vacancies in the Court of Session were an object of your Lordship, and that last week you had committed to the Post Office the transmission of a letter or packet by express to your friend in London upon that subject, could you in such a case approve of the pursuers being obliged to discover your Lordship's secret and confidential affairs?" The Sheriff, however, notwithstanding of this personal appeal, remained firm, and assoilzied the defenders and found them entitled to expenses. Upon this Mr. Jackson thought proper to present a bill of advocation, which, having been passed, came, in course of the rolls, before the Lord Ordinary, who, upon advising the memorials, made avizandum with the cause to their Lordships. The Court of Session confirmed the interlocutor of the Sheriff, and thus an end was put to the system in Glasgow of the Post Office sending off private expresses under the cloak of the Post Office seal, and under the pretence of their being sent on Government business.

A SHIP INSURANCE ANECDOTE.

In connection with this subject of express despatches, one or two interesting incidents may here be related.

During the French War, the premiums of insurance upon ships sailing without convoy, were very high, in consequence of which several of our Glasgow shipowners were in the practice of allowing the expected time of arrival of their ships closely to approach before they effected insurance upon them, thus taking the chance of a quick passage being made, and if the ships arrived safe, the insurance premium was saved. Mr. Archibald Campbell, about this time an extensive Glasgow merchant, had allowed one of his ships to remain uninsured till within a very short period of her expected arrival; at last, getting alarmed, he attempted to effect an insurance in Glasgow, but found the premiums demanded so high, that he resolved to get ship and cargo insured in London. Accordingly, he wrote a letter to his broker in London, instructing him to get the requisite insurance made on the best terms possible, but, at all events, to get the said insurance effected. This letter was dispatched through the Post-office in the ordinary manner—the mail at that time leaving Glasgow at two o'clock P.M. At seven o'clock the same night Mr. Campbell received an express from Greenock, announcing the safe arrival of his ship. On receiving this intelligence, he instantly despatched his head clerk in pursuit of the mail, directing him to proceed by post-chaise and four with the utmost speed, until he overtook it, and then to get into it; or if he could not overtake it, he was directed to proceed to London, and to deliver a letter to the broker, countermanding the instructions about insurance. The clerk, in spite of extra payment to the postilions, and every exertion to hasten his journey, was unable to overtake the mail; but he arrived in London on the third morning, shortly after the mail, and immediately proceeded to the residence of the broker, whom he found preparing to take his breakfast, and before delivery of the Glasgow letters. The order for insurance was then countermanded, and the clerk had the pleasure of taking a comfortable breakfast with the broker. The expenses of this express amounted to £100; but it was said that the premium of insurance, if it had been effected, would have amounted to £1,500, so that Mr. Campbell was reported to have saved £1,400 by his promptitude.

Another remarkable case happened in this manner. At the period in question, a rise had taken place in the cotton market, and there was a general expectancy among the cotton dealers that there would be a continued and steady advance of prices in every description of cotton. Acting upon this belief, Messrs. James Finlay & Co., had sent out orders by post to their agent in India, to make extensive purchases of cotton, on their account, to be shipped by the first vessels for England. It so happened, however, shortly after these orders had been despatched, that cotton fell in price, and a still greater fall was expected to take place. Under these circumstances, Messrs. James Finlay & Co. despatched an overland express to India, countermanding their orders to purchase cotton. This is said to have been the first overland express despatched from Glasgow to India, by a private party on commercial business.

Before the plan was adopted, of conveying the mail by a mail coach, protected by a guard, Glasgow was very ill supplied with the means of sending parcels, or light boxes of goods to London or Edinburgh in a safe and quick manner. When forwarded to London by stage coaches there was frequently not only great delay, but also considerable risk of loss or theft; for they required on the route to be transferred from one coach to another—there being independent coach proprietors at different stages. On one occasion a small box sent to London by stage, value £100, did not arrive for six months, having been carried on to Bristol, and there it lay disregarded, although the address was so plain and legible that a school boy might have read it.

When the mail coaches were introduced, a great improvement took place in the despatch with which light parcels were carried, and there was much more traffic in these parcels and other goods. "Senex" remembers on one occasion when travelling from Edinburgh to Glasgow, he was surprised to find the whole of the top of the coach occupied by early lambs for the Glasgow market; and he was informed on two occasions that the whole places of the mail coach, both outside and inside, had been taken, and that the coach had been entirely loaded with early lambs for Glasgow. The fares at that time were 16s. for insides and 10s. for outsides, and he left it to those curious in these matters to calculate what should be the price per pound of lamb so carried. But the Glasgow merchants were becoming wealthy in those days, and they were rather famous for their love of good eating as well as hard drinking.

Soon after the establishment of the London mail coach to and from Glasgow, a daring attempt was made to rob it at a place near Tollcross. A little way east of that village the road passed through a small wood of fir trees; and as the coach was expected to pass this place early in a winter morning, a strong rope had been tied from one tree to another, athwart the road, at the height of the seats usually occupied by the coachman and guard, so that in the course of the coach proceeding rapidly along, both of these men would have been thrown down by the rope, and then the coach could have been easily robbed. It fortunately happened, however, that a waggon of hay was accidentally coming to Glasgow early in the morning, and was stopped by the rope, which extended across the road, and thus the intended robbery was frustrated.

In the month of February, 1831, a great snowstorm was recorded in the *Glasgow Herald*. Mails were stopped for several days, and the guard and driver of the Dumfries and Glasgow mail coach, which had stuck in the snow near Beattock, lost their lives in attempting to carry on the mail bags themselves. Another interesting item appears in the *Herald* of 12th March, 1832, as follows:—" We learn from good authority that it is now settled that a two-horse light mail coach, carrying four inside passengers only, is to run from Carlisle to Glasgow at the rate of 11 miles an hour. We suppose that the Edinburgh mail will bring in the London bags to Carlisle. The horses are to be changed every 6 miles, and the coach is to reach Glasgow at half-past one. The present mail coach is to be continued, and is to arrive in Glasgow at the same time as at present." This was the greatest achievement in the way of speed attained in these good old days, and would be looked upon, no doubt, somewhat in the same light as we now regard our "Flying Scotchman."

To illustrate the efforts for speed in those days, and also to indicate the zeal of our forefathers in the cause of reform, it may here be stated that the great Reform Bill was read a second time in the House of Lords at an early hour on the morning of Saturday, 14th April, 1832, by a majority of nine. The result was given in the *Glasgow Herald* on Monday morning, the 16th. "After announcing this result," says the *Herald* leader, "we must stop to explain how we have been able to give the news so early. At half-past seven o'clock last evening (Sunday) a post-chaise and four arrived at Glasgow with copies of the *Sun* newspaper (the old *Sun*) to Mr. Atkinson's newspaper agent, dated on Saturday morning at seven, containing no less than twenty-two and a half columns of the debate commenced on Friday evening, and which must have concluded a few hours before the date of the express. By this extraordinary and liberal exertion we have had the news here in thirty-six and a half hours, anticipating the news in regular course by nearly twenty hours. We understand it was Mr. Young, the editor of the *Sun*, who came down with such express to Glasgow."

Nor was this the only exertion put forth to bring early news of the important event to the great Radical city; for we are also told that copies of the *True Sun* came to Mr. M'Phun, newsagent, at half-past ten the same evening, being only three hours later than the arrival of the elder but swifter luminary.

Before this date, and during the time of the French war, it was quite exhilarating to observe the arrival of the London mail coach in Glasgow, when carrying the first intelligence of a great victory, like the battle of the Nile or the battle of Waterloo. The mail coach horses were then decorated with laurels, and a red flag floated on the roof of the coach. The guard, dressed in his best scarlet coat and gold ornamented hat, came galloping at a thundering pace along the Gallowgate, sounding his bugle amidst the echoings of the streets; and when he arrived at the foot of Nelson Street, at Mr. Bain's office, he there discharged his blunderbuss in the air. On these occasions a general run was made to the Tontine Coffee-room, to learn the great news; and long before the newspapers were delivered, the public were informed by the guard of the particulars of the glorious victory, which flew from mouth to mouth like wildfire. When the papers were delivered all was bustle and confusion to learn what the *Courier* or the *Sun* said—for these were the leading papers of the day; and Walter Graham was usually called for to mount a chair and read the despatches aloud for the general benefit. This he did with great glee, and afterwards, dismounting from his rostrum, he went about the room shaking hands with every one he encountered, and this was almost every subscriber in the room; for Walter was a great favourite, and knew all our towns-folks, great and small.

At this period, says "Senex," there was a curious custom in the Tontine Coffee-room at the delivery of the newspapers. Charles Gordon was then the waiter at this establishment, and being a bit of a wag, he, after collecting the newspapers, made them up into a heap, and making a sudden rush into the middle of the room, tossed up the whole lot as high as the ceiling. Now came a grand rush and scramble of the subscribers, every one darting forward to lay hold of a falling newspaper, pushing and driving each other about without mercy; and as the old saying goes, before you could have said "Jack Robinson" a dozen or two of the *élite* of Glasgow merchants might have been seen sprawling upon the floor playing at "catch who can." On these occasions quite a *humploc* of gentlemen would be seen sprawling on the floor, or riding upon each other's backs like a parcel of boys.

In course of time, however, this rough-and-ready method of distribution of newspapers became toned down and more decorous—perhaps brought about by some of the merchants getting some of their teeth knocked out in the *melee*—and they were laid out in order on the forms. Charles Gordon, the waiter, then delivered the Tory papers to the one form, and the Liberal or Radical papers to the one opposite; and so it became known of what opinions the readers were by the forms they occupied.

As indicative of the mental activity of early days, it may be stated that about the year 1796 a Mr. John Austin, muslin manufacturer, promulgated a plan of having the mail despatched between London and Glasgow through the medium of iron tubes or pipes, to be laid from the one city to the other. He suggested that a rope should be carried on rollers along the line inside of the tubes, to which the waggon containing the mail should be attached; and this rope being at certain stations coiled round large drums or cylinders, the waggon would be drawn from station to station by fixed steam engines, now called *stationary engines*. This plan was, however, considered so visionary that little attention was paid to it; indeed, it was spoken of as a mere piece of castle building, fit only to be laughed at.

It may not be out of place, in this chapter about mails and mail coaches, to relate an anecdote in connection with the coaches running between our city and the metropolis of Scotland, which gives a good illustration of the enterprise and determination of our Glasgow men of the past generation. A Glasgow gentleman fell deeply in love with a beautiful young lady of the city, who, in addition to her personal charms, was a rich heiress. It would appear that this young lady fought shy of her lover, and did not give him that amount of encouragement which he desired. It happened that on one occasion he found himself in Edinburgh at a time when his fair *inamorata* was there on a visit to some friends; and by making careful inquiries he ascertained the day and the hour at which she intended returning to her home in the West. Our ardent Lothario then speedily devised a daring scheme by which he might attack with success the citadel of the lady's heart. Having learned that she had booked for herself a seat in a certain coach, he went to the coach office and bought up all the remaining inside seats, so that he had the pleasure of travelling in her company alone all the way to Glasgow. And he made such good use of this favourable opportunity that, by the time the coach rattled up to the Tontine Hotel he had overcome her scruples, and obtained the pledge of her heart and hand! Our Glasgow men never did things by halves in those good old days.

To give our readers an idea of the rate of travelling in former days, it may be stated that when "Senex" made his first trip to Edinburgh, in 1784, he started in the "Edinburgh Diligence" from the Saracen's Head Inn, Gallowgate, at seven o'clock in the morning, and arrived at Edinburgh at eight o'clock at night. Travelling at the rate of six miles an hour, the coach arrived at Cumbernauld shortly after nine o'clock, where a stoppage of an hour and a half took place to allow the passengers to partake of breakfast and the horses to rest and feed. About two o'clock they arrived at Linlithgow, where a comfortable dinner was leisurely partaken of; and then, in the old jog-trot fashion, the coach proceeded for a couple of hours or so, when another halt took place for rest and tea at a roadside inn; and finally the party were set down safely in the Grassmarket about eight o'clock, thoroughly wearied and worn out with their tedious journey.

The journey from Glasgow to London in the earlier days of coaching occupied a week; while the carriers' covered waggons for the conveyance of merchandise were three whole weeks upon the road; resting, however, on the Sabbath days in accordance with our good old Scottish custom. In course of time, however, as we have seen above, by means of frequent change of horses, the journey for passengers to London was greatly accelerated, and in cases of urgency could be accomplished within three days.

CHAPTER VIII.

THE TOBACCO LORDS AND EARLY MERCHANTS.

> "To catch dame Fortune's golden smile
> Assiduous wait upon her;
> And gather gear by every wile
> That's justified by honour;
> Not for to hide it in a hedge,
> Nor for a train-attendant;
> But for the glorious privilege
> Of being independent."—*Burns.*

THE City of Glasgow is *par excellence* a mercantile and manufacturing city, and to give an adequate history of the rise and progress of its trade and commerce would not only be foreign to our purpose, but it would take a volume many times the size of this to do anything like justice to the subject. All we can attempt in this chapter is to cull a few characteristic incidents and stories relating to the men who were engaged in raising the mercantile importance of the city, and to their manners. We may, however, preface these incidents by a very brief summary of the origin and development of the various principal branches of the city's business from the earliest to the latest times.

There can be no doubt that the many able and eminent bishops and monks of Glasgow were active agents in originating the early trade and commerce of the city. For example, it was through the exertions of the worthy Bishop Rae that the old Glasgow bridge was erected in 1345-50, and this would doubtless throw the city open to communication with the country on the south side of the river, and facilitate the egress and ingress of merchants and merchandise. It would also appear that even before that time, Bishop Joceline, in or about the year 1190, obtained a charter from King William the Lion for the institution of an annual fair; which was afterwards resuscitated by a friar of the convent of the Grey Friars in the fifteenth century. And it is highly probable that for many years, the ecclesiastical superiors of the cathedral would give their advice and encouragement to the early traders, even though they might not personally engage in the work themselves.

One of the first promoters of trade in Glasgow was Mr. William Elphinston, a younger brother of the noble family of that name, and the father of an eminent prelate to whom we refer in another part of this work. He was engaged as a curer of salmon and herrings for the French market, for which brandy and salt were imported in return. In the reigns of James VI and Charles I also, a considerable traffic was carried on by traders carrying goods of home manufacture from Glasgow into England, and bringing home "merchand waires." During the liberal administration of Cromwell, Scotch vessels were at liberty to carry cargoes to Barbadoes, and to bring sugar back from that port. Speaking of the merchants of Glasgow, Franck says that in 1650 their commerce was extensive. "Moreover," he adds, "they dwell in the face of France with a free trade. The staple of the country consists of linens, friezes, furs, tartans, pelts, hides, tallow, skins, and various other small manufactures and commodities;" and Tucker, in 1656, reported to Cromwell that Glasgow was "one of the most considerable burghs as well for the structure as the trade of it."

But it was after the Union with England in 1707 that Glasgow really developed that great trading and commercial enterprise which has ever since characterized it. The great tobacco trade began in that year, and that trade may be regarded as laying the foundation of the prosperity of our city. The tobacco trade continued down till the revolt of the American Colonies in 1775. Dr. Strang informs us that Sir John Dalrymple, writing shortly before 1788, says,— "I once asked the late Provost Cochran of Glasgow, who was eminently wise, and who has been a merchant there for seventy years, to what cause he attributed the sudden rise of Glasgow. He said it was all owing to four young men of talent and spirit who started at one time in business, and whose success gave example to the rest. The four had not £10,000 amongst them when they began." These four young men were Mr. Cunninghame of Lainshaw, Mr. Speirs of Elderslie, Mr. Glassford of Dugaldston, and Mr. Ritchie of Busbie—the estates here named being all purchased out of their acquired wealth. These gentlemen were at the head of the great tobacco lords, who strutted on the *plain stanes* on the Trongate, dressed up with scarlet cloaks, silken hose, powdered wigs, cocked hats, and buckled shoon, and looked down upon all but themselves with supreme contempt. Shortly after this, the banking system was instituted in Glasgow ; and this business produced its own particular class of notabilities, such as the Dunlops, the Houstons, the Dennistouns, the Blairs, the Buchanans, and above all, that *facile princeps* in the banking world of our city—Robin Carrick, of the famous Ship Bank.

On the decline of the tobacco trade, our citizens turned their attention and directed their talents and energies to other fields. They commenced to trade with the West and East Indies, in cotton, sugar, coffee, molasses, rum, tea, brandy, &c. ; and soon the India merchant princes took the place of the tobacco lords. Amongst these may be mentioned the names of Bogle, Gordon, Alston, Buchanan, Craigie, Ewing, Corbet, Stirling, and Finlay, some of which are even yet well known names amongst us. Then, in the beginning of the present century came the coal and iron trades, with the familiar names of Dixon, Colquhoun, Baird, Merry, Cunninghame, Neilson, and others at their head. Alongside of these enterprises, we have the discovery and application of the steam engine, of which the most notable representative is the immortal Watt ; then followed the river Clyde improvements, which opened our port to vessels of all sizes, giving an immense impetus to the commerce of Glasgow. Then we have the developing of the manufacture of cotton and woollen goods, with the Monteiths, Dales, Finlays, Macintoshes, Dunns, Houldsworths, and several others as the leading spirits; the rise and progress of the chemical trade, of which the Tennants of St. Rollox and Charles M'Intosh were the chiefs; and last, but not least, the great shipbuilding enterprise, with the eminent shipbuilders, Napier, Elder, Randolph, Todd, M'Gregor, and a few others, as its principal originators and promoters.

It will thus be seen that Glasgow has drawn to itself, a great variety of the principal trading interests of the kingdom, the result of all which has been not only the amassing of large fortunes by individual citizens, but the rapid growth and importance of the city itself, the drawing within its boundaries of an immense population from all parts of the country, and placing Glasgow on a sure foundation as a manufacturing and commercial city, and as a great labour market that cannot easily be shaken.

Prior to the time of the Union of England and Scotland in 1707, the trade and commerce of Glasgow, as we have seen, was on a comparatively small scale, but even then it gave evidence of the enterprise and energy of the Glasgow merchants. One of these early merchants was one William Simpson, a native of St. Andrews, who, about the latter half of the seventeenth century, built two ships at the "Bremmylaw," and brought them down the river during a great flood tide. The place of our shipping in those days was the bailliary of Cunninghame, on the Ayrshire coast. Simpson traded to Flanders, Poland, France, and Dantzic; and so successful was he that he was able to build great houses in Glasgow, within the Trongate, with orchards, barns, and gardens behind. He also built a large tenement in the New Wynd. Another contemporary merchant was Archibald Alcorn, who was the first to build two tenements in the Bridge Street—as it was then called—now Bridgegate. Another merchant of note was Matthew Turnbull, who was a Dean of Guild, a great trader to France and Holland, and a man of known integrity and distinction. He built a large tenement of houses in Gallowgate.

About this period, 1664, a war broke out between England and Holland, and some of the Glasgow merchants fitted out privateers, and sent them out to sea in pursuit of His Majesty's enemies. The following paragraphs from the *London Gazette* will show of what stuff these Glasgow men were made :—

"A privateer, of Glasgow, one Chambers, has lately brought in a Dutch caper of 8 guns, with a prize ship laden with salt."—*London Gazette*, Nov. 8th, 1666.

"A merchant ship of Glasgow of 300 tons, laden with wines from Spain, was in her return attempted by a Dutch man-of-war, for which encounter finding himself too weak, though sufficiently manned, the master commanding his men to conceal themselves, himself and only seven men appearing upon the deck, who immediately struck sail in token of submission, which the man-of-war perceiving, sent twenty-two of his men aboard her, himself leaving her to pursue another vessel discovered to leeward; but, at the close of the evening, the concealed men finding their advantage, set so vigorously upon the Dutchmen, that making them prisoners, they regained the possession of their vessel, and returned safe to Glasgow."—*Ibid*, Feb. 18th, 1667.

Here is another incident that indicates the nature of the trade of Glasgow in those days. "Walter Gibson, eldest son of the deceast John Gibson of Overnewtoun, merchant and late provost of Glasgow, his first appearance was in malt making, and his stock being improven that way, he left that trade, and betook himself to merchandizing, and began first with the herring fishing, and in one year he made, packed, and cured 300 lasts of herring at six pounds sterling per last, containing twelve barrells each last, and having fraughted a Dutch ship, called the St. Agat, burdened four hundred and fifty tuns, the ship, with the great cargo, arrived safely at St. Martin's in France, where he got for each barrell of herring, a barrell of brandy and a crown, and the ship at her return was loaded with salt and brandy, and the product came to a prodigious sum, so that he bought this great ship, and other two large ships; he traded to France, Spain, Norway, Swedland, and Virginia. He was the first that brought iron to Glasgow, the shop keepers before bought the same, with dying stuffs from Stirling and Borrowstounness." (M'Ure's *History of Glasgow*.)

It is also said that about the beginning of last century there were some 10,000 Scots merchants and pedlars going up and down England, on horseback or otherwise, selling cloth; and no doubt the Glasgow lesser merchants would be well represented among that number. In those primitive days the shops or business premises of our Glasgow merchants were on rather a diminutive scale, and were chiefly located about the Trongate, Saltmarket, Princes Street, Bridgegate, &c. In the majority of instances they consisted of one or two small apartments situated on the ground floor, and the merchants themselves resided on the upper floors. They were a somewhat independent class of men; they attended personally to their business, conducted their own sales, and were not too civil to their customers. They shut their shops during the dinner hour—generally from one to two or three o'clock—and during that time no purchaser could be served. The following anecdotes will illustrate the manners of the merchants of our city even at a much later date:—Towards the end of last century a well known hardware merchant, Mr. James Lockhart, who had his shop in the Saltmarket, was one of the best specimens of the good old fashioned morality of bygone times. One day a country girl came into his shop to buy a pair of garters. Having asked the price, Mr. Lockhart told her they were fourpence. The girl said, "I will not give you a farthing more than threepence for them." "Weel, lassie, you'll no' get them," replied the shopkeeper. Shortly afterwards the girl returned and said, "I'll noo gie ye fourpence." "Gang awa', lassie, gang awa'," replied Mr. Lockhart, "an' no' tell lees."

A story is told of the late Bailie John Mitchell, who died only a few years ago. He had been long in business as a corkcutter, and in this trade had acquired a considerable fortune. He had a large connection with France and Spain, so that he was able to keep up a considerable style. But his business was conducted in a small shop in the Stockwell, and although a man of means, he did not disdain to attend to the shop himself. On one occasion two gentlemen in high positions in France came to Glasgow on some public business, and having had large dealings with Mr. Mitchell, they called upon him to secure his assistance in their inquiries. They were rather taken aback at the small and insignificant appearance of the place of business which they were conducted to, and could scarcely believe that this was the place of their extensive correspondent. They observed a plain, homely-looking man assorting goods in the window of the shop, and taking him for a mere shopman or porter, they inquired if Mr. Mitchell were on the premises. They were answered in the affirmative, that Mr. Mitchell was no other than the person before them, and if they would but wait for a few minutes till he finished the sorting of his goods, he would be at their service. This being done, the distinguished visitors proceeded to state the object of their visit, and said they would be glad to have Mr. Mitchell's aid and advice. Whereupon the worthy corkcutter replied that if they would come and dine with him that evening he would do his utmost to promote their mission, and then courteously bowed them out of the shop. Rather dubious of the assistance that could be rendered to them by such a commonplace looking individual, the French magnates nevertheless resolved to keep their appointment. Mr. Mitchell at that time resided in a fine, large, elegant mansion house in Carlton Place (now occupied as the chambers of the Govan Combination Parochial Board), which was at one time one of the most aristocratic parts of the city. Here they presented themselves at the hour fixed. To their surprise the door was opened by a tall powdered footman, who ushered them into a splendidly furnished apartment. The host speedily made his appearance in full evening dress—a very different looking person from what they had seen in the morning; and by and by they were entertained to a sumptuous banquet, graced with all the choicest dishes and wines of the period. And in the matter of their business they found the Stockwell Street merchant everything that could be desired.

In his later years Bailie Mitchell, having realized a large fortune, had a much higher estimation of his own importance than he had in his earlier days. It is said that on one occasion, when being examined before a Parliamentary Committee in London, he was asked by one of the bewigged counsel what his business was. "I am a cork merchant," replied Mr. Mitchell; but as if he thought that would convey but a poor idea of the extent of his business, he added, "but on a large scale." "Oh, then," said the learned counsel, "you will be a *bung* merchant?" And the roar of laughter that followed this query rather disconcerted our worthy magistrate.

But we must return to the tobacco lords, or Virginian dons, who, as already stated, were the founders of the trade of Glasgow in the larger and more important sense of the term. After the union of England and Scotland, Gibson informs us that so sensible were the people of Glasgow of the advantages which they had procured by that union, that no sooner was the treaty signed than they began immediately to prosecute the trade to Virginia and Maryland. They chartered vessels from Whitehaven; they sent out cargoes of goods, and brought back tobacco in return. The method adopted was certainly a prudent one:—A supercargo was sent out with every vessel, who bartered his goods for tobacco until such time as he had either sold all his goods or procured as much tobacco as was sufficient to load his vessel. He then returned immediately, and if any of his goods remained unsold, he brought them home with him. "Happy would it have been for Britain," adds the worthy historian, "if she had always traded with America in this manner."

The merchants of Glasgow continued to proceed in their trade after this method. They were of great advantage to the country by the quantity of manufactures they exported, and their own wealth began to increase. They purchased ships of their own, and in 1718 the first vessel belonging to Glasgow crossed the Atlantic. The imports of tobacco were considerable, and Glasgow began to be looked upon as a respectable port. The tobacco trade at the ports of Bristol, Liverpool, and Whitehaven was observed to dwindle away as the Glasgow merchants began to send tobacco to these places and to undersell the English even in their own ports. A rigid frugality governed the merchants of Glasgow in everything at this time; they were therefore able to bring their goods cheaper to market. Jealousy and envy took possession of the English traders, and every scheme was tried by them to destroy the trade of Glasgow. False representations were made to Government against our traders. A Commission was appointed to investigate these charges, but they were found to be groundless. The Glasgow merchants overcame all opposition and carried everything before them.

To give the reader an idea of the great proportions to which the tobacco trade attained in Glasgow, the following figures from Gibson's *History of Glasgow* may be quoted. They show the imports and exports of Glasgow, Greenock, and Port-Glasgow, for the year from 5th January, 1771, to 5th January, 1772. In a footnote Gibson states that "the share of these imports and exports belonging to Greenock and Port-Glasgow is very trifling:"—

Tobacco imported from Maryland, 11,313,278 lbs.; from Virginia, 33,986,403 lbs.; from North Carolina, 755,458 lbs., or a grand total of 46,055,139 lbs.

Tobacco exports from Glasgow:—To Italy, 170,853 lbs.; to Minorca, 140,854 lbs.; to France, 20,774,843 lbs.; to Holland, 14,932,543 lbs.; to Germany, 3,868,027 lbs.; to Denmark, 320,249 lbs.; to Sweden, 163,503 lbs.; to Norway, 596,037 lbs.; to Ireland, 3,125,101 lbs.; to Barbadoes, 23,846 lbs.; or a total export of 44,125,856 lbs., besides a considerable quantity of roll and manufactured tobacco sent back to America and elsewhere.

Denholm also in his *History of Glasgow* says that in 1772 out of 90,000 hogsheads of tobacco imported into Great Britain, Glasgow alone imported 49,000, or considerably more than the one half, and in the year before the declaration of American Independence (1783), the quantity imported into Glasgow was 57,143 hogsheads, of which only 16,000 were used for local consumption; the remainder being despatched all over the kingdom and to the Continent of Europe.

It is somewhat remarkable that the four great Virginia magnates who have been referred to above, were not originally men of family or aristocratic descent, except possibly Mr. Cunninghame, who is supposed to have been related to the family of Caprington. However, in old times the Glasgow traders belonged in many instances to some of the oldest and best families of the landed aristocracy. Among many families that might be named, the late Lord Gray and the last Earl Hyndford but one, were Glasgow apprentices in their youth. We have already referred to Mr. Elphinstone as being also connected with the nobility; and in addition, there was Mr. Archibald Lyon, son of the Earl of Strathmore, who is spoken of as the second trading merchant after Elphinstone, and undertook great adventures and voyages in trading to Poland, France, and Holland, through the success of which he acquired considerable lands in and about the City of Glasgow, and built for himself and family a mansion or "great lodging, about the middle of the sixteenth century, on the south side of Gallowgate Street." By marriage, the Campbells of Blythswood became connected with families of rank in Scotland, such as the Douglases, the Cunninghames, the Colquhouns of Luss, and others. These merchants, as we have seen, held a very high head, and looked upon themselves as men of great consequence. To such a degree did the mercantile aristocracy during the last century carry their proud and haughty demeanour, that while they, arrayed in white wigs and wide scarlet mantles, strutted along the pavement at the Cross, no inferior trader, however respectable, durst venture to approach them. If any of this class was desirous of speaking to one of these proud merchants, he had to wait patiently until he caught the great man's eye, and was granted an audience.

Mr. Cunninghame, the first of the great tobacco lords, purchased the great estate of Lainshaw from the ancient house of Montgomerie. He had many successive wives, and a numerous progeny. One of his wives was a near relation of Lord Cranstoun, and sister of the accomplished judge, Lord Corehouse. One of the daughters married the second Lord Ashburton. He disinherited his eldest son, and was succeeded by his second son, William Cunninghame of Lainshaw, who was a very extraordinary man. He possessed distinguished abilities and great talent for business. After spending his earlier manhood in India, he, on his father's death, returned and settled at Lainshaw, which he greatly improved and beautified. In later life, he devoted much attention and means to the diffusion of religious knowledge, and became himself somewhat of a recluse, and engaged in deep studies in sacred chronology, prophecy, and kindred subjects.

The Glasgow mansion of the elder Cunninghame stood on the site of the present Royal Exchange, and was then quite in the country. It was a large and elegant building. In our previous work, we related an anecdote showing how he had acquired a large portion of his fortune by purchasing the whole of the tobacco held by his firm at 6d. per pound, at the time of the American Revolution, when it rose by degrees to 3s. 6d. per pound. Here is another story showing that he was not of a selfish disposition. There was in those days a small tobacco merchant named John Rankin, who had his dwelling house, shop, and tobacco manufactory in the Bridgegate, immediately opposite to the Blythswood mansion house. Mr. Rankin died shortly before the American War broke out in 1776, and when this latter event caused a sudden rise in the price of tobacco, Mr. Cunninghame, as a friend and old acquaintance of the family, called on Mrs. Rankin, and strongly advised her to lay in a stock of tobacco forthwith, as he was sure there would be a still greater rise in the market. (It had by this time risen from 3d. to 6d. per pound.) Mrs. Rankin, however, hesitated to speculate, but being pressed to do so by Mr. Cunninghame, she at last rather unwillingly agreed to buy one hogshead, but she refused to venture on any greater purchase, considering the risk too great. She had scarcely concluded the bargain, when tobacco rose to 9d. per pound, then to 1s., and thus continued to rise step by step till it reached the extraordinary price of 3s. 6d. per pound; so that ultimately, by the purchase of this single hogshead of tobacco, Mrs. Rankin cleared £1,500. This lady's eldest daughter, Janet, was married to Humphrey Ewing, Esq., the brother of Walter Ewing Maclae, Esq., of Cathkin, and uncle to James Ewing of Strathleven.

Another of these great tobacco lords was Mr. Alexander Speirs, who purchased the great estate of Elderslie, once the inheritance of Sir William Wallace, and became one of the landed magnates of Renfrewshire. Mr. Speirs, the tobacco lord, was the son of John Speirs, merchant in Edinburgh. His mother was Isabel, only daughter of John Tweedie, Provost of Peebles. He was born in 1714. He became one of the leading partners of Speirs, Murdoch & Co., bankers in Glasgow, his bank being the famous "Glasgow Arms Bank," which commenced business in the Bridgegate in 1750, and thereafter removed to King Street, and lastly to Miller Street. Mr. Speirs married Mary, daughter of Archibald Buchanan, of Silverbank and Auchentorlie, Dumbartonshire, also a Virginian don. Portraits of Mr. and Mrs. Speirs were placed in the directors' room of the Merchant's House, to the funds of which they were both liberal contributors. The town residence of Mr. Speirs was the "Virginia Mansion," situated at the head of Virginia Street, and was one of the most splendid houses then in

Glasgow. It was built by George Buchanan, of Mount Vernon, and was purchased by Alexander Speirs in 1770. Mr. Speirs erected Elderslie House, the building of which occupied five years, and was completed in 1782; but its owner died on the 10th December of that same year, so that he does not appear to have enjoyed his new residence beyond a few months. His son, Archibald, was for many years M.P. for that county, and allied himself to the great English family of Fitzwilliam by marrying Miss Dundas, daughter of Lord Dundas and sister of the Earl of Zetland and of Lady Milton. The eldest son of Archibald was Alexander, third of Elderslie, who became Lord-Lieutenant of Renfrewshire and M.P. for Richmond. In 1836 he married Eliza Stewart (daughter of Thomas C. Hagart, of Bantaskine, and his wife—a famous beauty of her day—Miss Stewart, of " the field "), and died in 1844, leaving one daughter, married to Colonel Alexander, of Ballochmyle, late M.P. for Ayrshire, and one son, Archibald Alexander, fourth of Elderslie, who must only have been a child of four or five years old when his father died. For sixteen or seventeen years the estates were managed by trustees and his able and enterprising mother.

The name of Speirs does not frequently occur in the history of Glasgow, and the family have not been notable, as many of our other merchants were, for devotion to municipal interests. A somewhat remarkable fatality has attended this family in connection with Elderslie House. The late Captain Speirs, M.P., shortly after attaining his majority, married into the noble English family of the Bouveries (Lady Ann Bouverie, daughter of the Earl of Radnor), and great rejoicings took place at Elderslie on both of these occasions. But, alas! his auspicious career was speedily cut short. Within a year after his marriage, and ere his son and heir was born, he was cut off with a fever, and the family estates have for nearly twenty years been under trustees. The mansion house and grounds of Elderslie, near Renfrew, were afterwards let to the notorious Mr. James Morton, whose connection with the failure of the City Bank is still fresh in the memory of the citizens of Glasgow; and after that disastrous event the active brain of Mr. Morton devised a scheme for retrieving his fortunes by turning the property of this aristocratic family—greatly to the disgust of its representatives—into a huge dairy farm and milk shop! The lease expired, however, and Mr. Morton was relegated to much humbler premises.* But from the fact just narrated, and the now suspected unhealthiness of the site, with the sad associations above referred to, it is very doubtful whether the Speirs family will ever occupy Elderslie House again.

Of Mr. Glassford, the third of the great tobacco dons, we are told that he also turned his tobacco into broad acres by the purchase of the estate of Dugaldstone from the family of Graham. His town mansion was situated at the west end of Trongate and corner of what is now Glassford Street—the famous Shawfield House, formerly occupied by Mr. Duncan Campbell, M.P., and later as the no less famous Black Bull Inn. Mr. Glassford appears to have been a man of versatile talent and genial spirit. He was a member of the "Hodge Podge" Club, and his mental photograph was taken by Mr. James Murdoch, one of the poetasters of that fraternity, in the following lines :—

"Squire, lawyer, and merchant, and soldier comes next,
Not fictitious in song, but true as the text ;
In Glassford these characters mix and agree,
And surely no better Hodge Podger than he."

Mr. Glassford was allied by marriage to two ancient families, his first wife having been a daughter of Nesbitt, Baronet of Dean, and his second wife having been a daughter of the Earl of Cromarty. His eldest son was for some time the much respected member for the County of Dumbarton, and his second son tried unsuccessfully to dispossess of the Cromarty estates his cousin, Mrs. Hay Mackenzie, grandmother of the Marchioness of Stafford.

The fourth of this celebrated quartette of Virginia magnates—Mr. James Ritchie, of Busbie—was, like his companions in trade, infected with the "earth hunger" and with aristocratic leanings. Besides the estate of Craigton, he acquired extensive estates in Ayrshire. He was one of the founders of the celebrated Thistle Bank, and was succeeded by his son Henry, an active, shrewd man of

* Mr. Morton died in deep poverty a few months ago, leaving an insurance upon his life to the extent of upwards of £100,000 ! Such are the vicissitudes in the life of a speculator !

business, who married a sister of Hugh, Earl of Eglinton, although this last acquisition has been rivalled by a living Glasgow merchant in the person of Mr. John Cross, who recently married a daughter of the present earl. Mr. Ritchie seems to have been of a jovial and social disposition, for we find his name recorded in the list of members of the "Hodge Podge," which was apparently *par excellence* the club of the tobacco lords. But the following anecdote does not present him in the most favourable light, bringing out, as it does, the worst features of the haughty spirit of his class:—At a dinner party of his Glasgow neighbours he was guilty of giving way to a somewhat domineering spirit, and among other assumptions claimed the merit of having benefited his native city by introducing into it, to take a lead in its society, a lady of distinguished birth and connections, or, as he termed her, "a real lady!" A vulgar little bailie, provoked by this speech, told Mr. Ritchie that they all thought as much of *their* wives as he did of his. On this the offended magnate replied, "Sir, as one of His Majesty's county magistrates, I could sign a warrant to put you in prison." "Aye," retorted the citizen, "but do ye no' ken that, as a bailie of the town of Glasgow, I could clap *you* in prison without a warrant?"

Here is a delineation of Mr. Ritchie from the pen of Dr. Moore, the talented father of the hero of Corunna :—

"What precise dapper gentleman now treads the scene?
How sagacious in look and how formal in mien!
Why, Ritchie runs counter the general rule—
Though he always looks wise, yet in faith is no fool."

The mansion house of Craigton, on the Paisley Road, which was built by Mr. Ritchie in 1746, afterwards came into the possession of Mr. Henry Dunlop, M.P., who was a merchant in Glasgow, and for two years Lord Provost of the city. A few years before his death, in 1867, Mr. Dunlop sold it to Mr. Graham Hutchison, whose heirs are still the owners of the property. But this fine old mansion house was unfortunately burned to the ground on the morning of the 21st January in the present year. The occupant of it at that date was Mr. James Spencer, shipowner, and it may be stated here—as an instance of the fact that there is still scope in Glasgow for men rising from poverty to affluence by industry and perseverance—that Mr. Spencer was in his early years an ordinary "stevedore," or loader and disloader of ships' cargoes, in a very humble way.

As another instance of the aristocratic connections of our old Glasgow merchants, the following narrative will be interesting to our readers:—On the death of Lady Mary Lindsay Crawford, Mr. Hamilton Dundas became, along with the Earl of Glasgow, co-heir of the line of the Earls of Crawford and Lindsay, in right of their grandmothers, who were daughters of that great family. But the heir of the line of the family, and also the inheritor of the large estates in Fifeshire and Ayrshire, would, if he had survived, have been young Bogle, of Hamilton Farm, son of Peter Bogle, one of the most noted men in Glasgow more than a century ago. This gentleman, who was a hard liver and man of pleasure, married one of the most beautiful young women in Scotland of her day, the Hon. Graham Lindsay Crawford, daughter of Viscount Garnock, and only sister of the twenty-first Earl of Crawford and fifth Earl of Lindsay. The issue of this union was an only son, who was handsome, gay, wild, and thoughtless, and who, after a short and dissipated career, died prematurely. If he had lived and married and had issue, his descendant would now have been one of the greatest proprietors in Scotland. The Bogles were of French origin, but had long been settled in Glasgow, where they were among the principal citizens for several generations.

As we have in this chapter made several references to the celebrated "Hodge Podge" Club, we may here give another short story from the delightful work of the late Dr. Strang:— "Among the hundred annual lists of toasts regularly entered in the minute book of the club, that of 1809 contains a perfect galaxy of beauty, all of whom we remember to have seen in our boyhood. It was of one of those lovely young ladies belonging to that period the following anecdote was told:—Being one day talking with a strange gentleman from a distance about Glasgow and its gaieties, the conversation turned about balls and those who attended them, when the stranger laughingly asked this fair toast of the Hodge Podge, 'Have you many *beauties* in Glasgow?' On which the young belle *naïvely* replied, 'There are five of us!'"

The Campbells of Blythswood.

The Campbells (afterwards of Blythswood) are descended from one of our oldest mercantile families, for they seem to have been traders in Glasgow during the reign of Queen Mary, when the city only contained 4,500 inhabitants. They resided in an elegant mansion house called Silvercraigs, situated in the Saltmarket opposite the Bridgegate, and in this house Oliver Cromwell took up his abode when he visited Glasgow in 1650. One of the members of the Campbell family was left the estate of Mains by his mother's father, in consequence of which he changed his name to Douglas, and became Douglas of Mains. The family mansion house of the Douglases was in the Bridgegate, a little to the west of Blythswood's house. The last Duchess of Douglas seems to have belonged to the Mains branch of the Campbells of Blythswood. She was a Miss Douglas of Mains, and lived in the family mansion in the Bridgegate. The following story is told of the manner of her first introduction to the Duke of Douglas. A Glasgow party had been made up to take an excursion to see Bothwell Castle and its pleasure grounds, and among this party was Miss Douglas of Mains, a very lively rattling girl. The Duke of Douglas was a man of very retired habits, and saw little company, living generally at Bothwell Castle. Upon the Glasgow party reaching the Castle, and finding that the Duke was there, they sent a message requesting liberty to take a view of the Castle and pleasure grounds, which was readily granted. The Duke himself very politely received them, and not only made them welcome, but accompanied the party himself through the Castle and grounds. On this occasion Miss Douglas rattled away with his grace, and chatted with him in so easy and lively a manner, that the Duke was quite taken with her. The Glasgow party, after viewing the Castle and pleasure grounds, were about to depart, when Miss Douglas said to the Duke—"Please, your Grace, everything here is most beautiful, and very fine indeed; but I think this place might be wonderfully improved." "How so?" said the Duke quickly. "Why," answered Miss Douglas, "just by your Grace taking a wife." Of course, this passed off with a laugh. However, the Duke returned the call, and ultimately married the lively young lady.

The last of the Blythswood Campbells who resided in the Bridgegate was James Campbell, Esq., father of Major Archibald Campbell, M.P. for Glasgow. James appears to have been in somewhat reduced circumstances before his death, for beyond the entailed estates belonging to his family, he left little or no real or personal estate behind him. There is a story told of him, that being short of cash he let his large garden in the Bridgegate to David Lillie, wright, as a timber yard at the yearly rent of £5; but afterwards thinking that he could get a little more of the needful by dividing the garden into lots, he, in 1770, parcelled it out into three parts, granting leases of nineteen years, with breaks at seven years, first to John Robertson, a cooper; second, to William Martin, a wright; and third, to Linn Dillon, a plasterer. In the leases granted to these tenants he designed himself *heritable proprietor of the yard aftermentioned*, and the stipulated rent, in all, was £20. None of these tenants were aware that Mr. James Campbell was only a life-renter of the subjects, and they proceeded to make erections on their respective lots, on the faith of a clause in their leases, which bound the landlord at the end of the tacks or leases to take them over at a valuation. The erections on each lot amounted to something like £300, and they were erected with the consent and under the eye of Mr. Campbell himself.

James Campbell of Blythswood died in 1773, and his eldest son, John, afterwards Colonel Campbell, succeeded to the Blythswood entailed estates. In 1776 Mr. Dillon, one of the tenants of the yard, having entered into another line of business, gave regular intimation that in the following year he would quit the subjects; and at Whitsunday, 1777, he renewed the intimation, at the same time requesting a proper person to be named to ascertain the value of the buildings, so that he might be recouped for his outlay according to agreement. Colonel Campbell, however, paid no attention to these communications, and Dillon raised an action against him in the Court of Session for £300 as the value of the subjects. The result of this action was unfortunate for poor Dillon, the Court, after long litigation, having found that Colonel John Campbell, being merely heir of entail in the said estate, "does not represent the late Blythswood in any other manner." Dillon's case, of course, decided the two others, and thus Colonel John got all the back erections on his Bridgegate garden for nothing!

It is said that Colonel John Campbell was a remarkably handsome man, although some of our readers may be inclined to exclaim, "Handsome is that handsome does." He was killed at Martinico in 1794, and was succeeded by his brother Archibald, then Captain Campbell, who was a prisoner at Toulon, where the news reached him of his having succeeded to the large entailed estates of Blythswood. About the beginning of this century Archibald Campbell, M.P., obtained powers to purchase the annexation lands of Blythswood Holm, and also the Bridgegate family mansion and garden, at a valued price. In 1802 he sold the Bridgegate mansion house, with all the back buildings before mentioned. The Blythswood Holm lands, as our readers are all aware, have proved a perfect mine of wealth to the modern representatives of this family. Archibald Campbell died in 1838 without issue, upon which the estates fell to Archibald Douglas, Esq., of Mains (son of his cousin-german), who assumed the name and title of Campbell of Blythswood. This gentleman, who was the father of the present laird—Sir Archibald Campbell, Bart., M.P.—was a man of excellent character, a good landlord to his tenantry, a large-hearted and generous benefactor in the neighbourhood in which he resided, and also a humble, sincere Christian. He died in July, 1868.

The Firm of James Finlay & Co.

One of the most enterprising firms of Glasgow merchants during the last century, says a writer in the *Glasgow Herald* of 17th April, 1884, was that of James Finlay & Co., and that firm, with its various members and varied enterprises, may be regarded as a worthy type of a race of merchants who have not only made Glasgow one of the foremost mercantile cities in the world, but have made merchandise honourable and ennobling. Without unduly reflecting upon the character of our modern merchant citizens—for we have many noble men still amongst us—we may safely say that the merchant princes of Glasgow in the eighteenth century were conspicuous among their compeers in other cities and other lands for their energy, their daring enterprise, their high-toned mercantile morality, their public spirit and private munificence. They were, many of them, men of genius, devoted to trade and commerce, and their genius cast a halo of actual romance round all their operations. To trace the rise and progress, the achievements, of these men would in itself be an education; and they have left an impress upon the mercantile mind of Glasgow which has not yet been, and probably never will be, effaced while the good old city continues to exist.

The founder of the eminent firm of James Finlay & Co.— viz., James Finlay—was born in the Buchanan country, at Moss, on the Blane Water, near Killearn there, in 1727. His ancestors had been small lairds in that district for 200 years. He came to Glasgow in his early manhood, and settled there as both a manufacturer and merchant. In the first *Glasgow Directory*, published in 1783, he appears as "James Finlay, merchant, Bell's Wynd." But he was designated both "manufacturer and merchant" in the second *Directory* of 1787. Of course he had been long in business before either of these dates. He was an able, energetic man of business, and an enthusiastic Celt and citizen. The *Glasgow Mercury* of 29th January, 1778, gives a long account of a procession through the town to beat up for recruits to serve against the American rebels. Among those who supplied the musical stimulants were "two young gentlemen playing upon fifes, two young gentlemen beating drums, and a gentleman playing the bagpipes." Tradition has it that James Finlay was the person who tramped the streets playing on the bagpipes. And in the public subscription towards the expenses of the corps, "James Finlay & Co." are down for fifty guineas—a substantial sum, which only four citizens exceeded. This subscription in a few days was over £10,000, and a fine regiment, 900 strong, was piped together. Good old James Finlay died in or about the year 1790, and was succeeded in the business by his second son, the famous Kirkman Finlay, afterwards the owner of Castle Toward, who was born in 1772, and was long the head of the firm.

Kirkman Finlay was a man of great energy and enterprise. He had been trained to the manufacturing business in the office of James Buchanan in the Stockwell, who foretold that "that laddie would either mak' a spoon or spoil a horn." Under his management, the business of James Finlay & Co. took new shape and bulk. His quick eye caught the future, opened up by the inventions of Hargreaves and Arkwright, Crompton and Cartwright, and he threw himself with energy into the cotton trade. In company with his friends the Buchanans, he acquired works at Deanston on the Teith, Ballindalloch on the Endrick, and Catrine on the Ayr; and these works, with Glasgow as headquarters, he carried on to the day of his death with varying success, but with unvarying spirit, and with such care for good honest work, as gave Glasgow cottons a name both for make and finish.

But it was as an East India Merchant that Glasgow owes most to Kirkman Finlay. If our City has more than its own share of the great trade to the East, she may thank Kirkman Finlay for it. He had been one of the keenest and ablest opponents of "John Company's" monopoly, and as soon as the India trade was thrown open, he pushed in, and led the way to others. The first ship direct from the Clyde to India, the van of a vast fleet, was freighted by him, the "Buckinghamshire," of 600 tons, for Calcutta direct. Mr. Finlay was, however, more than a mere man of business. He took a broad view in all civic and public matters. He was a man of thought and culture, and when he was in Parliament his opinions were carefully listened to, and quoted after he left it. Always a busy man, he still found time for much public and charitable work. He was a liberal and kindly man, a genial companion, a generous master, and a fair opponent; and his word was as good as his bond. He was greatly esteemed by his fellow-citizens, and they conferred upon him all the honours they had to bestow. He was Governor of the Forth and Clyde Navigation; President of the Chamber of Commerce; Lord Provost; Member of Parliament; Dean of Faculty; Lord Rector of the University—a rare accumulation of honours, which yet left him the simple straightforward gentleman it had found him. When he was gone, the citizens raised a statue to his memory and placed it in the vestibule of the Merchants' House.

The day of Kirkman Finlay's election to Parliament was a great day in Glasgow. His opponent was Archibald Campbell of Blythswood, the Tory manager of the West,

Blythswood always had Renfrew in his pocket. He had also Dumbarton, Finlay had Glasgow and Rutherglen; and Glasgow having, on this occasion, the casting vote, he won. He was well known and well liked, and had done the City good service. He was a citizen, and no citizen had sat for Glasgow since Neil Buchanan in 1741; he was Provost, and no Provost had been M.P. since Robert Rodger in 1708; and the good people "tin't their reason a' thegether." He was franked of all expenses. Medals were struck, inscribed "Faith, Honour, Industry, Independence, Finlay, 1812." There was cheering, and toasting, and clinking of glasses in front of the Town Hall. Finally his constituents seized their Member's carriage, and dragged him along the Trongate to his house in Queen Street. This was on 30th October, 1812. They paid him a second visit on 7th March, 1815. It was well they found him not at home; they attacked his house, broke his windows, and were only dispersed by the soldiers, horse and foot. Their Member had voted for "Prosperity," Robinson's Corn Bill. In a subsequent Parliament he sat for the borough of Malmesbury.

Kirkman Finlay was a member of one of the famous Glasgow clubs—*The Gaelic*—and had often joined in the Gaelic toast to the "Horn, corn, wool, and yarn" at their hospitable board. Under his presidency twenty members turned out to give a welcome to the officers of the 42nd Highlanders after their return from the Battle of Waterloo, pursuant to the following resolution unanimously passed at a previous meeting:—"That a more than ordinary mark of respect was due to the Standard of the Royal Highlanders, in acknowledgment of their national attachment, and of the high sense which each member entertained of the military glory early acquired and maintained by a series of gallant achievements, down to the last most brilliant service at Waterloo." To add to the hilarity of this festive gathering, the band of the regiment, alternately with the club piper, discoursed martial music, and on the relative merits of the performers the following extract from the club minutes bears significant testimony:—"While the band is at first to be decidedly preferred, still as *judgment ripens* by experience, intrinsic worth is seldom permitted to remain long unnoticed, for, *late in the evening*, the bagpipe became the favourite." While speaking of this famous club, the following anecdote may here be related:—One of the members was so proud of his Celtic origin, that on one occasion he exclaimed in the hearing of the fraternity—"I thank God that there is not a single drop of Lowland blood in my veins!" On hearing which Samuel Hunter, editor of the *Glasgow Herald*, who happened to be present, at once rejoined—"You are certainly thankful for sma' mercies!"

Kirkman Finlay died at Castle Toward on 4th March, 1842, in his 70th year, and lies in Blackadder's Aisle in our noble cathedral. By his wife, Janet Struthers, he had four sons—James Finlay and John Finlay of Deanston, both of James Finlay and Co.; Thomas Finlay, of Thomson, Finlay & Co., Liverpool; and Alexander Struthers Finlay of Castle Toward, of Ritchie, Stewart & Co., Bombay, and M.P. for Argyleshire. Of these, James, John, and Thomas are dead, and there are now no Finlays in the old firm. Kirkman Finlay of Dunlossit, Islay, eldest son of John Finlay, is now the representative of his grandfather, *the* Kirkman Finlay, of old James, the founder of the firm, and of their far-back forebear, the tacksman of Spittal, Killearn.

The Buchanan family are now also passed away from the connection of James Finlay & Co. But in other hands the old firm still survives, and well on in its second century shows no signs of old age. Long may it live to keep up the old Finlay tradition of "Faith, Honour, Industry, Independence!"

The Monteiths of Anderston.

The history of the rise and progress of some of our notable Glasgow families possesses an interest little short of the romantic; and that of the eminent family of Monteith is not the least remarkable. The forerunner of the Glasgow family—James Monteith—was a small "bonnet laird" near the *clachan* of Aberfoyle, and was born about the close of the seventeenth century. He was an active and industrious man; and, in addition to his agricultural pursuits, he was a dealer in black cattle. But he lived in the stirring days of "Rob Roy," and other Highland reivers; and was on several occasions brought to the brink of ruin by the raids of these depredators; and at last died of a broken heart. He left a family of three daughters and one son. The latter, Henry, who was born in 1710, finding his father's affairs in such a sad plight, made his way to Glasgow, then a town of some 17,000 inhabitants. He took up his abode in the village of Anderston, a mile out of the city, where he began business as a market gardener. He began on a small scale, and brought the produce in to the city on the market days only. But he was of a resolute character, and soon took an interest in public affairs. During the Jacobite rebellion of '45 he joined the Glasgow regiment of volunteers, and fought bravely at the battle of Falkirk. He died some years afterwards, leaving one son, James, who was born in 1734, and who became the founder of the great manufacturing business with which the family name was afterwards associated. He was the first to introduce the fabrics of cotton-yarn, woven in imitation of the East India muslins, which became a most successful enterprise. He caused a dress of it to be made and embroidered with gold, which he presented to Queen Charlotte.

A romantic story has been told in connection with another branch of manufacture, after the French style of cambrics. Mr. Monteith had considerable dealings with a Monsieur Mortier, a yarn dealer in Cumbray (hence the word cambric); and, about the year 1780, M. Mortier paid a visit to Glasgow, bringing with him his son, a fine youth of twelve or thirteen years. They were most hospitably entertained by Mr. Monteith; and so pleased was the Frenchman with his reception, that he left his son behind him, for the purpose of finishing his education at our University. Young Mortier remained three years in Glasgow, under the kindly care of his father's friend; and, after his return to his native country, a correspondence was kept up for some time between the two families, which, however, owing to alterations in the mode of manufacture, came gradually to a close. But about twenty years after this, a young Glasgow merchant named Patrick Falconer, of the firm of Monteith & Falconer—afterwards of the famous house of Dalglish, Falconer & Co. (of which our late respected M.P., Robert Dalglish, subsequently became a partner), was sent on a business mission to Germany. The Continent was at that time being overrun with the armies of Napoleon, and great difficulty was experienced in travelling. Mr. Falconer proceeded in the first place to Holland, as the easiest route to his destination. But, on his arrival there, he found it occupied by the French, and he was arrested on the suspicion of being a spy, and carried to the headquarters of the French general in command, where he was interrogated in French by that officer.

Mr. Falconer was somewhat surprised at the minute inquiries the general made to him regarding the city whence he had come. As he replied to these queries, and mentioned some of the more notable places, such as the College, the High Street, and of the leading men, such as the Dales, M'Ilwhams, Carricks, &c., a broad smile gradually appeared on the stern countenance of the French officer; and at last he broke out in "guid braid Scotch" with the astounding query, "But, my frien', do ye ken auld James Monteith o' Anderston?" Mr. Falconer, though taken completely by surprise, nevertheless had presence of mind enough to reply in similar style, "Ou aye, general, I ken him brawly, for he's my ain pairtner's faither." Then a hearty laugh followed, and it soon transpired that the distinguished General Mortier, one of Napoleon's famous generals, and afterwards Marshal of France, was no other than the young man who had received part of his education in Glasgow College, and the protegé of our Anderston manufacturer. After a long talk about Glasgow and its "bodies," Mr. Falconer was allowed to pass on his way through the French ranks unmolested. General Mortier was afterwards slain, along with several others, in the streets of Paris, in 1835, on one of the festival days in commemoration of the restoration of the Orleans family, by an infernal machine, fired by a Corsican assassin named Fieschi, who was himself severely wounded by the bursting of his own machine.

James Monteith became the owner of the Blantyre cotton mills, and made a large part of his fortune out of that undertaking. But there is a curious story connected with that acquisition which illustrates not only the indomitable enterprise of our old Glasgow merchants, but also the apparently fortuitous manner in which great fortunes have been realized.

In 1792, the spinning of cotton was a very profitable business, and in that year Mr. Monteith purchased the

Blantyre mills from David Dale, at what was considered a fair price; but almost immediately afterwards the war of the French Revolution broke out, which was followed by the commercial panic of 1793. In that year three of the Glasgow banks failed, and even the Royal Bank trembled, although the sagacity and firmness of auld Robin Carrick, saved it from the general fate. A fall of 45 per cent took place in the price of yarns, and Mr. Monteith saw only ruin staring him in the face. In his trouble he went to Mr. Dale and tried to persuade him to cancel the bargain, but without success; old David stuck to the cash. Mr. Monteith then, from sheer necessity, proceeded to manufacture his own yarns, and to send them to a firm in London, which did a large business in selling the East India imitation fabrics in that city. Mr. Monteith had no idea of obtaining anything like a full profit from his goods; but to his surprise and delight, he found that not only was he getting his yarns disposed of to advantage, but he was realizing a large profit from the manufactured cloth, which was mostly book muslins dressed as lawns. Within five years, Mr. Monteith had made a fortune of £80,000 by this trade. Mr. Dale afterwards seeing the success of Monteith's adventure, set about manufacturing the same class of goods, but for once he was too late; the tide had turned, and was in full ebb. Here is a description of Mr. Monteith about the period referred to, as he appeared on the "plain stanes," near the Glasgow Cross, in the hey-day of his prosperity:—
'Figure to yourself a portly gentleman of forty; 5 feet 9 inches high, walking with a slow and rather heavy step, dressed in a neat round hat, powdered hair and long cue, white neckcloth, Duke of Hamilton striped vest, blue coat and gilt buttons, yellow buckskins, and top boots. Such was James Monteith, who may be considered the first of our cotton lords, and who made a fortune nearly as rapidly as our former tobacco lords; but not like many of them, by holding large stocks at an important crisis, but by fortunately holding no stock at all at a similar crisis."

ANECDOTES OF DAVID DALE.

No book relating to the merchants of Glasgow in the last generation would be at all satisfactory that did not make some reference to this worthy man. He was born in Stewarton, Ayrshire, on 6th January, 1739. His ancestors are said to have been farmers in that district for several hundred years; but his father, William Dale, was a grocer and general merchant in the town. David was apprenticed to the weaving trade in Paisley, but disliked this sedentary occupation, and came into Glasgow while a young man, and became clerk to a silk mercer. With the assistance of some friends, however, he shortly afterwards went into business on his own account in the linen yarn trade, and after being twenty years in this business he entered into an agreement with Sir Richard Arkwright for the use of the patent invented by the latter for the improvement of cotton spinning, erected the New Lanark Cotton Mills, and subsequently became sole proprietor of that concern, still, however, carrying on an extensive yarn trade. He also at the same time (1783) became sole agent in Glasgow for the Royal Bank of Scotland, and thus the erstwhile herdboy at Stewarton and weaver in Paisley was now sole proprietor, or connected as a managing partner with, several of the most extensive mercantile, manufacturing, and banking concerns of the country, the proper conducting of any one of which would have absorbed the entire powers of most other men. Not so, however, with David Dale, for besides conducting successfully and with strict commercial integrity all these important enterprises, we find him devoting time and money to various benevolent schemes, and discharging the onerous duties of a magistrate of the city of Glasgow, to which he was elected, first in 1791, and again in 1794; moreover every Lord's Day, and sometimes on other days, preaching the Gospel to a Congregational Church in Greyfriars Wynd, afterwards called the "Candle Kirk," of which he was one of the pastors or elders. From an early period, also, he regularly visited Bridewell for the purpose of preaching the Gospel to the convicts, and his example in this respect was long followed by his colleagues in the church.

Mr. Dale had a short, corpulent figure, a good humoured homely face, wore a kind of cocked hat, a long ample frock coat, short breeches, with hose and buckled shoon. He carried a stout staff, and altogether bore a comfortable, well-to-do appearance. Among the many stories told in illustration of his short, stout figure is the following:—

Having stated to a friend that he had slipped on the ice and fallen all his length, "Be thankful, sir, it was not all your breadth," was the apt reply. As illustrating his benevolent disposition, the following anecdotes may be related:—A young man called at the Royal Bank, and presented a draft for discount which Mr. Dale considered to be a forged document. He sent for the young man, and in private informed him of his suspicions. The fact was acknowledged. Mr. Dale then pointed out to him the risk he put his life in by such an act, destroyed the bill that no proof of his guilt should remain, and finding that he had been led to it by pecuniary difficulties, gave him some money and dismissed him with a suitable admonition.

In a sermon preached by Mr. Andrew Fuller of Kettering, sometime after Mr. Dale's death, when enjoining on his hearers *who have* to give of their abundance, and to do so liberally, he says—"The poor people of Glasgow used to say of a late great and good man of that city, 'David Dale gives his money by sho'elsful, but God Almighty sho'els it back again.'"

Mr. Dale seems to have been regarded with esteem and confidence by all classes in the community. A widow named Mrs. Mary Brown, who, strange to say, became one of the principal cotton brokers in Glasgow in those days, applied on one occasion to Mr. Dale for his advice in the following circumstances:—Her husband had been a shoe-maker in pretty extensive business. At his death Mary was at a loss how to dispose of his stock to advantage, and she had recourse to Mr. Dale. He advised her to work up the raw materials into shoes suitable for the West India mar-ket, and then to consign the whole to a respectable house for sale in the West Indies. Mary, however, said that this was too great a venture for her to engage in; but Mr. Dale told her, that if she was pleased with the proposal, he would run *halves* in the adventure. Mary at once jumped at the offer, and accordingly the whole of Mr. Brown's finished stock was shipped to the West Indies, upon joint account, with instructions that the produce of the sales should be remitted in cotton. When the cotton arrived, Mr. Dale proposed to put it into the hands of a cotton broker for sale; but Mary did not approve of this plan, saying that she would sell it herself, and thereby save the broker's commission. Mary was very successful in selling the cotton at a good price, and immediately thereafter she commenced the business of a cotton broker. But, like many others in similar circumstances, she was carried away with a zeal for speculation, and in 1794 her name appears in the *Edinburgh Gazette* as a bankrupt.

Mr. Dale built, in 1783, a spacious house at the north-west corner of Charlotte Street, which, with its large garden, has since been turned to many strange purposes, and had many odd tenants. In 1777 he married Miss Ann Caroline Campbell, daughter of John Campbell, W.S., Edinburgh. She was the mother of seven children, whom she trained up in the fear of the Lord. Mrs. Dale died in 1791. Mr. Dale did not again marry. His eldest daughter married Mr. Robert Owen, who had become a partner with Mr. Dale in the New Lanark Mills, and became famous in after days for his socialistic opinions and schemes.

A somewhat interesting story is told in connection with Mr. Dale and his city residence in Charlotte Street. It seems that on the 18th November, 1795, on which date a great flood took place, by which the River Clyde overflowed its banks, Mr. Dale had invited a large party to dinner, and expected William Simpson, cashier of the Royal Bank; the great millionaire, Gilbert Innes of Stowe, and the whole posse of the Royal Bank Directory to come from Edinburgh to meet Scott Moncrieff, George M'Intosh, and a few others of the Glasgow magnates at dinner. Great preparations were made for this important feast, and everything had been got ready, when lo, the waters of the Clyde began gently to ooze through the chinks of the kitchen floor, and by and bye to increase till the servants were wading ankle deep. At this critical moment the Monkland Canal burst its banks, and like an avalanche the waters came thundering down by the Molindinar burn, carrying all before it, and filling the low houses in the Gallowgate, Saltmarket, Bridgegate, &c., with a muddy stream. The Camlachie burn, too, which ran close by Mr. Dale's house, rose to an unusual height, and, with a crash, rushed into his kitchen, putting out the fires, and causing the servants to leave everything behind and flee for their lives. Then came the question—What was now to be done? The dinner hour was fast approaching, and the great Edinburgh visitors were already whirling to Glasgow in their carriages. In this cruel dilemma Mr. Dale applied to his opposite neighbour, Walter Wardlaw, Esq. (father of Rev. Dr. Ralph Wardlaw), for the loan of his kitchen, and also to another neighbour, Mr. Archibald Paterson, for a like accommodation, both of whom not only granted the request, but also gave the use of their servants to help cook another dinner. But still the question remained—How were the wines, spirits, and ales to be got from the cellar which now stood four feet deep of water? After much cogitation a porter was hired, who, being suitably dressed for the occasion, was to descend to the abyss and bring up the liquids. To guide him in his quest, Miss Dale, then sixteen years of age, was perched on the porter's shoulders, and, descending into the cellar, she pointed out to her chevalier the different articles required for the dinner. After receiving his directions, the porter landed his fair charge in the lobby of the house, and returned to the cellar for the other and scarcely less precious cargo. All things now went on in a satisfactory manner. The dinner was cooked and placed on the table in the best style, and the whole party passed the evening in mirth and jocularity at the odd circumstances which had preceeded this merry meeting.

As a retreat from the bustle of a city life, about the year 1800 Mr. Dale purchased Rosebank, a small landed property on the banks of Clyde, about four miles east of Glasgow. But, whilst gradually withdrawing from business, he most unaccountably, through the influence of Mr. Owen, became a partner in the Stanley Cotton Mill Co.—a connection which cost him a great deal of uneasiness during the latter years of his life, and is said to have involved him in a loss of £60,000. He died in his house in Charlotte Street on the 17th March, 1806, in the 68th year of his age, and was buried in St. David's (Ramshorn) church burying ground.

THE STORY OF CHARLES TENNANT OF ST. ROLLOX.

As another illustration of the humble origin of many of the eminent mercantile firms of Glasgow, and of the intense energy and industry of their founders, the story of the rise of the great chemical firm of St. Rollox is both interesting and instructive.

In the early part of last century there lived at "The Mains," on the banks of "bonnie Doon," a worthy farmer named William Tennant, who had a son, John, who became factor or manager to that Countess of Glencairn who was daughter of a poor fiddler in Ayr, named "Willie Macrae," but became the rich heiress of her uncle, Governor Macrae, of Madras. It was this Governor Macrae who presented to our city the well known statue of William III, which stands at Glasgow Cross, and whose remarkable story we give a sketch of in another part of this volume. John Tennant and "Leezie" Macrae, the fiddler's daughter, had been playmates at school, and, it has been surmised, were also sweethearts; but, at all events, the widowed Countess had great faith in her former playfellow, and entrusted the management of her estates to him. And he appears to have been worthy of her confidence, for it was of him the poet Burns gave the character, "that ace and wale of honest men." Mr. Tennant was twice married, and had a family who all appear to have distinguished themselves. The eldest son, James, was the miller of Ochiltree, and was the bosom friend and companion of Burns. The poet addressed to him that characteristic and racy epistle beginning with the words, "Auld comrade dear, and fellow-sinner." In many of the editions of Burns' works this epistle is addressed to "James Tait," but there is little doubt that it was in reality addressed to James Tennant, and it is so headed in Gilfillan's edition; and the editor there states that it was James Tennant who assisted Burns in the choice of Ellisland Farm, near Dumfries. In this epistle Burns refers to the other members of James Tennant's family, his brothers and sisters. According to Mr. Stewart, in his "Curiosities of Glasgow Citizenship," the line, "my auld school-fellow, preacher Willie," refers to James' brother, Rev. W. Tennant, LL.D., "who went to India, and there instituted a movement for the educational and moral improvement of the natives." "The manly tar, my mason billie," became a naval officer, who lost his hand in the French war. He was at one time offered a knighthood, but declined it, as, like the worthy wife of the Provost of Paisley, "he regarded the title as little better than a nickname." The couplet—

> "An' Lord, remember singing Sannock,
> Wi' hale breeks, saxpence, an' a bannock,"

refers to Alexander, who went to Cape Colony, and whose descendant, Sir Hercules Tennant, was for many years Speaker in the Colonial Parliament there.

But the member of the family with whom we have most to do was Charles, who is thus referred to by the poet:—

> "An' no forgettin' wabster Charlie,
> I'm tauld he offers very fairly."

Charlie was then a lad of only seventeen years, and serving his time as a weaver in Kilwinning. After this he was established in business as a bleacher at Darnley, in the parish of Eastwood. His business was of course on a very small scale, and he was his own principal workman, rising early and working late. One of his neighbours at Darnley was the late Mr. Wilson of Hurlet, who was then one of our leading Glasgow merchants. His house overlooked the bleachfield of Charles Tennant, and he became greatly interested in the industry and perseverance of the young bleacher, who might have been seen going about at daybreak with a watering-can in his hand, sprinkling his yarns and cloths till they became as white as snow. His sympathies were aroused towards the enterprising young man, and he sought his acquaintance and introduced him to his family circle. Here Charles succeeded equally in awakening the admiration and affections of Mr. Wilson's lovely daughter, Margaret, and in due time she became his wife.

All this time Charles Tennant was busily engaged in trying to discover the secrets of chemical science, with the view of devising a speedier and more effective method of bleaching than the homely watering can. And so successful was he in this pursuit, that by the application of "oxymuriatic gas" (chlorine), along with that common substance "lime," he produced a wonderful revolution in the process of bleaching. The advantages of the discovery were so great that it was calculated in the first year of its introduction, 1789, no less a sum than £168,000 was saved by the process in Ireland alone.

Mr. Tennant in course of time migrated to Glasgow, where he established (in 1799) the chemical works at St. Rollox, which business was rapidly extended till it became the largest in Europe. In addition to his business, Mr. Tennant took a lively interest in the public affairs of our City. He was not an orator, nor a very demonstrative man, but he was a man of great business capacity, clear understanding, and much enterprise. He was one of the projectors of the first railway in Scotland—viz., the Garnkirk Railway; and he also assisted in the establishment of the Edinburgh and Glasgow line, and other similar enterprises. Mr. Tennant died suddenly at his own house in Abercrombie Place in the year 1838, at the age of seventy. The *Glasgow Argus*, at the time of his death, published a high eulogium on his character and influence. It said :—"The loss of Mr. Tennant will be widely and deeply felt. He was an earnest and indefatigable promoter of economical and educational improvement, an uncompromising friend of civil and religious liberty. His own inborn energy of character and clear intellect placed him among the foremost of that class which, by wedding science to manufactures, has at once extended their field of action, and elevated them to the rank of a liberal profession. . . . In every respect—as a domestic man and a citizen—a more pure and upright soul we have not known than his, whom society, and still more, his family, have lost."

On the death of Mr. Tennant, his son John carried on the works. He also was a man of uncommon energy and ability, and was highly esteemed as one of the most honourable of our City merchants. He greatly interested himself in labours for the relief of the poor and destitute, and allied himself to most of the charitable institutions of the City. During the Indian Famine, he contributed most generously to the relief fund. Mr. John Tennant died in 1878, aged 82 years, and his son, the present Sir Charles Tennant, Bart., of the Glen, late M.P. for Peebles-shire, became the head of the great firm at St. Rollox, and is in all respects a worthy representative of the honourable name he bears.

Some idea of the extent of the works belonging to the firm of Charles Tennant & Co. may be formed, when it is mentioned that they are estimated to cover 180 acres of ground, and to absorb about £120,000 of yearly wages. St. Rollox, or, as it is more familiarly called, "Tennant's" Stalk, is regarded with more pride by the citizens of Glasgow than any merely ornamental monument in the city. It was erected in 1842, and its measurements are as follows :—

	Feet.	Inches
OUTER CONE—		
Total height from foundation,	455	6
From surface to top of cone,	435	6
Outside diameter at foundation,	50	0
Do. at surface,	40	0
Do. top of cope,	13	6
INNER CONE—		
Total height from foundation,	263	0
From surface to top of cope,	243	0
Inside diameter at foundation,	12	0
Do. top of cope,	13	6

It may be interesting to note here the following facts relating to the great rival chimney stalk of Glasgow, erected at Port-Dundas by Mr. Joseph Townsend in the years 1857-8-9 :— The foundation consists of thirty courses of brickwork, the lowermost course 47 feet in diameter, the uppermost 32 feet 6 inches in diameter. The height above the foundation is 454 feet. The diameter at the base is 32 feet, and at the top 13 feet 6 inches. A 9-inch lining built inside, distinct from the chimney, with a space between the walls, is carried up to a height of 60 feet. It will thus be seen that Townsend's stalk is the higher of the two.

. . . .

We regret that our space will not permit us to dwell longer on this interesting aspect of our city's history. The mercantile is by far the largest and most prominent side of its character, and many incidents of a highly instructive nature could be given, showing how fortunes have been made through industry, perseverance, and honesty; and, alas! also, how fortunes have been lost and characters ruined, by reckless speculation, overreaching rapacity, dishonesty, and fraud. For all our merchants have not been of the honourable type, although that has, we verily believe been the prevailing characteristic. The failures of the Western and City Banks in modern days were almost unparallelled in the United Kingdom for their magnitude and disastrous consequences; and it were folly to deny that these mercantile calamities were brought about by recklessness and grasping selfishness on the part of a few unprincipled men. But even these failures, black and gloomy though they were, became blessings in disguise; for they were the means of bringing out in luminous and beautiful colours the very highest and best qualities of our great community, in arousing into action a spirit of deep, warm sympathy for the oppressed, and a princely generosity that not only turned the darkness into light, but shed a halo of glory round the character of our city that aroused the admiration of the whole United Kingdom. Let us trust that these disasters have also had the effect of permanently purifying the entire texture of our mercantile morality.

We have already indicated that the acquisition of large fortunes by men in humble positions has not been confined to the period of the tobacco and cotton lords of the last generation, but has extended even to the present day. Many interesting instances of that fact could easily be related did our space permit. One or two may, however, be allowed, although, for obvious reasons, we cannot mention names.

Just a few months ago one of the best known and most respected of our city merchants, who was foremost in every good work for the benefit of the citizens, died at an advanced age, leaving behind him a fortune of £100,000. That sum might have been much larger had the gentleman referred to been a hard, miserly man, who kept all his means to himself. But he was liberal and charitable, and gave to private and public benefactions many hundreds a year. Well, this gentleman was at one time a common porter in the establishment of which he afterwards became the head, and might have been seen by many still alive wheeling a barrow with his employer's goods through the streets of our city.

A recent Lord Provost of the city—who was honoured by Her Majesty with a knighthood, who has a fine estate and mansion house in the country, and whose wealth is great—was, at a not very distant period, a humble grocer in Cowcaddens. And it is gratifying to know that his success was achieved by honest and honourable industry, and was the means of benefiting his fellow-citizens as well as enriching himself.

And have we not all observed within the last few months that one of our great captains of industry—who gave employment to not hundreds, but thousands of workmen—has left behind him a fortune of upwards of a million pounds sterling, made within the brief space of twenty years. For that gentleman began his career in Glasgow as a foreman mechanic, and we believe resided in a common tenement house of three or four apartments on the south side of the river.

Let our young citizens, then, not think that the former days were better than these. There are yet fortunes to be made if the proper qualifications are brought into play. And in any case, and perhaps best of all, there is scope for an honourable livelihood being earned by all who will adopt the grand old motto of the Finlays—" Faith, Honour, Industry, Independence."

With one short anecdote we close this long, but we trust not uninteresting, chapter. A company of Glasgow merchants found themselves gathered together one night at a dinner party, and, warmed and put in good humour by the excellence and abundance of the viands provided for them, they grew loquacious and confidential with each other, and proceeded to relate the history of their success, which in every case was considerable. Nearly all of them had begun their city life in humble circumstances. One had come from a lowland parish with the proverbial half-crown in his pocket; another had come from the Highlands with all his effects in a bundle carried over his shoulder; a third had come over from the Green Isle with nothing but a shillelagh in his hand; and so on they went. At last one of the company arose, and with solemn visage declared that his record could beat all the others. His companions bent their ears eagerly to hear what that record could be. "Why, gentlemen," continued the speaker in deep thrilling tones, "I came to Glasgow without a shirt on my back." Every one expressed the utmost surprise at this revelation, for the speaker was one of the most prosperous of the company. They had no idea that he had been so far down. But the story was not yet completed. "Yes, gentlemen," said he, "my story is perfectly true, for I was born in Glasgow!"

CHAPTER IX.

ON THE MANNERS AND HABITS OF OUR FOREFATHERS.

" When this old cap was new,
  'Tis since a hundred year ;
No malice then we knew,
  But all things plenty were :
. . . .
The neighbours were friendly bidden,
  And all had welcome true ;
The poor from the gates were not chidden,
  When this old cap was new."
          —TIME'S ALTERATIONS—*Anon.*

NOTWITHSTANDING the great wealth of our merchant princes, and the industrious well-to-do condition of our working classes of a past generation, the mode of living adopted by both classes was, on the whole, of a remarkably natural, frugal, and unaffected description. True, the Virginia dons and India merchants bore a high head, kept up a considerable state, dressed well, and in their leisure hours were addicted to conviviality and boisterous social enjoyment. Yet, compared with our present luxurious modes of living, theirs were simplicity itself. As we have seen, their residences were either situated within the city, or in its immediate neighbourhood ; and it was no uncommon thing for our opulent merchants to have a house in town, and a country house at a distance of not more than 6 or 10 miles. They dined at the primitive, plebeian hour of one o'clock, and latterly at three o'clock, on the most substantial fare ; all the dishes were set upon the table at once—no such a thing as *courses* being known in those days. They drank port, sherry, and Madeira, rum punch or hot spiced ales ; and while they, too frequently, perhaps, drank deeply, yet the cost of their bibulations was not great. Even at their nightly or weekly clubs, Dr. Strang informs us, the cost of their supper and potations did not exceed two shillings a head, at most, and sometimes a good deal less. But what they lacked in gentility and refined luxuriance they made up in exuberant mirth and jollity, in racy jokes, puns, quips, and cranks, and in abundant laughter and high animal spirits. Here is a picture of the manner of living of the better classes of a century ago. "The houses, with the exception of those occupied by the leading men and merchants of the city, were chiefly in flats; and the furniture of these, although very inferior, both in taste and elegance, to that of the present day, was nevertheless good and comfortable. The dinner table on party days was, as at present, invariably covered with a fine white double damask tablecloth, which, however, was removed so soon as the repast was ended. There were, however, no table napkins placed before the guests at dinner; although, sometimes these modern comforts were sported at the tea table; and such articles, if ever seen, were certainly not fringed with *lace*, which some upstarts have lately been attempting to introduce. There were no silver forks then in use; and forks of steel, with more than two prongs, were even a rarity. It was the common practice, even among the higher circles, that the dinner should be put upon the table, and the ladies placed at the dinner board, before the gentlemen were called or allowed to enter. And this custom was felt to be the more necessary when, as frequently the case, a bedroom was the only reception room in the house. Most of the small company dinners were placed on the board at once, after which there might be a remove of upper and lower end dishes, but nothing more. In addition to the wines already noticed, oat cake and small beer were to be had in every family; the former was presented even at state parties, and the latter was always placed in two or more china jugs at the corners of the table, for any guest who might wish to quaff such a luxury. Drinking water at an entertainment was altogether unpractised. Cheese was invariably produced at the close of every repast, and was always accompanied with London porter. Ices and finger-glasses were still in the womb of fashion; and each person generally carried in his pocket a small silver dessert-knife, which was unhesitatingly brought from its hiding-place, if a golden pippin or a moorfowl-egg pear by any chance called for its aid. The retiring of a male guest to the drawing-room was a rare occurrence indeed; and hence the poor lady of the house, when there were no ladies invited, was generally left to sip her tea in solitude, while her husband and friends were getting *royal* over their *sherbet*. The fact is, that drinking and swearing were characteristic of the dinner parties of last century, not only in Glasgow, but everywhere else. It was, at that time, an exception to the general rule for a man to be either willing or capable of joining the ladies after dinner. The ladies, however, had some consolation in their frequent evening tea parties. These entertainments—which were ever redolent of cookies and shortbread—were generally held about six, and concluded about eight o'clock, at which time "the lass with the lantern" was formally announced—the constant companion of every lady (whether protected by a gentleman or not) who might, in those gasless days, be out after nightfall. There does not appear to have been the same formality in the matter of invitations as is now observed. The friends of the hostess lived within a radius of a few hundred yards, and the maid would be sent round to invite the guests, perhaps, on the previous day. There was a custom of numbering the tea spoons, so that the hostess was able to return to each guest the cup that he or she had before. It was quite a common thing for the lady of the house to wash her own tea things in presence of her guests, partly for the sake of preventing her china being broken by a careless servant, and partly because servants were not so numerous as now; and no lady in those good old days was ashamed to do a part of her own household work. It would have been considered a piece of intolerable pride for her to summon a servant from her duties in the kitchen to mend the fire in the parlour, as is now too frequently the case."

A few words now on the domestic habits of the working classes. Towards the close of last century Glasgow was not considered a cheap place for a working man to live in, prices being higher than in other towns. But according to *Gibson*, although the wages of mechanics were, upon an average, only about 7s. per week, yet, by their frugal mode of living, they were able to meet their expenditure and to save a little money besides. Their ordinary breakfasts and suppers were, from choice, oatmeal porridge, with a little milk or small beer, and their dinner often consisted of barley broth. Two other articles of food, we are told, were much made use of by the poor people in Glasgow. These were potatoes and salted white herrings, which were cheap, potatoes being at the rate of 7d. per peck of seven English gallons heaped, and salted herrings at 4s. 2d. per 100. Three pounds of these potatoes boiled with a couple of salted herrings did not exceed in value three halfpence, and were a sufficient dinner for any labouring man whatever. Honest Gibson adds that there was no set of people in the world more healthy than the mechanics of Glasgow, and yet potatoes and herrings were daily made use of for a considerable time of the year. Scarce any such thing as an apoplexy was then known in Glasgow. By the bill of mortality for the year 1776 only one person died of that disorder, whereas in the bills of mortality for a town of the same size in England, the numbers who died of apoplexy in one year were great. We are further told that seldom did a year pass in England without complaints about the high price of provisions, and the English mechanics were recommended to try the fare of their Scottish compeers, not only for the sake of their health and their pockets, but with a view to the encouragement of our herring fisheries, by which a hardy race of seamen would be trained and fitted for the defence of their country when the occasion demanded.

This worthy old historian, who was at the same time a merchant in Glasgow, had a keen eye to business as well as to historical research, although some of his ideas were of a somewhat primitive and quaint order, as the following sentences will show. He had been dealing with the subject of the manufactures of the city, which were evidently at that time in a depressed state:—"While the industrious inhabitants of Glasgow and Paisley," he says, "were lately exerting themselves to improve, bring to perfection, and extend the manufactures of cambric and lawn, the greater part of the women of Scotland were wearing muslin, a fabric of the Indies. Nay, so great is the influence of fashion, that the very wives and daughters of these men were wearing this exotic themselves. Surely we are void of thought! People prone to start difficulties will naturally say, Who is to lead this fashion, and which way is it to be brought about? My answer is, that there is nothing more easy. Let the people who fix the fashion be such whose quality and fortune elevate them above the rest of mankind, and let this fashion be changed three times every year in the following manner:—Let there be a public breakfast in Edinburgh upon the 14th February annually. Let the different manufacturers produce before this assembly the respective kinds and patterns of the goods which they can manufacture, and let it be determined by the company present what species of goods are to be in fashion for the whole dress of both men and women, to commence on the 4th of June and to continue to the 11th of November. Let there be another breakfast upon the 12th November which shall direct the goods to be in fashion from the 13th of February to the 4th of June. Let the woman of the highest quality present always preside in these assemblies. Let her appoint some gentleman to take the sense of the company, and let their determination be published in the Edinburgh newspapers. Let the ladies treat every gentleman who does not give obedience to the mandates of these assemblies as an unfashionable creature, and as one inimical to the welfare of his country. Let the gentlemen look upon every lady who does not appear dressed in the manufactures of her country as an extravagant woman, unfit to attend to the concerns of a family. An institution of this kind would, in a very short time, have a surprising and salutary effect, and would certainly tend to the good of our country."

The simplicity and ingenuousness of the foregoing views are in themselves a good illustration of the homely and unsophisticated manners of those days.

The external character and appearance of the city towards the close of last century, as described by various historians, will be interesting to our readers, and will give a further indication of the manners of our forefathers. With the exception of the market day—when there was a more than ordinary bustle in the leading thoroughfares, and when the sides of the High Street were encumbered with a profusion of wooden dishes, such as churns, tubs, pails, bowls, &c., and when the south side of the Trongate was also crowded with shoe and other stalls—there was on other days little or nothing in the streets to attract particular attention, far less to create any risk of detention or of damage. Indeed, during the last ten years of the past century there was scarcely anything so striking as the stillness of the city, at least when compared with the continued hum and hurly-burly of the present day. The rattle of a coach or a carriage was then a rare sound, and as to carts going at the present high pressure speed, that was altogether unknown, and if tried would certainly have been put down by the magistracy, not only as dangerous to the lieges, but as hurtful to animals! Time then appeared to be no object, and the day was felt to be always sufficient for all its wants. The populace loitered along the streets without the fear of anything to molest them, and stopped in knots to gossip and to *claver* in the busiest thoroughfares without the risk of at all incommoding the passenger traffic. In short, nothing of the universal turmoil, noise, and jostling which now characterize the city was heard, and consequently when any one either raised his voice to cry or sing, he was at once heard and listened to; and an announcement by the city crier was then held to be more effective for most things than an advertisement in the *Mercury* or *Journal*. The city bell—then rung by *Bell Geordie*—always secured a good audience, for no sooner was the triple tinkle of his skellat heard than each house in the neighbourhood was sure to despatch a messenger to hear what he had to communicate.

In those early days the watchmen of the city assumed a discretion in the performance of their duty which would look rather queer at the present day. It was nothing uncommon then for a watchman to take a man to the office and lock him up for a few hours, and then let him out again, without any charge being entered or any record kept of the proceedings. There was a stern old pensioner named "Jaikey Brown," who at one time about this period officiated as an officer. "Jaikey" had a mortal antipathy to Irishmen, and whenever, in the case of a street disturbance, he heard the *brogue* uttered, he was sure to take the unhappy owner of it into custody, whether he was the assaulting or assaulted party, holding it to be sufficient evidence of guilt that the man was a *Patlander*. In fact, it was alleged that many a poor fellow was locked up for no other offence than that he was an Irishman. "Jaikey," as a good patriot, did all he could to discourage and suppress the "Eerish" by locking them up in the cells and *cracking* their *croons* with his truncheon; but the effect was like that of Dame Partington sweeping out the Atlantic with her besom. The Huns overspread the land notwithstanding. Each watchman had a wooden box, called a sentry box, for resting in when he felt fatigued or when the weather was cold and rainy. The wild youths of the town used often to lock "Dogberry" in his nest altogether, and sometimes they even tumbled the box over on its face, in which position the poor fellow lay till relieved by his fellow-watchmen. In those days there was no regulation to prevent all the watchmen in the city being in their boxes at one and the same time, and it was well known that many a snooze they took in their retreats while the city took care of itself. This system would be considered the height of absurdity now-a-days; but later on, when it was resolved that not more than every alternate watchman should take shelter in the sentry boxes, this modified arrangement was considered to savour of inhumanity!

That our Glasgow citizens of the past generation were more addicted to conviviality, fun, and frolic than to gentility in their manners, the following anecdotes will illustrate:—A party of gentlemen once dined with a person who had a bleaching green and residence a few miles from the city. The night was wet both within and without doors, and about two in the morning, when a proposal was made to break up, the host got a large covered cart, usually employed in carrying cloth to and from Glasgow, into which the guests gladly consented to go, for want of anything better, in order to be conveyed to their quarters. On driving up to the Cross with this strange load, the servant, a very whimsical old fellow, stopped, and coming round to the door, which was behind, inquired to what point he was now to proceed. The few who could speak bawled out their respective lodgings—some in one part of the city, some in another—while others could only utter such sounds as showed how unable they were to take care of themselves. Quite perplexed with the contrary orders he received, and altogether hopeless of being able to see the whole safely housed, the man, to use a popular saying, resolved to "let the tow go with the bucket;" and going to the other end of the cart, deliberately upset the whole into the street, as if they had been only a parcel of old sacks, remarking, "My braw sparks, gin your tongues hing sae loosely in your heads as no' to be able to say whaur your hames are—though it's maybe mair frae punch than pride—just try if your feet will find them."

Provost Aird, a worthy citizen of Glasgow, who lived in the earlier part of last century, was honoured on several occasions with high municipal offices. Among other good actions, he devoted a good deal of his time and abilities to the promotion of religious movements; and the Ramshorn Church was built under his dictatorship. His death occurred about fourteen years after the erection of that church. The worthy provost during his lifetime was wont, along with his brethren in the Council, to frequent a comfortable tavern or hostelry at the head of the Saltmarket, kept by one Mistress Neps Denny. At one of the meetings, shortly after the good man's decease, it was proposed that an epitaph should be composed by one of the members of the club; but whether it was that the magistrates of those days were less poetical than their successors, or that this is an office not easily assimilated to the ordinary duties of a civic functionary, it was found that the assistance of the buxom landlady was necessary. Perfectly familiar with her subject, and under no fears of severe criticism, Neps produced the following lines :—

" Here lies Provost Aird,
He was neither a great merchant nor a great laird;
At biggin' o' kirks he had richt gude skill;
He was five times Lord Provost and thrice Dean o' Gil'."

It would be a piece of unpardonable neglect in a volume on Glasgow, to overlook the abilities of the ingenious and witty JOHN DOUGLAS of Barloch, writer in Glasgow. His well known convivial powers and readiness of repartee made him a welcome guest at all social parties. On one of these occasions he happened to occupy the next seat to the hostess, to which, according to the laws of etiquette, was assigned the office of carving for the lady. Mr. D., with his usual politeness, proffered his services. The joint had not been prepared by the butcher, and it required some strength, as well as art, to separate the parts. In pressing the carving knife on a tough ligament, it missed, and a quantity of the gravy was thrown upon the gown of the hostess. " Mr. Douglas," she said, " I beg a thousand pardons, the fault is entirely mine; the piece ought to have been better prepared for the knife." " Oh, ma'am," replied Mr. Douglas, " yours is all the grace, and mine is all the gravy."

When the popular walk on the banks of the Clyde was thrown open to the public by a decision of Supreme Court, after the long period of interruption caused by the erection of "Harvey's Dike," great numbers of people crowded thither, attracted by the celebrity of the case. Mr. Douglas happening on one occasion to meet the gentleman who had taken the most active part in conducting the plea on behalf of the public, waggishly declared to him, in the most serious manner, that he must surely be a most dangerous person, as he had aimed a severe blow at the security of the mercantile world. "How?" asked the gentleman, in the utmost astonishment. "Because," said Mr. Douglas, "you have created a very great run upon the banks."

When Dr. Thomson's famous work on chemistry was published a very severe review of it appeared in a London magazine. Dr. Thomson, in as severe a reply, ascribed the authorship of the review to Dr. Ure. In allusion to which, Mr. Douglas said, "If this were the case, it was merely a very fine specimen of *Uric Acid!*"

Mr. Douglas was a very handsome man; for which reason he received the name of "Adonis"; but on account of an infirmity in his lower extremities, he always wore very broad cloth pantaloons; and he used to remark they were his "loose habits." One day, on entering the Tontine reading room, at the Cross, he was followed by a little cur. "Is this your dog?" inquired the keeper. "No," replied the wit. "You should know I am *Dogless* (Douglas)." He took great interest in furthering the agitation preceding the Reform Act of 1832. He was the foremost in many processions, and an orator at mass meetings held on the Green. He had a stentorian voice, and his usual exordium was in the style of Brutus—"Britons, countrymen, and lovers, hear me for my cause, and be silent that you may better hear."

Here is a sample of the *genus* "Dominie" in the olden times.

Mr. Andrew Taylor, though a good teacher, became, in after-life perhaps, rather too fond of social enjoyment, and consequently his classes fell off. It was his invariable practice to dine out on Saturday; and he rarely reached home on that day by the most direct route; and when he did so, it was with some difficulty that he found his way into bed. It appears, too, that he had little recollection next day of how he had done so; and, accordingly, it is scarcely surprising that, on one occasion, after returning home, and going to bed on Saturday night, well "refreshed," he happened to wake up in a hurry, on hearing the clock strike in the morning, and forgetting the day of the week, rung his bell violently, and on his servant coming, cried out, "Jenny, Jenny, bring shaving water as fast as possible; what 'll the boys says, an' me no at the schule?" "Oh! Maister Taylor," said the domestic, "it's the Sawbbath day!" "The Sawbbath day!" quoth the dominie; "glorious institution the Sawbbath!" and forthwith turned himself round for another snooze.

There was a good deal of the form of religion and of severe orthodoxy among our forefathers, however lax their morality and rough their social habits. And the mixture of religion and worldliness was sometimes rather grotesque. Sound doctrine has generally been regarded in Scotland as of more importance than good works. The following anecdote will serve to illustrate what may be termed the straight laced orthodoxy of the time:—One of the tradesmen employed at the erection of a Unitarian chapel in Glasgow—probably the one situated on the site in Union Street now occupied by the *N. B. Daily Mail* office—went into an ironmonger's shop to make a purchase of single-flooring nails for the woodwork; and having paid and got delivery of the nails, the shopman, struck at the quantity wanted, inquired, "Whaurto are ye gaun to drive a' thae nails, man? They micht sair ane o' the toun kirks." "An' they're just for a kirk! though no ane o' the toun anes," was the reply. "Maybe ane o' our meeting houses?" was the next query. "They're for the woodwork o' the Unitarian chapel," replied the tradesman. "Say ye sae?" said the man of metal; "and had ye the impudence, sin' I maun say sae, to try to get them frae me! there's your siller to you, an' gie me back my nails. I'll no sell a pin to prop up the tabernacle o' Sawtan."

Another anecdote of a similar kind is related by Robert Gray of Carntyne, who, in his day, was a deputy-lieutenant and active magistrate of the county of Lanark. It refers to the Presbyterian zeal of his aunt, an old lady of the Hamilton of Newton family. When the Episcopalian chapel, near the Green of Glasgow, was in the course of being built, Mrs. Hamilton happened to be walking in the Green during the hour when the workmen were absent at dinner. She accordingly took advantage of their absence, and lifting up one of their mallets, she deposited it in her ample muff and carried it off, muttering, "If ilka ane would do as I am doing this day, the House of Baal would not be biggit for twelve months to come."

Here is an example of the rude manners of even the ministers of the olden times. The Rev. Mr. Thom, of Govan, an eccentric, but worthy divine who flourished in the latter half of last century, was requested on one occasion to preach a sermon in the Tron Church of Glasgow, and being uncertain as he said what would best suit a Glasgow audience, he brought with him on Saturday evening about half-a-dozen MS. sermons in his pocket. He thought if he had the opinion of a few friends, it might serve as a key to guide him in his choice. He accordingly asked a few acquaintances to join him in a pipe and tankard of ale in a favourite howff. "I'm invited to preach a sermon to you great folks in Glasgow," said he, "and really I maun after this think myself a man of some consequence, when I have had such an honour conferred upon me. But as I'm ignorant of what will please your nice preaching palates in this big town, I have brought a few sermons with me, which I'll read over to you, that I may judge which will be the most suitable." He read over one by one, accordingly, until he came to the last, and with each they were equally well pleased. Taking up the last one he proceeded until he came to a passage that fairly puzzled his auditors. "Stop," said they, "read that passage over again, Mr. Thom." "Wait a wee till I get to the end," said Mr. T., and he continued till another halt was made for explanation. "I'll tax your patience nae langer" said the orator; "this will suit ye exactly, for you Glasgow folks admire most what ye least understand."

It is of the same worthy and on the occasion of the service in Glasgow, alluded to, that the story is told that during the service, a gentleman in front of the gallery took out his handkerchief to wipe his brow, forgetting that a pack of cards was wrapped up in it; the whole pack was scattered over the breast of the gallery. Mr. T., who had risen to engage in prayer, could not resist an expression of sarcasm, solemn as the act was in which he was about to engage—"Oh man, man!" said he, "surely your psalm-book has been ill bun!"

We do not for a moment doubt that during the whole of its history there was much genuine religion and morality in Glasgow, and many of its ministers and people were of the very salt of the earth, but a century ago or less, their manners were rude and unpolished, and even occasionally approached the profane.

But a more earnest religious spirit, and a more fervent zeal for the improvement of the morals of the people were shortly to be infused into the community, as will be related in a subsequent chapter.

CHAPTER X.

A MEDICAL CHAPTER.

" Helpers of men they're called, and we confess
Theirs the deep study, theirs the lucky guess.
We own that numbers join with care and skill
A temperate judgment, a devoted will;
Men who suppress their feelings, but who feel
The painful symptoms they delight to heal.
. . . .
Glad if a hope should rise from nature's strife
To aid their skill and save the lingering life ;
But this must virtue's generous effort be,
And spring from nobler motives than a fee."
—THE PHYSICIAN— *Crabbe.*

THE FACULTY OF PHYSICIANS AND SURGEONS
was incorporated by Royal Charter granted by King James VI in the year 1599. At that time the population of Glasgow was about 7,000, and the medical men in the city consisted of a few ordinary practitioners and their apprentices. The well informed and well educated medical practitioner did not come into existence for many years afterwards. The law was somewhat lax in those days in respect to the practising of medicine; so much so that Dr. Peter Low, Dr. Robert Hamilton, and one or two more medical men of standing thought it necessary for the safety of the public and the dignity of a noble profession that more

stringent laws should be formed in regard to the right to practise medicine. Dr. Peter Low—himself an eminent practitioner, having been "chirurgeone to King James VI, and chief chirurgeone to his dearest son the Prince; a doctor in the Faculty of Chirurgerie at Paris; and ordinary chirurgeon to the French King and Navarre;" and having had great practice, both civil and military; and who prided himself in being a "Scottishman"—was the first to take the very important step of making application to King James for a charter to form a Medical Corporation. The charter was readily granted "to Peter Low, surgeon, and Robert Hamilton, professor of medicine, and their successors." According to this charter, "all ignorant, unskilled, and unlearned persons, wha, under colour of chirurgeons," made havoc with the lives of His Majesty's lieges, were prevented from doing so any longer, and none but those who passed through the portals into the sacred profession by examinations of a searching nature, conducted by Peter Low and Robert Hamilton, were allowed to practise medicine or surgery. In those days, on the Continent, throughout Europe, in London, and in Edinburgh, the barber was closely associated with the surgeon, performing the more menial offices of shaving, hair cutting (which were called surgical operations), and of bleeding, administering clysters, &c. But in the charter granted by King James VI no mention is made of barbers, nor had they any connection with the new faculty until the year 1656, when they jointly obtained from the magistrates of the city a seal of cause constituting them an incorporation, which existed for about seventy years, in 1722 the surgeons falling back upon their original gift, and the barbers upon their seal of cause. They have ever since continued separate and distinct. Mr. Peter Low, who may be considered the founder of the Faculty, was a very famous surgeon during the latter half of the sixteenth century, and practised in Glasgow for some years previous to his death. He was the author of a book on the *Art of Chirurgerie*, in the dedication of which he addresses the friendly reader in the following words:—"I impart to you my labours, hidden secrets, and experiments by me practised, and daylay put in use, to the great comfort, ease, and delight of you, and such as have had occasion to use my help in France, Flanders, and elsewhere, the space of 22 years: thereafter being Chirurgian Maior to the Spanish regiments at Paris, 2 years; next following the French King, my master, in the warres 6 years, where I took commoditie to practise all points and operations of Chirurgerie. Upon which occasion, I endeavoured myself to collect my practices, at vacant houres, into the booke, according to the opinion of the ancient and learned practitioners in Physick and Chirurgerie, in such plaine termes as I could, for the use of the common sorte; which now I do offer to thee newly corrected and enlarged for thy greater comfort." To his book on the *Art of Chirurgerie*, there is a quaint and curious dedication "to my very Worshipfull, learned, and well experimented good friends Gilbert Primrose, Sergeant Chirurgian to the King's Maiestie; James Harvie, Chiefe Chirurgiane to the Queene's Maiestie; those of the Worshipfull Companie of Chirurgians in London and Edenborough, and all such well experimented men in this Kingdom who are licensed to professe the Divine Art of Chirurgerie, Peter Low wishes all happinesse of life." In this dedication he declaims at great length and grand style against all quack doctors, and such "as do their worke unskillfulley, . . . like as cosoners, quacksalvers, charlitans, witches, charmers, and divers other sortes of abusers," which latter he denounces as poisoning and killing the lieges in "divers ways." Dr. Peter Low died at a ripe old age, and his remains were interred in the old burying ground of the High Church. The stone erected to his memory (which is the property of the Faculty) bears the following inscription :—

"1612.
M.
P.   L.
IOHN LOW.   IAMES LOW.
"Stay passenger and view this stone,
For under it lyis such a one,
Who cuired many whill he lieved,
So gracious he no man grieved,
Yez when his physick's force oft failed,
His plesant purpose then prevailed ;
For of his God he got the grace
To live in mirth, and die in peace,
Heaven hes his soul—his corps this stone,
Sigh passenger and soe be gone.
. . . .

> Ah, me ! I gravell am and dust,
> And to the grave deshend I must ;
> O, painted piece of liveing clay,
> May be not proud of thy short day."

The Andersonian University.

John Anderson, F.R.S., Professor of Natural Philosophy in Glasgow University, born in 1726 in Roseneath, died in 1796, willed that all his effects, of every kind, should be devoted to the establishment of an educational institution, to be denominated the Andersonian University. His will was carried into effect on the 9th of June, 1795, by the Magistrates granting a charter of incorporation to the proposed institution. The design of the founder was that there should be four colleges—for arts, law, medicine, and theology. Anderson's University is a wonderful example of what one man may do for his kind. The private fortune of one professor of the original College of Glasgow has been found sufficient to produce a new fount of learning, not unworthy to rank with the old, and of great practical utility to the public. It has, perhaps, been most noted as a school of medicine, and its allied subjects. In the long roll of its students may be found names indicating all nationalities, and at the present time, many who are possessed of its honourable surgical qualification of L.F.P.S.G. fill important public and private positions in all parts of the world. The world renowned African explorer, David Livingstone, was at one time a humble and devoted medical student within its walls. In regard to teachers or professors, it has served as a stepping stone to higher careers in more distinguished Universities. Several of the medical and surgical professors in our venerable, though revivified *alma mater* can look back with pride to the Andersonian as the place where they, for the first time, with a little trepidation, doubtless, delivered prelections under the new and high-sounding name of professor. Many of our distinguished students and practical medical men, of professorial proclivities, would still count it no mean honour to be ranked among its staff of teachers.

GLASGOW UNIVERSITY FACULTY OF MEDICINE.

This Faculty is much indebted to the celebrated Dr. William Cullen for giving it a primary and very powerful impulse, and for organizing a more extended and important course of study. Dr. Cullen was born in the parish of Hamilton, 15th April, 1710. He studied in Glasgow University, and was apprenticed to John Paisley, M.F.P.S.G. He had no regular course of medical study at this time, as, although there were professors whose business it was to give lectures on medicine, these were on a small scale. His education was chiefly derived from observing his master's practice, and reading such medical books as he could procure. Dr. Cullen gained the high esteem of his master, who, in after years, when Cullen had distinguished himself as a teacher, opened his extensive library for the use of his students. He was slow to speak when any speculation or debate was started by his fellow-students; but when they met again, if the same subject came up, he never failed to show that in the interval he had acquired a more intimate knowledge of the subject than any of his companions. He studied in Edinburgh during the sessions of 1734-5-6. The doctrines of Boerhaave, which were taught in the University, were subsequently contested in the Medical Hall by Cullen and his associates. Many years after, the doctrines of Cullen were as keenly contested in the same hall. The onward progress of knowledge and science is fatal to all theories chiefly based on speculation. Dr. Cullen practised in Hamilton in company with Dr. William Hunter, with whom he was on intimate terms, and was twice elected magistrate. In 1741 he married a Miss Johnstone, who was beautiful, had great good sense, sweet temper and disposition, and elegant manners, and who brought him a little money, which was of much service to him in his investigation after knowledge. Dr. Cullen removed to Glasgow, and became a professor in the University in 1746. He was the first to establish a systematic course of instruction in medicine. No lectures were delivered previous to his connection with the University. He arranged with the other professors to give lectures, and he himself lectured on *Materia Medica*, physic, and botany. His lectures were not written, but were delivered extempore in a plain familiar style. He deviated from the usual custom, and lectured in English—except on botany. Dr. Cullen introduced the Linnaen system of botany into the University. He also taught chemistry. He was the founder of a new era in the medical school in the University of Glasgow. He had an extensive, but not lucrative, practice in Glasgow during the period of his busy connection with teaching in the University. About 1751 he removed to Edinburgh, where he thought he would have more leisure and opportunity for prosecuting his investigations. There he succeeded the celebrated Dr. Plummer as Professor of Chemistry in the University, and was the contemporary of the noted and distinguished Dr. Gregory. In Edinburgh he wrote and published in eight volumes his important work, *Synopsis Nosologiæ Methodicæ*, a work which did much to systematize and facilitate the acquirement of medical knowledge, as they express or classify the leading and characteristic signs of certain diseases. In 1775 he published the first edition of his *Practice of Physic*, which spread rapidly throughout Europe, and produced the author £3,000—a very considerable sum in those days. It was translated into French, German, and Italian. His doctrine is based principally upon that which had been previously promulgated by Hoffman—viz., that the nervous system has a powerful and extensive influence in producing and modifying the diseases to which the human body is liable. Both in Edinburgh and Glasgow, Dr. Cullen took great interest in his work and in his students. He was employed from five to six hours daily in seeing his patients, and in prescribing for those who consulted him at a distance in writing; and when the College was open, delivered two and often four lectures of an hour each during five days of the week. Yet he never seemed in a hurry, and had an easy, cheerful, sociable demeanour; and in a private party of whist, for sixpence a game, he could be as keenly engaged for an hour before supper as if he had no other employment to mind, and as if he had a thousand pounds depending on the game. With the attentive and diligent of his students he formed an early acquaintance, and invited them in two's, three's, and four's, to sup with him, and freely and with much ease, conversing with them on many topics. By such means, he soon became acquainted with the most deserving of them ; and as there were many in those days whose circumstances were much hampered for want of money, he found many delicate excuses for making these circumstances easy, by placing himself under trifling obligations to them. Dr. Cullen lectured in Edinburgh till he was 79 years of age; and on his retirement, the provost, town council, and magistrates, and the different public societies of Edinburgh conferred upon him many honourable testimonies of their regard. He died on 5th February, 1790, in his 80th year, and was interred in the churchyard of Kirknewton near Edinburgh.

WILLIAM HUNTER, M.D.

Closely associated with Dr. Cullen was William Hunter, M.D., the founder of the valuable and famous Hunterian Museum. He was born at East Kilbride, 23rd May, 1718. He studied at the University of Glasgow, and was designed for the church, but hesitated from conscientious scruples to subscribe to all the articles of faith. He became acquainted with Dr. Cullen, who was in practice in Hamilton, and such was Cullen's influence over him, that he turned his attention to medicine, which he studied at the Universities of Edinburgh and London, and gained a position of great eminence in the profession. His connection with Glasgow is chiefly through the Hunterian Museum. A Dr. Sandys, who was at one time professor of anatomy at Cambridge, had formed a valuable collection of preparations, which, on his death, fell into the hands of Dr. Bloomfield, and was afterwards purchased by Dr. Hunter for £200. This was the nucleus from which the Hunterian Museum was formed.

MATTHEW BAILLIE, M.D.

Dr. Baillie was the son of the Rev. James Baillie, D.D., Professor of Divinity in the University of Glasgow. He was born in Shotts, 27th October, 1761, where his father was then minister. His mother was sister to the celebrated Dr. William and Mr. John Hunter, and one of his two sisters was Miss Joanna Baillie. He was educated in Glasgow, and studied medicine in Baliol College, Oxford. He was assistant and successor to his uncle, Dr. William Hunter, who appointed him by will to have the use of his splendid anatomical preparations so long as he continued an anatomical lecturer, after which they were to be transferred to Glasgow College. Dr. Baillie added no less than 1,100 articles to his uncle's museum. He obtained the highest distinction in London as an anatomical lecturer.

Joseph Black, M.D.

Dr. Black, though born in 1728 in France, was of Scotch extraction, and studied in Glasgow under the celebrated Dr. Cullen, whose assistant he became in chemistry. He, however, completed his studies in Edinburgh. He devoted his attention chiefly to chemistry, and succeeded Dr. Cullen as professor of that science in Glasgow University. He obtained this position by his discovery in chemistry of what was called *fixed air*, or the part which carbonic acid plays upon pure lime—a very important discovery in those days, and which not only was the means of the advancement of that then comparatively unknown science, but through him reflected credit upon the chair of chemistry in the University. Dr. Black was also the discoverer of *latent heat*, another most important discovery in chemistry ; and his prelections on the subject of evaporation were of great advantage to James Watt, and may be said to have laid the foundation of the great practical use of steam. His principal friend was Dr. Adam Smith, author of the *Wealth of Nations*, who was professor of moral philosophy at that time. Dr. Black also succeeded Dr. Cullen as lecturer in chemistry in Edinburgh University. He died, 26th November, 1799, in the 71st year of his age, without any convulsion, shock, or stupor, to announce or retard the approach of death. Being at table with his usual fare—some bread, a few prunes, and a measured quantity of milk, diluted with water, and having the cup in his hand, when the last stroke of the pulse was to be given he had set it down upon his knees, which were joined together, and kept it steady with his hand in the manner of a person perfectly at ease, and in this attitude, expired without spilling a drop, and without a writhe in his countenance, as if an experiment had been required to show to his friends the facility with which he departed. His servant opened the door to tell him that some one had left his name, but getting no answer, stepped about half way towards him, and seeing him sitting in that easy posture, supporting his basin of milk with one hand, he thought that he had dropped asleep, which he had sometimes seen happen after his meals. The man went back and shut the door, but before he got down stairs, some anxiety that he could not account for, made him return and look at his master. Even then he was satisfied, after coming pretty near, and turned to go away, but again returned, and coming quite close, found his master without life.

William Hamilton, M.D.,

Was a celebrated surgeon and lecturer on anatomy in Glasgow University. He was born on 31st July, 1758, in Glasgow, and was a son of Thomas Hamilton, surgeon in Glasgow, and professor of anatomy and botany. He studied in Edinburgh under Cullen, and in London under Dr. William Hunter, who formed a very high opinion of him. He had an extensive and lucrative practice in Glasgow, and extended to the poor much of his time and great talents. He died in the 32nd year of his age, in the midst of a promising and brilliant career. As a lecturer, his manner was free from pomp and affectation. His language was simple and perspicuous, but so artless that it appeared flat to those who place the beauty of language in the intricacy of arrangement or the beauty of figures. His manner of speaking corresponded with his style, and was such as might appear uninteresting to those who think it impossible to be eloquent without violent gestures or frequent variations of tone. He used nearly the tone of ordinary conversation, as his preceptor, Dr. Hunter, did before him. aiming at perspicuity only, and trusting for attention to the importance of the subjects he treated.

Allan Burns, M.D.

Allan Burns, brother to James and George Burns, the largest owners of steamships in Europe, an eminent anatomist and medical writer, was born in Glasgow, 18th September, 1781. His father, the Rev. John Burns, was minister of the Barony Parish for 69 years, and died in 1839, aged 96 years. He was early sent to study for the medical profession, and such was his proficiency that, two years after he had entered the classes, he was, at the age of 16, enabled to undertake the sole direction of the dissecting rooms of his brother, Mr. John Burns, at that time lecturer on anatomy in Glasgow. In 1804, having gone to London with the view of entering the medical service of the army, he received and accepted of the offer of director of a new hospital, on the British plan, established at St. Petersburg by the Empress Catherine, to whom he was recommended by His Excellency Dr. Crichton; and accordingly proceeded to Russia, where he did not remain above six months. On his leaving the Russian capital in January 1805, he received from the Empress, in token of good will, a valuable diamond ring. In the winter, after his return to Glasgow, he began, in place of his brother, to give lectures on anatomy and surgery. In 1809 he published "Observations on some of the frequent and important Diseases of the Heart," illustrated by cases. In 1812 appeared his second publication, "Observations on the Surgical Anatomy of the Head and Neck," also illustrated by cases. Both of these works, which embrace all his separate publications, are held in the highest estimation by the profession. Early in 1810 his health began to decline, and although he continued for two years longer to deliver lectures, it was often amid great personal suffering. An edition of his "Surgical Anatomy of the Head and Neck" was published in America, with a life of the author, and additional cases and observations by Granville Sharp Pattison,* Professor of Anatomy in the University of Maryland. Mr. Burns also contributed to the *Edinburgh Medical and Surgical Journal.*

Dr. John Moore.

During Dr. Moore's time Glasgow was a very clubable city. There were many clubs in Glasgow, and the names by which they were distinguished were varied and ingenious. They were conducted on strictly honourable, yet convivial and generous principles; and the frequent concourse of such

* Mr. Granville Sharp Pattison distinguished himself some years previously as a medical student in Glasgow, and as the daring leader of the "Resurrectionists."

individualities which composed them, under the influence of the punch bowl, and the often strained interchange of thought and opinion, as well as wit and humour, to which they gave rise, did much to develop that sagacious shrewdness which has generally characterized our enterprising townsmen. Dr. Moore was the originator of the once famous Hodge Podge Club. He was also the author of "Zelucco," and other well known works. For many years he made Glasgow his home, and in it long and ably practised the therapeutic art. He was born in Stirling in 1729, and on the death of his father (Rev. Chas. Moore) he removed into Glasgow with his mother. He was apprenticed to Mr. John Gordon, a surgeon of extensive practice; and while under his tuition he attended the lectures of Drs. Hamilton and Cullen. He afterwards served in the army on the Continent under the Duke of Argyll; attended the lectures of Dr. Hunter of London; and afterwards in Paris, where he became surgeon to the household of the Duke of Albemarle, who was ambassador at the Court of France. After residing in the French capital two years, he returned to Glasgow, and became partner to his former master, Mr. Gordon. Mr. Gordon becoming a consulting physician, Dr. Moore continued to act as surgeon; and acquiring such an extensive practice, he chose Mr. Hamilton, professor of anatomy, as his assistant. He married a daughter of Rev. Mr. Simson, professor of divinity in Glasgow University. He was a great favourite in the city and neighbourhood, and was much courted for his wit and lively humour. He afterwards became medical travelling attendant to Douglas, Duke of Hamilton; and accompanied the young duke, who was in delicate health, all over the Continent. In 1787 he commenced his remarkable correspondence with Robert Burns. He was also the biographer of Tobias Smollet, the noted author of "Roderick Random." He died in Richmond, near London, in 1802, aged seventy-three years. He was the father of General Sir John Moore, whose monument (with his martial cloak around him) stands in one of our squares, and whose memory Campbell has made dear to every Scotchman in imperishable verse. Dr. Moore was one of the most noted members of the Hodge Podge Club, many of whose members he has characterized and registered in verse. On Dr. Thomas Hamilton he wrote—

"He who leads up the van is stout Thomas the tall,
  Who can make us all laugh, though he laughs at us all;
But *entre vous*, Tom, you and I, if you please,
  Must take care not to laugh ourselves out of our fees."

On Dr. Stevenston.

"An obsequious Doctor appears next in view,
  Who smoothly glides in with a minuet bow;
In manner how soft, in apparel how trig,
  With a vast deal of physic contained in his wig."

On Dr. Colin Douglas.

"Despising all airs, detesting all art,
The thought bursts spontaneous from Douglas's heart.
Of the dregs of his vigour the best let us make,
He may do for a leech—tho' he's done for a rake."

On Dr. Moore, himself.

"The surly companion who brings up the rear,
Who looks so morose, and still speaks with a sneer,
Would fain have you think he's a poet and wit,—
But indeed, Mr. Moore, you're confoundedly bit."

Dr. Moore resided for many years in the Trongate, opposite the Laigh Kirk Steeple; and it was in this house where his son, the celebrated Sir John Moore, was born. Among those whom death cut off from the convivialities of the Hodge Podge Club at a rather early period were Dr. Colin Douglas and Dr. Stevenston, two very eminent physicians, and who, by the elegiac poet of the fraternity, Mr. John Dunlop, were honoured with the following epitaphs:—

On Dr. Colin Douglas.

"The plain, good man, who lies beneath this stone
Detested flattery. Let us give him none.
Endowed with probity and manly sense,
With genuine knowledge, void of vain pretence;
No sneaking caution, nor low venal art,
Checked or disguised the dictates of his heart;
Free from his lips his sentiments did flow,
Unawed by wealth or power, by friend or foe.
Reader! if thou canst boast as firm a friend,
As true, sincere, and void of private end,
With thy best care endeavour to retain
What kings can't give, nor Eastern treasures gain."

On Dr. Alexander Stevenston.

" Let hireling bards on splendid marble tell
How kings and heroes lived, and how they fell ;
To private worth this humble stone we raise,
Inscribed by friendship with no venal praise.
The man whose hallowed dust lies here enshrined
Was bountiful, beneficent, and kind ;
From honour'd path he never did depart ;
Mild were his manners, tender was his heart ;
Joy and good humour filled his honest soul,
When mirth and fancy sparkled round the bowl ;
And when dull care sat brooding on the brim,
The recreant fled his merriment and whim.
Friendship shall mourn, and Medicine deplore
The heart that glows, the hand that heals no more ;
While every reader joins the general tear,
For gentle, generous Stevenston lies here."

The Medical Club.

There were few members of the Faculty when the Medical Club was formed, and it was even more difficult to become a member of the Club than the Faculty. The aspirant after this honour required to be no mean man, but a high minded and social boon companion. It was composed only of the leading members of the profession, and existed from 1800 to 1814. It held its meetings once a month in Mrs. Pollock's, Princes Street, and latterly in the aristocratic "Prince of Wales," in Brunswick Street. The usual hour of meeting was four o'clock, and ten o'clock struck before any of its members showed any disposition to leave such good cheer and company, unless called away by any unforeseen summons for professional assistance. It was the most social of the then social and clubable city of Glasgow, and no cantankerous individual was on any account allowed to become a member. One black ball was sufficient to exclude any one. The Medical Club was not recruited from the younger members of the profession, and during the period of its existence serious havoc was made even in the ranks of its founders.

Doctor Drumgold,

was the originator of another of the Glasgow clubs—the "What you please Club." The doctor (although not much else is known of him) occupied at that period the situation of Inspecting Medical Officer of the Glasgow Recruiting District—a situation which, in those warlike days, was certainly no sinecure, though on that account it necessarily poured some supplementary cash into his pocket. Busily employed, no doubt, as the doctor must have been, in examining and passing his recruits during the forenoon, he naturally resolved to have the evenings to himself, and, as he perhaps wisely judged that, for a bachelor, there was no better mode of obtaining the news and gossip of the town, than by a reunion of talkative companions round a comfortable board, with somewhat thereon to wash down the conversation, he, along with some of his brother officers of the recruiting corps, resolved to parade every night, as the clock struck eight, in a comfortable tavern situated near the head of the west side of Saltmarket Street, which not long afterwards was exchanged for several others, and lastly was transferred to Henderson's Oyster House, at the south end of the Candleriggs, then the most fashionable rendezvous for the lovers of *Pandores* and other shell fish. Never was an individual better calculated, it may be truly affirmed, than Dr. Drumgold, from buoyancy of spirit, good temper, and unaffected loquacity, to become the nucleus of such a numerous and mixed fraternity, as this club so speedily became. To many excellent social qualities, he added a strong love of crambo, and had a salutation in rhyme on every possible occasion, for all who ever came within the boundaries of the club sanctum. The fact is, he seemed to have the rhyming dictionary at his tongue end, for never was he at a loss to find a couplet for the oddest names in the directory. As a proof of this, he was wont to say—

"Pray, good Mr. Milligan,
Take off your glass, and fill again."

a call which the worthy member, we believe, scarcely ever required to be made so bread in order to be obeyed.

William Mackenzie, M.D.

Dr. Mackenzie was the son of James Mackenzie, muslin manufacturer, and was born in Queen Street, April, 1791.

Died in July, 1868. He studied in the Grammar School of Glasgow, and in the University, and was intended for the church; but this intention was given up on conscientious grounds; and he selected the medical profession as an outlet for his aspirations and talents. This profession he studied first in the Glasgow University and Royal Infirmary, and after obtaining the degree of F.F.P.S.G., went to London, and studied under the celebrated Dr. Abernethy. He also studied two years on the Continent. He early devoted his attention to the study of eye diseases, and was stimulated and encouraged by Dr. Rainy. He visited France, Italy, and Pavia, where he was introduced to Scarpa, who impressed him more than any of the other great men with whom he had come into contact ; and who, while on a visit to London having met with Potts, Hunter, and others, told Mackenzie there was no necessity for leaving England to learn surgery. In 1817, he went to Vienna, then the most celebrated school of Ophthalmology, and became pupil to the celebrated Beer, in whose practical class he performed his first operation on the eye, and whose teaching and practice approved themselves more to him than those of any other schools he had visited. In 1818, he practised in London as an oculist and lecturer on the eye. After eight years' study under the most celebrated teachers, his success as a lecturer and teacher was not encouraging, and, in 1819, at the age of 27, he returned to Glasgow, and engaged in general practice. In concert with Dr. George Monteath, then the chief oculist in Glasgow, he opened subscriptions for the establishment of an eye infirmary, and its success developed under the professional ability and careful and economical supervision of Dr. Mackenzie. In 1828, he was appointed Waltonian lecturer in the University, and was distinguished for his lucid and elegant style of diction. He was accurate even to finical minuteness, and jocularly said it was necessary to teach in order to learn thoroughly. In 1830, he published his "Practical Treatise of the Diseases of the Eye," which attracted much attention, and spread his fame throughout Europe. In 1833, Dr. Mackenzie unsuccessfully contested the Chair of *Materia Medica*. He also edited for two years the first series of the *Glasgow Medical Journal*, and contributed many important articles on the eye to its pages. He was shy and reserved, and took no part in public affairs; but was genial and pleasant in private, and was possessed of an inexhaustible fund of quaint humour. His inestimable services to the Glasgow poor were recognised and appreciated.

George Cunningham Monteath, M.D.,

Was the first practitioner in Glasgow who devoted particular attention to diseases of the eye. He studied in Glasgow University, and practised for some years in Glasgow as a surgeon and oculist with remarkable success. In 1821, he published a "Manual of the Diseases of the Human Eye," and soon become celebrated all over Scotland. His manner was soothing, and his politeness fascinating.

Andrew Buchanan, M.D.,

was born in Glasgow 10th December, 1798, and died in 1882. He was taught in the High School, and entered College when he was twelve years of age, and after a course of ten years' medical instruction and study, took his degree in 1822. He also studied two years abroad, and was three years in the Royal Infirmary. He said, "I left the hospital with a more ample experience of disease in every form, and a more thorough knowledge of the practical resources of the healing art, than I could have acquired from a whole lifetime of ordinary medical practice." His object in studying medicine was "to afford me a liberal and congenial occupation, as I believed myself to have very little need to cultivate it from any other motive." This, he adds, "turned out ultimately to be a mistake, and I was thus compelled in my later years to toil unremittingly at a business so little remunerative as medical practice was at that time in Glasgow." By his voluntary practice among the poor of the wynds he contracted fever on three occasions, and nearly lost his life. In 1828 he projected and established the *Glasgow Medical Journal*, and was editor, along with Dr. Weir; but some of his contributions about the poor got him into trouble, and caused him to resign his editorship and his post as poor's doctor. He rendered invaluable services to

the city during the time of cholera. At one time he taught
Materia Medica in the Andersonian, and from 1839 to 1876
he held the chair of Institutes of Medicine or Physiology in
the Glasgow University. While a surgeon to the Royal
Infirmary he was closely associated in his friendship and
career with Professor Lawrie, and it was held that Buchanan
had the best head and Lawrie the best hands in the hospital.
Dr. Buchanan was a ready and effective writer, but his
modesty and sensitiveness prevented him from becoming
widely known, and others reaped the credit of work which
he alone performed. He was a fine specimen of the best
class of professional men of the good old school ; cultured,
well read, gentle mannered, he was, in its truest sense, a
gentleman. With highest intellectual powers, he was as
guileless as a child. Dr. Buchanan never acquired a large
practice. He was perhaps wanting in decision, and in the
enforcement of trivial matters, but which invalids are apt to
overestimate the value of. In serious or difficult cases his
advice was eagerly sought by his professional brethren, who
deeply mourned his death as that of an old, sagacious,
honest, and trusted friend.

The Resurrectionists.

About the year 1813 a number of medical students
banded themselves together for the purpose of studying
pathology and anatomy. The scarcity of dead bodies for
dissection was a difficulty in the way, and they resolved to
overcome it. Their leader was a Mr. Granville Sharp
Pattison, who, on account of the dangerous notoriety he
gained at the time, was compelled to flee to America, where
he became a very eminent physician and surgeon, and
enjoyed a lucrative practice down to the day of his death.
He was zealously fond of anatomy, and inspired twenty or
thirty students to form themselves into a secret brotherhood.
They hired a suite of rooms in College Street. Each had a
private key by which he could gain access to the anatomy
den by night or day. They had a noble end in view, and
were not actuated by motives of mere devilry. When they
heard of the death of any important person, where the
symptoms were so obscure as to baffle the profession while

he was living, these students gathered up all the particulars, mode of treatment, &c., and when the burial took place, would draw lots for lifting the body from the grave to discover, if possible, the precise nature of the disease. From three to four students went forth under cloud of night to dig up the body, and carry it to the place referred to. The students thus called themselves Resurrectionists, a name which became notorious throughout Scotland. Many circumstances favoured their nefarious work in those days. There was no gas, and few policemen. Duncan and Donald were more disposed to doze in their little wooden boxes, than attend to the safety of the lieges, dead or living. Moreover, there was a considerable tinge of superstition in the bosoms of these old Highlanders; and while many of them would have the courage to face the devil if he would only appear in palpable human form, they were slow to move in what related to the mysterious dead. So, in dark and cloudy nights these young, but unhallowed devotees of science, ran little risk of being detected in their nefarious work. At first the students were cautious, and were careful to cover up any marks which would lead to their detection. But they became more daring and reckless, which led soon to suspicion and discovery. The beadle of the Ram's Horn Church had his suspicion aroused by the lifting of a corpse there, and almost traced it to the dissecting rooms. His revelation caused a profound sensation in the city; and hundreds rushed to the graves of their departed relatives to see if they had been disturbed in their last slumbers by impious hands. Many took preventive measures; and the iron bars or railings which we still see in some of our old and venerable graveyards were speedily and carefully erected. About this time even a more ghastly traffic in dead bodies was discovered. Large numbers were being imported from Ireland as supposed goods into the Broomielaw. An Irish sloop arrived in the harbour laden with what was supposed to be linen or cotton rags, addressed to a huckster in Jamaica Street. He refused to take delivery of the goods because £50 for freight was demanded on delivery. The carters were ordered to take them back to the sheds, and very soon an awful stench began to emanate from the bags, which, when opened, were found to contain the putrefying bodies of men, women, and children huddled together in the most shocking manner. It transpired that, as a sufficient number of bodies for dissection could not be obtained in Glasgow, a chain of communication had been opened up by some Irish students. The bodies were ordered by the magistrates to be interred. It was subsequently found that the bodies brought from twenty to thirty guineas. The rag merchant had not been notified as to the *valuable* nature of the cargo till a post too late; and so, much to his chagrin, we have no doubt, lost the high commission which such a consignment would have yielded. These ugly discoveries at the Broomielaw, and the consternation of the citizens, which the beadle of the Ram's Horn had occasioned, alarmed but did not daunt these daring students; nor were they deterred from what had evidently become a passionate search after knowledge, though one of their number was shot while emerging from Blackfriars Churchyard, or though traps and gins were laid for them in all directions. Nothing could arrest their ingenuity or daring. Even the occupants of beautiful churchyards in hamlets distant several miles from the city did not escape having their last slumbers rudely disturbed. For instance, they heard of a striking case in the Mearns which had baffled the united skill of Drs. Cleghorn and Balmanno, and the best of the profession in Glasgow. The patient died in spite of all their efforts. This case aroused profound interest in the bosoms of this select and daring band of the disciples of Galen. *Cuts* were drawn, and two proceeded to the Mearns in a gig, dug up the body, dressed it in the most approved fashion, and returned to Glasgow with it propped up in the gig. They had to pass the Gorbals toll-bar, however, the keeper of which had a horrid aversion to all resurrectionists, and an eye like a hawk for their detection. Their boldness, cunning, and dexterity, baffled even this lynx-eyed official. They halted at his bar, and while one paid the toll, the other pretended to hold up the head of his *sick friend* (the dead man), and told him to be of good cheer, as they would soon breakfast in the High Street. The toll keeper, lantern in hand, looked up at the supposed sick passenger, and exclaimed, "Oh, puir auld bodie, he looks unco ill, drive cannily hame, lads, drive cannily." Shocking as this may appear, it is true, nevertheless, and vouched for by Dr. Richard Millar, Professor of Materia Medica in Glasgow University, who remarked "that these experiments in the Anatomy School of Glasgow lighted up the torch of science in this quarter of the world, and saved the lives of many invaluable human beings."

"To what base uses we may return, Horatio!"

These enthusiastic but unscrupulous anatomists were at length tracked to their den, and brought to justice. They were tried in Edinburgh, but by the cleverness of their senior counsel, by some legal irregularity or flaw in the prosecution, they were acquitted.

A Doctor and his Fee.

It is of a Glasgow doctor that the following spicy anecdote is related, in an almost forgotten work entitled "Northern Sketches, or Characters of Glasgow." A wealthy citizen who had the misfortune to require the services of this *leech*, was in the habit of having the gold always ready in his hand to electrify the doctor when he felt his pulse. One day, on the doctor making his stated visit, the servant said to him, "All is over!" "Over!" re-echoed the doctor, as the vision of his customary fee flashed before his mind, "impossible! let *me* see him: he cannot be dead yet; some trance or heavy sleep, perhaps." The doctor was introduced to the sable apartment; he took the hand of the pale corpse, applied the finger to that artery which once ebbed and flowed with life, gave a sorrowful shake of his head, while, with a trifling *legerdemain*, he relieved from the grasp of death *two guineas*, which in truth had been destined for him. "Ay, ay, good folks," said the doctor, he *is* dead; there is a destiny in all things!" and, full of shrewd sagacity, turned on his heel.

CHAPTER XI.

MODERN RELIGIOUS LIFE IN GLASGOW, OR SOME NOTABLE BISHOPS—WITHOUT THE MITRE.

> "Friend to the friendless, to the sick man health,
> With generous joy he views the *ideal* wealth;
> He hears the widow's heaven-breathed prayer of praise :
> He marks the sheltered orphan's tearful gaze ;
> Or, where the sorrow-shrivelled captive lay,
> Pours the bright blaze of Freedom's noontide ray."
> —*Coleridge*.

In our random sketches of Glasgow life we have seen that from its very origin the city was greatly indebted for its progress and prosperity to its bishops and other religious teachers; and it is only sober truth to say that the influence of the clergy has, all through its history, been a powerful factor in the continuance and extension and preservation of that prosperity and progress. Our city has never lacked men of the very highest ability and most earnest piety to lead its citizens into the higher regions of things, and to moderate and subdue, if not to suppress, the keen trading and worldly instincts that have also been so largely developed. And to the credit of our citizens be it said, these leaders of thought and life have never been without many devoted and self-sacrificing followers amongst our merchant princes and other business men. The few pictures we have given in the foregoing pages of our early traders will show that underneath their daring enterprize, their genius for money making, and their public spirit, there frequently breathed a strongly religious spirit, a warm Christian benevolence, and a wide earnest philanthropy. A whole series of volumes might be written on this aspect of our city's history, but in this chapter we must confine ourselves to a few desultory sketches and reminiscences of an illustrative character, to serve as an index to the whole religious life of the community. These sketches have been given in the biographical form, but contain incidental references to events and movements which may serve to give a more than merely personal interest to the subject now under consideration.

Dr. Thomas Chalmers—in Tron and St. John's Churches.

Among the most potent influences exerted in Glasgow in modern days, in the direction of religious, moral, and social reform, an influence which still exists and operates amongst us, may be reckoned the advent of Dr. Thomas Chalmers to the Tron Church in the year 1815. Born in the small town of Anstruther, Fifeshire, on the 17th March, 1780, Dr. Chalmers came to Glasgow in the prime of his early manhood, full of life and vigour, and with his whole soul burning with zeal for the advancement of the highest interests of humanity. In his student days, and for several years after he entered upon the sacred duties of his office, as minister of the parish of Kilmany in his native county, his chief ambition was to engage in scientific studies, and his pulpit prelections were of a cold, formal, and ineffective character. But through the occurrence of a series of sad bereavements, chief among which was the loss of an amiable sister, who passed away amidst such feelings of exultant hope and joy, as filled with astonishment and rivetted the attention of the young moral teacher, and opened his eyes to a sphere of things which had hitherto been unknown to him. The whole character of his being and ministry was changed. His ardent nature was stirred to its inmost depths by the power of the Cross, he saw the error of his past ministry, and his soul became filled with a consuming desire for the salvation of his fellow-men. This change in the heart and life of their minister was soon felt by his rustic and hitherto uninterested parishioners. They were quickened into newness of life; his church became crowded; people flocked from all the country round about to hear his burning eloquence, and listen to the story of redeeming love. His fame, too, soon spread over all the land, and it was evident that he would not be allowed to spend his life in his quiet rural parish. Among the first of his calls was that from the Tron Church. Dr. M'Gill, the minister of that church had been translated to the divinity chair in our University; the task of finding a successor devolved upon the Town Council, and after due consideration, the usual overtures were made to Dr. Chalmers. He was not at first greatly enamoured of the prospect held out to him. He was deeply attached to his rural flock. He loved the quiet pastoral beauties of his native shire; and he dreaded the noise, bustle, and innumerable duties that would devolve upon him in the great metropolis of the West. But his objections were overruled, his fears were quieted by the assurance that his people would lighten his secular duties as much as possible; and the prospect of greater usefulness in that larger sphere impelled him to make the change. He was inducted to his new charge on Friday, 21st July, 1815, by Rev. Sir Henry Moncrieff, and on the afternoon of the Sabbath following, he preached his first sermon to an immense crowd. His popularity not only continued unabated to the end, but increased from year to year.

It is interesting to note that Dr. Chalmers' first residence in Glasgow was situated in Rottenrow. Here he lived in solitary lodgings until his family removed to the City, when they took up their abode in Charlotte Street. He afterwards resided in Kensington Place.

Sooth to say, he did not "take" to Glasgow at first. Writing to a friend eight days after his induction, he says, "I can give you no satisfaction whatever as to my liking or not liking Glasgow. Were I to judge by my present feelings, I would say I dislike it most violently; but the present state of my mind is not a fair criterion—at a distance from my family, and in a land of strangers; and though beset with polite attentions, feeling that there is positively nothing in them all to replace those warmer and kindlier enjoyments which friendship brings along with it. . . . I have got about a hundred calls in the course of this week, and I foresee a deal of very strange work in the business of a Glasgow minister. What think you of my putting my name to two applications for licences to sell spirits, and two certificates of being qualified to follow out the calling of *pedlars*, in the course of yesterday?"

In a subsequent letter to the same friend, he says:— "This, sir, is a wonderful place; and I am half entertained and half provoked by some of the peculiarities of its people. The peculiarity which bears hardest upon me is the incessant demand they have upon all occasions for the personal attendance of the ministers. They must have four to every funeral, or they do not think it has been genteelly gone through. They must have one or more to all the Committees of all the Societies. They (the ministers) must fall in at every procession. They must attend examinations innumerable, and eat of the dinners consequent upon these examinations. . . . There seems to be a superstitious charm in the very sight of them, and such is the manifold officiality with which they are covered, that they must be paraded among all the meetings and all the institutions. I gave in to all this at first, but I am beginning to keep a suspicious eye upon these repeated demands ever since I sat nearly an hour in grave deliberation with a number of others upon a subject connected with the property of the Corporation, and that subject was a *gutter*, and the question was whether it should be bought and covered up, or let alone and left to lie open. I am gradually separating myself from all this trash, &c., &c."

We have rather improved our manners in the treatment of our ministers, still even yet, it is to be feared, we need a rebuke of this kind, for we still have a sort of "hankering" for the presence of these dignitaries on every conceivable occasion, and are apt to feel slighted if they do not respond to our numerous calls.

It is further interesting to note that one of the earliest Glasgow experiences of this eminent man, whose capacious mind grappled with some of the greatest religious and moral problems of the age, was a singular attachment to a youthful citizen, who was one of the first trophies of Dr. Chalmers' ministry in Glasgow. This was Mr. Thomas Smith, the son of a well known Glasgow publisher, and who was qualifying himself for the profession of a writer or attorney. The friendship between the two was of the most affectionate nature. Scarcely a day passed without their seeing each other, and in addition to that, scarcely a day passed without one or more letters being sent by the pastor to his young convert. A trysting place was appointed on the banks of the Monkland Canal, where each day at a set hour they met, and here "the general conversation of ordinary friendship soon flowed in that new channel into which it was directed by a heart yearning for the spiritual and eternal welfare of its object." Mr. Smith was unfortunately in delicate health, and died within a year of Dr. Chalmers' induction, and doubtless the premonitions of this event would give an earnestness and a pathos to the friendship between him and his pastor, of a peculiar and touching description. But we are so apt to connect the name and memory of the great Dr. Chalmers with large schemes of public and national interest, that it is refreshing to get such a glimpse into the heart of the man, and to learn that a deep and undying love to the human soul was the root principle out of which all his public zeal and enterprises grew.

Coming to his public services, we find that one of his earliest and most notable efforts was the delivery of the famous "Astronomical Discourses." At the time of Dr. Chalmers' settlement in Glasgow, it was the custom that the clergymen of the city should preach in rotation on Thursday in the Tron Church, a duty which, as their number was but eight, returned to each within an interval of two months. On Thursday, 23rd November, 1815, this week day service devolved on Dr. Chalmers. The entire novelty of the discourse delivered upon this occasion, and the announcement that a series of similar discourses was to follow, excited the liveliest interest, not in his own congregation alone, but throughout the whole community. He had presented to his hearers a sketch of the recent discoveries of astronomy—distinct in outline, and drawn with all the ease of one who was himself a master in the science, yet gorgeously magnificent in many of its details, displaying amid "the brilliant glow of a blazing eloquence," the sublime poetry of the heavens The discussion of this subject occupied all the Thursday services allotted to him during the year 1816. The spectacle which presented itself in the Trongate upon the day of the delivery of each new astronomical discourse, was a most singular one. Long ere the bell began to toll, a stream of people might be seen pouring through the passage which led into the Tron Church. Across the street, and immediately opposite to this passage, was the old reading room where all the Glasgow merchants met. So soon, however, as the gathering stream upon the opposite side of the street gave the accustomed warning, out flowed the occupants of the coffee room; the pages of the *Herald* or the *Courier* were for the while forsaken, and during two of the best business hours of the day, the old reading room wore a strange aspect of desolation. The busiest merchants of the city were wont indeed on those memorable occasions to leave their desks, and kind masters allowed their clerks and apprentices to follow their example. Out of the very heart of the great tumult, an hour or two stood redeemed for the highest exercises of the Spirit; and the low traffic of earth forgotten, heaven and its high economy, and its human sympathies and eternal interests, engrossed the minds at least and the fancy of congregated thousands.*

In January, 1817, this series of discourses was ready for publication. The publisher, Mr. Smith, was a little doubtful as to the success of a volume of sermons, which were generally a drug in the market, and hinted to Dr. Chalmers that recourse might require to be had to publication by subscription. But the success of this literary venture was beyond all expectation. The volume was published on 28th January, 1817. In ten weeks 6,000 copies had been disposed of, and the demand showed no symptom of decline. Nine editions were called for within the year, and nearly 20,000 copies were in circulation. The "Tales of a Landlord" had a month's start in the date of publication, and even with such a competitor it ran an almost equal race. Not a few curious observers were struck with the novel competition, and watched with lively curiosity how the great Scottish preacher and the great Scottish novelist kept for nearly a whole year so nearly abreast of one another. "These sermons," said Hazlitt, "ran like wildfire through the country, were the darlings of watering-places, were laid in the windows of inns, and were to be met with in all places of public resort. . . . We remember finding the volume in the orchard of the inn at Burford Bridge, near Boxhill, and passing a very delightful morning in reading it without quitting the shade of an apple tree."

The circumstances amid which these discourses were composed are most noteworthy, and show the intense energy and concentration of mind of their author. In a small pocket book, with borrowed pen and ink, in strange apartments, where he was liable every moment to interruption; at the manse of Balmerino, disappointed at not finding the minister at home, and having a couple of hours to spare; at the manse of Kilmany, in the drawing-room, with all the excitement before him of meeting, for the first time after a

* Hanna's *Memoirs of Dr. Chalmers.*

year's absence, many of his former parishioners; at the manse of Logie, into which he turned at random by the way, and found a vacant hour, "paragraph after paragraph was penned of a composition which bears upon it as much of the aspect of high and continuous elaboration as almost any piece of composition in our language." And at the very time when he was composing some of these discourses he, while on a visit to his aged parents at Anstruther, guided the tottering steps of his blind father through the street to the church, and submitted with all the humility of a child to his parent's strict and severe advice as to his moral character and manner of life. On one occasion, when preaching in Anstruther, his father would not leave his own place of worship and go to hear his son, so severe was his sense of duty, and so unwilling to countenance in the slightest degree the practice of "gadding about" from one church to another. On another occasion, when preaching in London, and when the entire metropolis was in a *furore* about his eloquence and power, there was one Scotchman— James Chalmers—who did not go to hear him, and betrayed not the slightest interest in the famous preacher. On being asked by a friend whether he had heard the great Dr. Chalmers, this worthy replied, "Oh, yes, I have heard him." "And what did you think of him?" was the next query. "Not very much," was the curt reply. "Indeed!" said his astonished interrogator; "and when did you hear him?" "Oh!" replied James, "about half an hour after he was born!" It was the great Doctor's elder brother. But James was rather a character in his way, and though a conscientious, respectable man, had no great love for ministers or churches, and could on occasion give vent to his disapproval of religious matters in language more forcible than polite.

The pastoral work of Dr. Chalmers in Glasgow was of the most laborious and thorough-going kind. In his day, the Tron Parish comprised that portion of the city which lies to the east of the Saltmarket and to the south of the Gallowgate. Its population was believed to be between 11,000 and 12,000, and included a large number of the worst classes of the city. It was Dr. Chalmers' custom to visit all his parishioners once every two years, to hold weekly evening meetings, in halls, class rooms, or other convenient places. He encountered all kinds of opposition from sceptical and dissolute persons, with patience and good temper; he wrestled in prayer for the souls of his people with intense agony and earnestness; and so filled with a sense of his own unworthiness was he, that he was frequently in despair, and thought of retiring from his work as an unprofitable servant! His anxious eye beheld the utter ignorance and neglect amidst which the young people of his parish were growing up, and he instituted a system of district Sabbath schools, over each of which he appointed a capable superintendent and teachers, who were to confine their labours to a limited area, so that more careful supervision might be exercised, and every child brought under the influences of Gospel teaching. Out of this system of Sabbath schools, grew the territorial day schools, in which he was greatly assisted by David Stow and other earnest men; and so successful were these schools, that though mostly attended by the poorer classes, and situated though they were in the most thickly populated districts of the city, yet the parents of the wealthy merchants sought to get admission to them for their own children. Time would fail us to tell of the multifarious schemes and arduous labours of this large souled, earnest man, in seeking to grapple with the ignorance, vice, and immorality of the city in which his lot was cast; and it is not too much to say that had the work of evangelization and teaching been taken up in other districts of the city and continued to this day, in the same spirit, and with the same earnestness of purpose and energy of execution, Glasgow would at this moment have occupied a far higher and better position, intellectually, morally, and spiritually, than it does.

Into his magnificient scheme of administration of relief to the poor in the parish of St. John's, to which parish he was transferred at his own request in 1819, it is impossible for us to enter here: suffice it to say that it was carried out with all the systematic thoroughness, earnestness, and zeal, with which his other schemes were conducted; and completely justified, by its results, the views and principles expounded by its founder. The deserving poor were carefully attended to, but the idle, the profligate, and the undeserving, were cast upon their own resources, and compelled to work for their own support, when able, or their relatives were forced to support them whenever that was possible; and all this was done at considerably less cost than even Dr. Chalmers himself anticipated.

With like energy and earnestness, Dr. Chalmers entered upon another great scheme—viz., that of church extension in the city and in the country at large. He saw, at an early period of his ministry, that even in his own parish of the Tron, there were not a third of the people who attended any church, notwithstanding the growth of dissent in the city. What he therefore demanded was, "20 more churches and 20 more ministers" for Glasgow alone, and this *desideratum* he boldly proclaimed in his sermon on the death of the Princess Charlotte in 1817. His demand was clamoured at and cried down on all hands, and even the addition of a single church, which the magistrates had agreed to a few months previously, was thought too much. But strong in the confidence of truth, Dr. Chalmers held fast to his much decried doctrine, until he had the satisfaction of finding his church extension principle generally adopted, and not 20 but 200 additional churches erected in our towns and cities to attest the soundness of his argument, and reward the zeal with which he had urged it.

His biographer, Dr. Hanna, thus summarizes the effect of Dr. Chalmers' eight years' labour in our city:—"When Dr. Chalmers came to Glasgow, by the great body of the upper classes of society evangelical doctrines were nauseated and despised; when he left it, even by those who did not bow to their influence these doctrines were acknowledged to be indeed the very doctrines of the Bible. When Dr. Chalmers came to Glasgow, in the eye of the multitude evangelism stood confounded with a drivelling sanctimoniousness or a sour-minded asceticism; when he left it, from all such associations the Christianity of the New Testament stood clearly and nobly redeemed. When Dr. Chalmers came to Glasgow, for nearly a century the magistrates and Town Council had exercised the city patronage in a spirit determinately anti-evangelical; when he left it, so complete was the revolution which had been effected, that from that time forward none but evangelical clergymen were appointed by the city patrons. When Dr. Chalmers came to Glasgow, there and elsewhere over Scotland there were many most devoted clergymen of the Establishment who had given themselves up wholly to the ministry of the Word and to prayer, but there was not one in whose faith and practice week-day ministrations had the place or power which he assigned to them; when he left it, he had exhibited such a model of fidelity, diligence, and activity in all departments of ministerial labour as told finely upon the spirit and practice of the whole ministry of Scotland. When Dr. Chalmers came to Glasgow, unnoticed thousands of the city population were sinking into ignorance, infidelity, and vice, and his eye was the first in this country to foresee to what a fearful magnitude that evil, if suffered to grow on unchecked, would rise; when he left it, his ministry in that city remained behind him a permanent warning to a nation which has been but slow to learn that the greatest of all questions, both for statesmen and for churchmen, is the condition of those untaught and degraded thousands who swarm now around the base of the social edifice, and whose brawny arms may yet grasp its pillars to shake or to destroy. When Dr. Chalmers came to Glasgow, in the literary circles of the Scottish metropolis a thinly disguised infidelity sat on the seats of greatest influence, and smiled or scoffed at a vital energetic faith in the great and distinctive truths of revelation, while widely over his native land the spirit of a frigid indifference to religion prevailed: when he left it, the current of public sentiment had begun to set in a contrary direction, and although it took many years, and the labour of many other hands, to carry that healthful change onward to maturity, yet I believe that it is not over-estimating it to say that it was mainly by Dr. Chalmers' ministry in Glasgow—by his efforts at this period in the pulpit and through the press—that the tide of national opinion and sentiment was turned."

With one or two anecdotes illustrative of the simple-mindedness, sincerity, and influence of this great man, we must draw this paper to a close:—

Mr. Thomson and Mr. Heggie, an elder and a deacon, went out one evening to Kensington Place, where Dr. Chalmers was living, to speak to him about some parish matters. They found him on the floor busy playing at bowls with his children. "Come away, Mr. Heggie," he exclaimed when they entered, without changing, however, his position; "you can tell us how this game ought to be played." Elder and deacon, minister and children, were soon all busy at the game together. "This is not the way," said Mr. Thomson, "we used to play bowls in Galloway." "Come along, then," said Dr. Chalmers; "let us see what the Galloway plan is." And to it they set again with keener relish than ever, till Mrs. Chalmers at last said, "What a fine paragraph it will make for the *Chronicle* to-morrow that Dr. Chalmers, and one of his elders, and one of his deacons were seen last night playing for a whole hour at marbles!" "Well, really," said Dr. Chalmers, starting up, "it is too bad in us, gentlemen; we must stop." Two hours of useful and instructive conversation followed, not made in any way the less so by the manner in which they were ushered in.

On one occasion, when near the close of his ministry in Glasgow, he was called to the death-bed of a Camlachie weaver. This man had been the only son of a pious mother, who was a widow. In his boyhood he had been apprenticed to a master who was an infidel, and who, with about twenty men under him, had sown so sedulously his own principles among them, that every one of them had been seduced into unbelief. Among the rest this unfortunate widow's son fell a victim to his arts, and when his mother saw him married to his master's daughter, who was as bold an unbeliever as her father, and when she heard him blaspheme that holy name in which she trusted, it was too much for her to bear—deprived of reason, she died in an asylum for lunatics. In the course of years, and when his own only child was grown up, consumption seized upon him. The near look at eternity, and perhaps the remembrance of his mother's instructions and prayers, threw him into spiritual distress. A minister was sent for, who attempted to reason with him, but he "was too deep," and the wound remained unhealed. It so happened that he was living at this time in the district of St. John's parish assigned to Mr. John Wilson, one of the most valued and beloved of Dr. Chalmers' elders, who soon brought his minister to see the dying man. The simplicity, the earnestness, the sympathy displayed by Dr. Chalmers won the man's confidence, and it was not long till he related the history of his unbelief. Weekly, during nearly three months, Dr. Chalmers' visits were repeated. The instructions given and the prayers offered at that bedside were blessed—a sinner was turned from the error of his ways, and a soul was saved from death. Very shortly before his death Dr. Chalmers visited this man. Both felt that the interview was to be the last. "Doctor" said he, lifting his Bible off the bed on which it lay, "will you take this book from me as a token of my inexpressible gratitude?" "No, sir," said Dr. Chalmers, after a moment's hesitation; "No, sir, that is far too precious a legacy to be put past your own son—give it to your boy." The dying man obeyed his instructor's last advice. He gathered up his remaining strength of body and mind; asking for a pen, he wrote the few lines quoted below, laid his head back upon his pillow, and expired.

> "To thee, my son, I give this book,
> In hopes that thou wilt from it find
> A Father and a Comforter,
> When I do leave thee here behind.
>
> "I hope that thou wilt firm believe
> That Jesus Christ alone can save—
> He bled and suffered in our stead;
> To save from death Himself He gave.
>
> "A strong desire I now do crave
> Of them to whom thy charge is given,
> To bring thee up to fear the Lord,
> That we may meet at last in Heaven."

These lines, with the date, 11th June, 1823, and the addition —"I am, your very sincere affectionate father, John Hastie," were found after Dr. Chalmers' death in one of his repositories where nothing but papers on which he put the utmost value were deposited. The lines were in Dr. Chalmers' own handwriting on a small slip of paper, and below them he had added—"This from a common weaver in Marlborough Street, inscribed on a Bible to his only child. He had been an infidel till within a few months of his death."

It may be stated here that one of the most devoted of Dr. Chalmers' office-bearers was the worthy publisher, Mr. Collins, father of our Ex-Lord Provost, Sir Wm. Collins. Mr. Collins was one of the very first advocates of total abstinence in Glasgow more than half a century ago.

Edward Irving in Glasgow.

For a period of nearly three years—viz., from October, 1819, till July, 1822, that strange, weird, erratic, but talented genius, Edward Irving, dwelt and laboured among the people of Glasgow, in the capacity of assistant to the great Dr. Chalmers, in the parish of St. John's. Irving had just completed his 27th year when he came to our city. He was then little known; he was not yet ordained as a minister, but only licensed as a probationer; and had hitherto been rather neglected and unappreciated. He had been unexpectedly requested to preach in the pulpit of Dr. Andrew Thomson, St. George's, Edinburgh, and was informed that Dr. Chalmers was to be present, and that he was in search of an assistant in the splendid labours he was carrying on in Glasgow. The sermon he preached seemed to have pleased Dr. Thomson, who said, "it was the production of no ordinary mind." But what Dr. Chalmers thought of it he was not to know for a time at least. The great man preserved an ominous silence; and for nearly a month the young probationer felt the bitterness of despair, and had given up all hope of succeeding to the ministry. He packed up his books and boxes, and sent them off to his father's house in Annan, and made up his mind to go abroad as a missionary, or seek some other daring enterprise. He went off to Greenock, meaning to pay a visit to his home before his departure. Sick at heart, and buried in his own thoughts, he took the wrong boat and had to come ashore again. At that moment another vessel was in all the bustle of departure. Struck with a sudden caprice, Irving resolved, in his half desperation, to take the first that left the quay, and leaping listlessly into this, found it was bound for Belfast. The voyage was accomplished in safety, but not without an adventure at the end. Some notable crime had been committed in Ireland about that time, the doer of which was still at large, and the authorities were suspicious of every stranger. Of all the strangers visiting that part of Belfast, perhaps there was none so remarkable as this tall Scotchman, with his knapsack and slender belongings, his large powerful frame, and his total ignorance of the place, who was travelling without any feasible motive or object. The authorities laid hands upon him, and he was only liberated by applying to the Presbyterian minister, Rev. Mr. Hanna, who obtained his release and took him to his own house. That visit was a jubilee to the children of the hospitable minister. Irving at once engaged their interest and affection. One of the boys was afterwards the Rev. Dr. Hanna, the son-in-law and biographer of Dr. Chalmers, and he never forgot the stories of the stranger thus suddenly brought to the fireside, and his genial presence which charmed the house. It was while here that he received a letter from Chalmers inviting him to go to Glasgow.

He was not received by the people of his new charge with great favour, although his remarkable appearance seems to have impressed everybody.

A lady, who was then a member of Dr. Chalmers' Church and a personal friend, tells how she herself, on one occasion, being particularly engaged, had given orders to her servants not to admit any visitors. Notwithstanding this, she was soon interrupted by the entrance of one of her maids, in a high state of excitement. "Mem!" burst forth the girl, "there's a wonderful grand gentleman called; I couldna say you were engaged to *him*. I think he maun be a Highland chief!" "*That* Mr. Irving!" exclaimed another person—"*that* Dr. Chalmers' helper! I took him for a cavalry officer!" "Do you know, Doctor," said a third, to Chalmers himself, "what things people are saying about your new assistant? They say he's like a brigand chief." "Well, well," said Dr. Chalmers with a smile, "whatever they say, they never think him like anything but a leader of men." Regarding the impressions made by him as a preacher, the following somewhat doubtful opinion was expressed:—"He was generally well liked, but some people thought him rather flowery. However, they were satisfied that he must be a good preacher, since Dr. Chalmers had chosen him."

While Chalmers was devising and carrying out his great parochial schemes which made his name famous, his assistant, who was of a much less practical turn of mind, was quietly engaged in preparing his "flowery" sermons, and visiting the families of the church in their homes, dealing with them individually in their spiritual interests. He was rather a strange and striking visitor. His tall, military appearance, excited much attention and curiosity. When he entered a house, he saluted it in Eastern fashion with the words, "Peace be to this house," and this unusual style of address awed and puzzled the people. He did still more than this. He laid his hands upon the heads of the children, and pronounced with imposing solemnity, the ancient benediction, "The Lord bless thee, and keep thee," over each of them—a practice startling to Scottish ears. The following story is also told of him:—A certain shoemaker, Radical and infidel, was among the number of those under Irving's care; silent and sullen, and turning his back upon such visitors. Approaching the bench one day, Irving took up a piece of patent leather, then a recent invention, and began to speak about it in skilled terms. The shoemaker worked away for a little without seeming to pay any attention; but, at last, roused and exasperated by the speech and pretence of knowledge, he demanded in great contempt, "What do *ye* ken about leather?" This was just what his assailant wanted, for although a minister and a scholar, Irving was a tanner's son, and could discourse learnedly upon that material. Gradually interested and mollified, the cobbler slackened work, and listened while his visitor described some process of making shoes by machinery, which he had carefully got up for the purpose. At last the shoemaker so far forgot his caution as to suspend his work altogether, and lift his eyes to the great figure stooping over his bench; and finally he exclaimed,— "Od, you're a decent kind o' fellow!—do *you* preach?" On the following Sunday, the shoemaker made a defiant, shy appearance at church. Next day, Irving met him in the Gallowgate, and hailed him as a friend. Walking beside him in natural talk, the tall probationer laid his hand upon the sleeve of the cobbler, and marched by his side along the well frequented street. By the time they had reached the end of their mutual way, not a spark of resistance was left in the shoemaker. His children henceforth went to school; his wife went to the kirk in peace. He himself got a suit of Sunday "blacks," so dear to the heart of every poor Scotchman, and became a regular churchgoer and respectable member of society; while his acknowledgment of Irving's power was conveyed in the self-excusing pretence—"He's a sensible man, *yon;* he kens about leather."

About this time a little legacy of a sum variously stated at between £30 and £100 was left to Irving. Such a little windfall, one might suppose, would be very acceptable to the poor probationer; and so it was; but after a fashion entirely his own. He changed his legacy into one pound notes, deposited them in his desk, and every morning as long as they lasted, put one in his pocket when going out on his visitations. The legacy lasted just as many days as it was pounds in value, and doubtless produced as much pleasure to its owner as ever was purchased by money. What Dr. Chalmers would have said to this barefaced alms-giving, in the very midst of his social economy, it would be curious to know. As to its destination nobody but Irving was any the wiser.

His reputation as a preacher, however, did not improve in Glasgow. He was too "flowery" and poetical for the hard-headed citizens of the busy town; and he was quite eclipsed by the rushing energy, eloquence, and brilliancy of his superior. It was quite a common thing to see people turning away from the church door on a Sabbath forenoon, exclaiming "it's *no himsel'* the day." And even Chalmers seems to have had only a half appreciation of the merits of his assistant. "Irving's preaching," he said, evidently not with great admiration of it, "is like Italian music, appreciated only by connoisseurs." And yet most people will agree with the opinion of Mrs. Oliphant, Irving's biographer, when she says, "That Chalmers was the greater intellect of the two I do not attempt to question; nor yet that he was in all practical matters the more eminent and serviceable man; but that Irving had instinctive comprehensions and graces, which went high over the head of his great contemporary, seems to me as evident as the other conclusion."

A few more characteristic incidents in the life of Dr. Chalmers' wonderful assistant may be interesting to our readers. On one occasion he was on his way to some Presbytery meeting in the country—probably some ordination or settlement in which he was interested, though not a member of the Court. The ministers of the Presbytery were to be conveyed in carriages to the scene of action, but Irving set off on foot, according to his usual custom. The "brethren" in their carriages overtook a tall, remarkable figure, which would have been undeniably that of Dr.

Chalmers' helper, but that he bore a pedlar's pack upon his stalwart shoulders, and was accompanied side by side by the fatigued proprietor of the same. To the laughter and jokes that hailed him, however, Irving presented a rather affronted indignant aspect. He could see no occasion for either laughter or remark. The pedlar was a poor Irishman worn out with his burden. "His countrymen were kind to me," said the offended probationer, recalling those days when, sick at heart, he plunged among the Ulster cabins, and got some comfort out of his wanderings. He carried the pack steadily till its poor owner was rested and ready to resume it, and thought it only natural.

It is also told of him that he was present at a dinner party in Glasgow, at which one of the company was a young man who permitted himself to talk profanely, in a manner now unknown, and which would not be tolerated in any party now-a-days. After expending all his little wit upon priestcraft and its inventions, this youth, getting bold by degrees, at last attacked Irving—who had hitherto taken no notice of him—directly, as one of the world deluding order. Irving heard him out in silence, and then turned to the other listeners. "My friends," he said, "I will make no reply to this unhappy youth who hath attacked the Lord in the person of His servant; but let us pray that his sin may not be laid to his charge;" and with a solemn motion of his hand, which the awe-struck diners-out instinctively obeyed, Irving rose up to his full majestic height, and solemnly commended the offender to the forgiveness of God.

Mr. Irving, as we have seen, was a deeply interested visitor of the poor and degraded in their own homes; and frequently he co-operated with David Stow, the educational reformer of Glasgow, in going down to the slums, and both by personal visitation and open-air preaching, sought to reclaim these classes to the paths of righteousness. He also visited the criminals in their cells; and on one occasion, being impressed with the strong assertions of innocence on the part of a man condemned for murder, he set on foot a strict and anxious enquiry in the dens of the Gallowgate, to make a last effort to discover whether any exculpatory evidence could be found. In this, however, he was unsuccessful.

In December, 1821, Irving received an invitation to preach in the Caledonian Chapel, London, which he accepted; and after some difficulty and delay, he was at length called to that church, and was ordained in the following July. Before leaving Glasgow, he was presented by the congregation of St. John's with a gold watch; and it was characteristic of the man, when he was consulted as to his fancy or liking in the matter, that he requested that it should be provided by a certain watchmaker, whose distinguishing quality was not that he was skilful in his trade, but that he was an Annandale man.

Into Irving's brilliant yet troubled career in London, it is beyond our purpose to enter. But it will be interesting to state that after the conflict was over he returned, weary and heart-broken, to Glasgow to die. Not that he thought so himself, for it appears to have been his intention to resume his labours in the Gospel in the place in which he commenced them. For a few weeks he was visible about Glasgow—now appearing against the sunshine in a lonely street, his horse's hoofs echoing slowly along the causeway, his gaunt gigantic figure rising feeble against the light; now in the room which his Glasgow disciples had found to meet in; walking home after the worship, fain to lean on the arm of the elder who had come hastily from London to be near him, while his wistful wife went mournful by his side, carrying the stick which was unable to support him in his feebleness,—sometimes pausing, as they trode the streets in this sad fashion to take breath and gather strength: a most sorrowful pathetic picture. His hearers were few in the Lyceum room, in comparison with former times; but in the street, as he passed along, many a sad glance followed him, and the people stood still with compassionate looks to point out to each other, "the great Edward Irving." And, by and by, the end came. At the dreary midnight hour at the close of a gloomy December Sunday in the year 1834, the last bonds of mortal trouble dropped asunder, and the saint and martyr entered into his rest. His last audible words were "If I die, I die unto the Lord. Amen." They buried him in the crypt of Glasgow Cathedral, like his Master, in the grave of a stranger—the same man who had first introduced him to London coming forward now to offer a last resting place to all that remained of Edward Irving. Surely we may be permitted to add that our grim, smoky, busy, mercenary city is hallowed and honoured by being privileged to be the scene of the labours of such a man, and to afford a last resting place to the dust of one so noble, so unselfish, and so devout.

Somewhat similar in character, though longer in duration, was the closing period in the life of that eminently pious and spiritually minded minister, John Macleod Campbell formerly of Row, the friend of Norman Macleod, and of all true men of unprejudiced mind who had the honour of knowing him. Expelled from the Established Church for his so-called heresy in regard to the nature of the Atonement, but which we think was only heresy to those who did not understand or who could not rise to the high spiritual elevation which Campbell occupied—he came to Glasgow, where, in comparative isolation and neglect, he ministered to a few earnest and devoted people in a humble building, till at length he died, leaving behind him a fragrant memory and a hallowed influence, which is even yet, unseen though not unfelt, working for good in the higher spiritual sense, in the heart of the community.

Anecdotes of Rev. Dr. Gillan.

It may not be out of place here to record a few anecdotes of another rather notable minister, but of a somewhat different type, who for many years occupied the pulpit that had been so well and ably filled by Dr. Chalmers and Edward Irving. We refer to the late Dr. Gillan, who after spending his best days in our busy city, retired in later life to the quiet rural parish of Inchinnan, near Renfrew, where he died not very many years ago at an advanced age. Dr. Gillan was an able and popular divine, discharged with great zeal and with good practical results his duties as a faithful preacher and laborious pastor. But he was also a humourist of the first water, and no one could be long in his company without being amused and entertained by his pawky, witty sayings, which however carried wisdom as well as wit in them.

He was one winter night sailing from Liverpool to Glasgow. A foppish youth resolved to enjoy some light conversation with the Scottish parson. "Pray, Doctor, can you tell me why that is called the dog-star?" said he, pointing to that luminary. "Because it's a Skye terrier, I suppose," was the Doctor's witty reply.

A gentleman, well known for his liberality, meeting the Doctor one day in the streets of Glasgow, when he was minister of St. John's, thus accosted him,—"Man, Gillan, that was a fine letter you wrote me acknowledging the coals I sent you for the poor of your parish." "Ou, aye," says Gillan, "I'll write any amount of letters for the same number o' cairts."

Before the passing of the Forbes Mackenzie Act, one of Dr. Gillan's members kept a public house in Gallowgate, which did a roaring trade on Sabbath evenings, greatly to the annoyance of the worthy Doctor, who passed the shop every Sabbath evening on his way to his Bible class. Resolving to show his displeasure, he one Sabbath evening walked into the public house, and found the publican's wife, Mrs. A., serving at the counter. In his usual quick, peremptory way, he called for "a gill and a bake." The woman was dumbfoundered, and could scarcely believe her own ears. She managed however to go into a back parlour, where her husband was engaged in conversation with a friend. "Here's the minister," she says, "an' he's ca'ing for a gill." Equally astonished, Mr. A. went to the bar, and on presenting himself, the Doctor repeated his demand, "I want a gill an' a bake." No movement being made to comply with the request, the Doctor sharply observed, "If you are ashamed to serve your own minister with a gill at the counter on a Sunday night, you should feel ashamed to sell it to others;" and, so saying, he turned on his heel, and left the shop. Mr. A. afterwards told a friend that he was so rebuked by Dr. Gillan's little but effective stratagem, that he never afterwards opened his shop on Sundays.

But the Doctor was not a teetotaller, and he once met with a rather sharp rebuke himself on the liquor question. He was one day standing in the Piazza at the Tontine, near the Cross, to get shelter from a shower of rain, when he observed a working man vigorously pulling away at a clay pipe during his meal hour. Desirous of improving the occasion, the Doctor walked up to him, and the following colloquy ensued:— *Doctor.*— "That's a good going pipe, mister." "Yes." "You'll go through a good deal of tobacco?" "O, no much; sometimes three and sometimes four ounces a week." "Well, my young man, see what a lot of money you could save by giving up that filthy habit. Four ounces in the week comes to 1s., and as there are 52 weeks in the year, that's £2, 12s. you might save in the course of a twelvemonth, which would be a grand nest egg in the Savings' Bank, or might buy you a splendid suit of clothes every year." "Doubtless, doubtless, sir; but as you have all the appearance of a well-to-do gentleman, I suppose you'll take a glass of wine at dinner?" "Yes, I generally have a couple of glasses of wine during the day." "And no doubt you'll have a glass of toddy before going to bed?" "I do generally indulge to that extent each night." "Well, that's 1s. a day at a very low estimate, and as there are 365 days in the year, that's £18, 5s. you might easily save every year by giving up that filthy habit!" It is needless to remark that the Doctor did not attempt any further to improve the occasion.

As specimens of the Doctor's ready wit, the following may be given :—

He was in the habit of visiting a foundry twice a year to see the castings made, one of his elders being the proprietor of the foundry. The Doctor had a dog called Cæsar, which accompanied him on these visits, but was greatly terrified for the molten metal, and used to fly off in the opposite direction of the cast, when the stentorian voice of his master would be heard through the foundry, "Get thee behind me, Cæsar," to the great amusement of the workmen, who relished the repeated joke.

When the Doctor proposed to his second wife, she said, "I am not able to fill the late Mrs. Gillan's shoes." "I ken that fine," replied the Doctor, "but ye maun just dae yer best."

When he went to occupy the manse at Inchinnan, his predecessor, Dr. Lockhart, left behind him, among other things, a number of MS. sermons and lectures, intending to remove them when he returned from a Continental tour. In a letter to Dr. Gillan he expressed a hope that the MSS. were kept free from damp. The Doctor replied that "the MSS. were all very dry, especially the sermons."

He was fond of gardening, and a friend passing by one day while he was so engaged asked him what he was doing?

"Oh, I'm just trying to raise my celery" (salary), was the ready response.

On another occasion he was working in his garden dressed in his old clothes when he observed Colonel and Lady Campbell of Blythswood driving up to pay him a friendly visit. Ashamed to be caught in such shabby attire, he knocked his soft felt hat over his eyes, struck out his arms straight, and assumed the attitude of a scarecrow till his distinguished visitors had passed into the manse, when he ran in by a back door, changed his apparel, and appeared in proper style to do honour to his guests.

When preaching at Kirkcaldy on one occasion, he prayed that the inhabitants of that town "might be zealous in business, which most of them are, and fervent in spirit, which most of them are *not*."

Rev. Norman Macleod, D.D., of Barony.

Never was minister or citizen of Glasgow more beloved and revered by his fellow-citizens of all classes and denominations, than Norman Macleod; and never since the days of Dr. Chalmers did one man exert such a powerful influence for good over the spirit of the entire community as did he. Nor was his influence confined to our city. His fame and his "good words" and good works spread over all the land, and moved all sorts and conditions of men and women from the Queen upon the throne down to the meanest of her subjects. He swayed with his earnest, heart-felt eloquence the highest dignitaries in church and state. He moved to laughter and to tears by his unbounded humour, his tender pathos, his broad brotherly sympathy and humanity, the roughs of the High Street, and the denizens of Anderston and Bridgeton, as well as the shepherds of Morven and Mull, the backwoodsmen of Canada, and the semi-heathens of Hindostan. In the darkest hours of his widowed Sovereign's sorrow, he was her chosen comforter and trusted friend; while into his great loving heart the pauper widow in Barnhill, and the dying patient in the Infirmary, poured their troubles and their fears; and to each and all of these he ministered the truest, the best, and the sweetest of consolation. Seldom is there found united in one human soul such a diversity of gifts and graces, such a wealth of human nature. In Norman Macleod there was combined the playfulness, simplicity, and tenderness of a child, with all the dignity and gravity of a devout Christian minister and leader of men ; the deep, poetic enthusiastic lover of nature and of solitude, with all the ease, grace, and polish of the courtier ; the delicacy and sensitiveness of a woman, with all the unflinching courage and resolution of a soldier or a martyr. More, perhaps, than any of his contemporaries, did he by his preaching, his writing, and above all, by his life, break down that narrow, bigoted, and pharisaic formalism, which had taken such a tenacious hold upon Scottish Presbyterianism, and he breathed into its dry bones the breath of Christian life and love. He was not by any means a perfect saint or a faultless man, indeed, he had a holy horror of such men. He was not by any means a man of great learning, or a profound theologian, but he was far more and better than these, he was an humble, earnest, trusting believer in the Great Father and Saviour ; and his big heart overflowed with love to all mankind. He cared little for the jots and tittles of ecclesiastical or ceremonial law, but he had a passionate love for the spirit of truth and righeousness, and like his Great Master, " His delights were with the children of men."

We regret that our space will only permit of us recording a very few brief incidents in the career of this remarkable man, and these chiefly relating to his life and labours in Glasgow. Norman Macleod was born in Campbeltown, on 3rd June, 1812. He was of Highland origin, his grandfather having been parish minister of Morven, in Argyleshire. " This minister of Morven was in many ways a remarkable man. Noble looking and eloquent, a good scholar and true pastor, he lived as a patriarch among his people. He had a small stipend, and, as its usual concomitant, a large family. Sixteen children were born in the manse, and a number of families—a shepherd, a boatman, and a ploughman—were settled on the glebe, with others who had come there in their need and were not turned away." Norman's father was also a minister, and was ordained to the charge of the Parish of Campbeltown in 1808. He married, in 1811, Agnes Maxwell, a daughter of the chamberlain to the Duke of Argyll, and tacksman of Aros in Mull, whose forefathers had fled from the Lowlands in the time of the

Covenanter persecutions. He afterwards became minister of Campsie, and later, and for many years, was the honoured pastor of St. Columba Church, Glasgow. Young Norman received his early education in the Burgh School of Campbeltown, but he usually spent a portion of his holidays in Morven, and was also for a time lodged with the schoolmaster there, one Samuel Cameron, a man of rare merit. It was here, in Morven, where young Norman imbibed his deep and undying love of the Highlands, where he developed his sturdy stalwart frame, and became an adept in the management of boats, the climbing of rocks, and the catching of fish. Here, too, he learnt Gaelic, and got his youthful spirit imbued with Highland tradition and romance, which tinged his thoughts till the end of his life. At the age of 13, his father removed to Campsie, and shortly afterwards the young lad was sent to study in the University of Glasgow. He was rather versatile in his tastes to become a great student. He was an inveterate punster and mimic, he overflowed with animal spirits, was full of fun and frolic. But he passed through his College career in a creditable manner, and in due time was licensed to preach. He was ordained to the parish of Loudoun, in Ayrshire, in March, 1838, where he spent five happy and useful years. Shortly after the disruption in 1843, he received calls from Cupar-Fife, Maybole, Campsie, St. Ninians, Tollbooth (Edinburgh), Greenock, and Dalkeith, so popular had he even then become. He chose the last named charge, and was inducted there in December, 1843. He was translated to the Barony in July, 1851, where he remained until his death on 16th June, 1872, having thus laboured in our city for the long period of 21 years.

A very interesting event in his life took place about a month after his induction to Barony—viz., his marriage to Miss Catherine Ann Mackintosh, daughter of William Mackintosh, Esq., of Geddes, and sister of his dearest friend, John Mackintosh, who was his companion in their student days, and between whom and Norman an affection like that which existed between David and Jonathan sprang up, and continued until it was terminated by death, and that too, spite of the fact that young Mackintosh felt constrained at the Disruption to attach himself to the Free Church, while Norman adhered to the Establishment. Dr. Macleod, after his friend's death, wrote a beautiful touching memoir of him, entitled "The Earnest Student," and it is very pathetic to find him ever and anon, in after years, turning aside from his engagements with Royalty, and from the glare and bustle of the General Assembly and its Moderator's chair, to shed silent tears over the memories of his departed friend, and to utter exclamations of deepest admiration and regard towards him. It shows the deep, tender, loving nature of the man, and the singleness and intensity of his personal attachments.

His ministry in Barony was very popular from the first, and continued unabated to the end. Every Sunday he preached to crowds that filled every seat and passage; yet by far the greater proportion of those actually connected with his church were not rich. They, however, were a most devoted flock, and heartily supported him in all his missionary and educational enterprises. In reading the biographies of the two men, we are struck with the close resemblance between the church labours of Dr. Chalmers and Dr. Macleod. The latter had been a student of the former in the Edinburgh Divinity Hall, and ever entertained towards his illustrious teacher feelings of the greatest respect and admiration. But we do not suppose that in his pastoral work Macleod merely followed the example of Chalmers. The one was as original and independent as the other. But the truth is, both men were animated with the same burning zeal for the glory of God, the same intense love for humanity; and each, in accordance with his own instincts and practical sense, threw himself into the work of evangelization as such work ought to be done. The first obvious duty of a minister is to become intimately acquainted with the members of his flock, and Macleod, like Chalmers, at once set about visiting these in their own homes, and this in such a parish as Barony was a work of no ordinary magnitude. His next task was, like that of Chalmers, to organize his agencies. He first formed a large Kirk Session of elders and deacons, and gave them charge over all the agencies he intended to employ. He established district meetings in the poorer districts of his parish. He held a meeting once a year in each of these districts—twelve in number. He instituted several day schools for the education of the young, personally going about raising funds for that purpose. He opened evening classes for adults; he opened the first congregational penny savings bank in Glasgow; he started a refreshment room in one of the busiest centres of labour, where working men could get cheap and well cooked food, and enjoy a comfortable reading room at their meal-hours, instead of being obliged to have recourse to the public-house; and he may almost be regarded as the founder of the system of cheap cooking depots for which our city has since become famous. He visited the paupers in Barnhill Poorhouse, and proposed the complete adoption of the boarding-out system for children which has been carried out with so great success in these later years.

In his diary for 1st January, 1853, there occur the following entries:—"God has been very merciful to me during the past year. I never had so unbroken a year of prosperity in the usual sense of that word. I have preached about 140 times, seven of them for public collections, many for chapels. I have addressed about 13 meetings for missions and other useful objects. Held 7 mission meeting in my own church. Published a sermon and edited magazine (*Edinburgh Christian Magazine*). Organized (1) schemes, (2) industrial aid, (3) female aid, (4) endowment, (5) education committees in congregation. Opened refreshment rooms for working classes. Opened three chapels with three missionaries. Suggested and helped to carry out a proposal for two new churches, for which £10,000 is now collected. About to build three new schools. Have commenced work in Barnhill Poorhouse. Visited in 22 days about 222 families. Have organized a congregational class of 110 from eight to fourteen years of age. Wrote paper on pauper education. I need to reform the schemes. Have had two large classes of young men and women for three months."

Surely here was a workman that needed not to be ashamed; and yet he is continually bewailing his inefficiency and unprofitableness!

In 1857 he began to hold evening services for the poor, to which none were admitted except in their every day working clothes. For the first winter, these services were held in the Martyr's Church, which was filled every Sabbath evening by the very people he wished to get; the following year they were transferred to the Barony, where they were continued till a Mission Church was built. The pews were filled with men in their fustian jackets, and with poor women, bareheaded or with an old shawl drawn over the head, and dressed, most of them, in shortgown and petticoat. Unkempt heads, faces begrimed with labour, and mothers with infants in their arms, gave a strange character to the scene. The police sometimes reported that several well known thieves were present. An old blind man sometimes acted as precentor to these meetings, tracing the lines with his fingers over the raised letters, and repeating two lines at a time in the old fashioned style. This worthy would sometimes get impatient when the Doctor would linger over the exposition of the Psalm, and strike his pitch-fork from time to time thinking he was finished. But at last the Doctor would look kindly down upon him and say, "You'll rise now Peter and begin."

The results of these services were remarkable. Many hundreds were reclaimed from lawless habits, some of the more ignorant were educated, and a large number became communicants. There was a nobility of character displayed by several of these working men and women which moved him to tears as he spoke of them, and gave him a deeper love than ever for the poor. The poor people themselves almost adored their minister. "A' kinds o' folk come to hear the Doctor," said one. "A' body likes the Doctor," said another. "I ken great lots o' folk that's been blessed by the Doctor, baith Scotch and Irish. I ken an Irish Catholic that wrought wi' me, o' the name o' Boyd, an' he cam' ae nicht oot o' curiosity, an' he was converted afore he raise frae his seat, an' he's a staunch Protestant to this day, every bit o' him, though his faither and mither, an' a' his folks, are sair against him for't." Such was the evidence of a third. On one occasion when he was about to descend from a cab at his father's door, after one of his meetings, a rough hand was pushed in at the window. Norman understood what was meant, and on taking what was offered, received a warm grasp from some unknown working man, who had come from the church a mile away to express by this act more thankfulness than he could find words to utter. So writes his brother and biographer who was an eye-witness of the scene. On another occasion a poor woman was suffering from small-pox or some other deadly infectious disease. She was one of Dr. Macleod's converts and fain would she have been comforted and consoled in her dying hours by a visit from her warm-hearted pastor. But she would not allow any one to send for him, for fear that he might carry the infection to some of his "bairns." Surely the man who inspired such unselfish and self-sacrificing love, must have been himself a good man, even though he had as was charged against him, in theory at least, given "a' the ten commands a screed ae day." An old woman in Ayrshire who was praising one of his sermons was rebuked by a neighbour for speaking so favourably of a *read* sermon, replied, "I wadna hae cared if he had *whustled* it!" How like a remark made by a hearer of Dr. Chalmers, "It was *fell* reading yon!"

Dr. Macleod was an extensive traveller. He was sent by his church on missions to Canada, India, and various places on the continent of Europe, and wherever he went he was received with open arms, and listened to with enthusiasm, by large and deeply interested audiences. He revived the spirits and kindled the hearts of all with whom he came into contact. The common sailors, with whom he freely conversed on his voyages, adored him, and Highlanders whom he met abroad and spoke to in their native Gaelic were surprised and delighted beyond measure. He was a true man, whose sympathies were with his fellow-men. He entered with zest into all their joys, and sorrows, and experiences, with the heart of a true brother, and nothing that concerned humanity was too high or too low to escape his keen insight and catholic interest and regard.

A notable feature in his character was his buoyancy of spirits and abounding humour. In his biography there are scattered many of the most exquisite illustrations of this characteristic. He was the most comical of correspondents, and in company he kept the table in a roar of laughter by his odd sayings, mimicry of queer characters, and exhibitions of human nature. A whole volume might be filled with examples of his humour, but we must content ourselves with the following extract from a letter written to his mother on his 57th birthday, and when that good lady was nearly 80 years of age (and which we give by permission of his biographer, Dr. Donald Macleod). The letter was dated 3rd June, 1868 :—

"I am quite safe in saying that I have written to you, say forty letters, on my birthday, and whatever was defective as to number in my letters was made up by your love. Now I begin to think the whole affair is getting stale to you. In short you anticipate all I can say, am likely to say, or ought to say; and having done so, you begin to read, and to laugh and cry time about, and to praise me to all my brothers and sisters, until they detest me till June 4th. Don't you feel grateful I was born? Are you not thankful? I know you are, and no wonder. I need not enumerate all those well-known personal and domestic virtues which have often called forth your praises, except when you are beaten at backgammon. But there is another side of the question with which I have to do, and that is—whether I ought to be so very grateful to you for the event with which June 3rd, 1812, is associated. As I advance in life, this question becomes more interesting to me, and it seems due to the interests of truth and justice to state on this day, when I have had fifty-six years' experience of life in its most varied forms, that I am by no means satisfied with your conduct on that occasion, and that if you fairly consider it, I feel assured you will justify me in demanding from you the only reparation possible—an ample apology, and a solemn promise never to do the like again! You must acknowledge that you took a very great liberty with a man of my character and position not to ask me whether I was disposed to enter upon a new and important state of existence; whether I should prefer winter or summer to begin the trial; or whether I should be a Scotchman, Irishman, or Englishman; or even whether I should be 'Man or woman born,' each of these alternatives involving to me most important consequences. What a good John Bull I would have made! What a rattling, roaring Irishman! What a capital mother or wife! What a jolly abbess! But you doomed me to be born in a tenth-rate provincial town, half Scotch, half Highland, and sealed my doom as to sex and country. Was that fair? Would you like me to have done that to you? Suppose, through my fault, you had been born a wild Spanish Papist, what would you have said on your 57th birthday, with all your Protestant convictions? Not one Maxwell or Duntroon related to you!—you yourself a nun called St. Agnese!—and all, forsooth, because I had willed

that you should be born at Toledo on June 3rd, 1812!
Think of it, mother, seriously, and say, have you done to me
as you would have had me do to you?

"Then, again, pray who is to blame for all I have suffered
for fifty-six years? Who but you? This reply alone can
be made to a thousand questions which press themselves on
my memory, until the past seems a history of misery endured
with angelic patience. Why, I might ask, for example, did
I live for weeks on insipid 'lythings,' spending days and
nights screaming, weeping, hiccoughing, with an old woman
swathing and unswathing me, whose nature retires from
such attentions? Why had I for years to learn to walk,
and speak, and amuse aunts and friends like a young parish
fool, and wear frocks? Fancy me in a frock now, addressing the Assembly! And yet I had to wear them for years!
Why have I suffered from mumps, hooping-cough, measles,
scarlet fever, toothache, headache, lumbago, gout, sciatica,
sore back, sore legs, sore sides, and other ailments, having
probably sneezed several thousand times, and coughed as
often since christened? Why? Because I was born!—
because you, and none but you, insisted I should be born!
Why have I had to be tossed about on every sea and ocean,
and kept in perpetual danger from icebergs, fogs, storms,
shipwrecks? You did it! Why have I had my mind
distracted, my brain worn, my heart broken, my nerves
torn, my frame exhausted, my life tortured with preachings
and preparations, speeches, lectures, motions, resolutions,
programmes; with sessions, presbyteries, and assemblies;
with all churches, bond and free; with all countries from
east to west; with good words and bad words; with Sunday
questions and week-day questions; with all sorts of people,
from trembling Jock to the Queen; with friends and relations, Jews and Greeks, bond and free? Why all this, and
a thousand times more, if not simply and solely because,
forsooth, of your conduct on June 3rd, 1812? No wonder
it is a solemn and sad day to you! No wonder you sigh,
and—unless all good is out of you—weep, too! I was told
my poor father, on the day I was born, hid himself in a
hay rick from sheer anxiety. He had some idea of what
was doing. But, dear soul! he always gave in to you, and
it was in vain for either of us to speak. I am told I yelled
very loud. I hope I did. I could do no more then and I

can do little more now, than protest, as I do, against the whole arrangement.

"An American expressed to a friend of mine a great desire to visit Siam, as he understood its people were all twins! The thought makes me tremble. What if I had been born like the Siamese twins! Think of my twin brother and myself going as a deputy to India; in the same berth, speaking together at the same meeting, sick together at sea, or both suffering from gout, and you concerned and anxious about your poor dear boys! What supposing my twin had married Mrs. ——?

"Mother, dear, repent! One good quality remains—I can forgive and do forgive you this day, in token of which I send you my love, big as my body, yea without limit, and as large a kiss as my beard and moustache will permit, &c."

An anecdote told of Dr. Macleod and the late Dr. Watson, of Dundee, may here be given. They were travelling together in the far north on some special mission, and happened to be crossing an arm of the sea from one island to another in an open boat, when the weather became very stormy and the sea so boisterous that there was the greatest danger of the boat being swamped. In these perilous circumstances Dr. Watson suggested that one of them should engage in prayer to the great Ruler of the elements. One of the two boatmen, who had been toiling at the oars till they were almost worn out, looked over at Dr. Watson, who was a man of small stature, and said, "*You* may pray if ye like, sir; but this ane," pointing to Dr. Macleod, "maun tak' an oar." We can imagine the worthy Norman taking a hearty laugh to himself at this practical remark, so much in harmony was it with his own ideas of praying and working.

Rev. William Anderson, LL.D.

Dr. William Anderson, of John Street U.P. Church, who has been characterized as one of the most remarkable men and ministers in Scotland during the nineteenth century, occupied a prominent position among the citizens of Glasgow for the long period of half a century, he having been ordained as pastor of his first and only charge on 7th February, 1822, and died on 15th September, 1872. He at an early period became one of the most popular ministers in the city, and retained that popularity undiminished till the end of his life. With the exception, perhaps, of the late Dr. Norman Macleod, of Barony, there was no minister in Glasgow during the half century who was so highly esteemed and so greatly beloved as "Willie Anderson." He was a prime favourite of the common people, for he was a stern foe to all wrong and oppression; a genial, kindly, pawky friend of humanity, and a man of rare and somewhat eccentric genius. No meeting held in Glasgow for the advocacy of any great public cause, or for the redress of any crying public grievance—at least in the domain of religion, morality, or liberty—would have been considered complete unless Dr. Anderson was numbered among the speakers. Many interesting and instructive anecdotes are related concerning him, of which we subjoin a select few, and we believe them to be all well authenticated.

Here is one regarding the period of his boyhood which is very suggestive of the highly sensitive and sympathetic nature of the future man.

When he went first to the parish school at Chapel Green, about two miles distant from Kilsyth (his birthplace), he found he was the only boy who wore shoes and stockings! Partly out of delicate regard for the feelings of his fellows, and partly to escape the charge of *"pridefu'ness"* so abhorrent to a Scottish boy, he used regularly to take off his shoes and stockings at the outside of the town, and concealed them in a hedge till he returned

Anderson entered Glasgow College in the session of 1811-12, being only 12 years and ten months old. One day Professor Richardson called on young Willie to construe some verses in Virgil, when his Kilsyth accent and shrill, ballad-singing voice stunned the class with astonishment till after he had read, not—as was common—four, but eight lines, the silence broke out into a loud roar of laughter, as the professor—himself considerably tickled—remarked, "Well *sung*, Gulielme." Afterwards he was for a while regularly called upon to "sing," but by and by, his good scholarship was discerned, and he became a favourite at once with his fellow-students and with his professor.

William Anderson gained a prize in almost every one of his classes. This fact is connected with a characteristic incident. Long years afterwards—in 1868—when he presented himself for the purpose of voting in the election of the first M.P. for the University of Glasgow, the officer would not receive his vote, unless he produced his tickets, which he had lost. When he failed to convince the man of the validity of his claim, he said somewhat sternly, "Well, I'll bring down my prizes!" and so the point was settled at once.

While attending the Moral Philosophy class, young Anderson read an essay on "Conscience," which Professor Milne, who was usually very chary of commendation, eulogized very highly, and the youthful student was greatly elated over his success, and began to fancy he was a genius of the first water. Going down soon afterwards to visit his grandfather in Falkirk, he attended a sacramental preaching, but the address given by the minister seemed to young Willie to be very poor stuff. He thought he could do much better himself. Thus, to use his own words, "Puffed up with self-conceit, I was coming home (it was a fine summer evening), and when passing by a short cut to grandfather's house, through Stenhouse Muir, I thought I could extemporise a Communion Address. Looking round first to make sure that not even a cow or a sheep should hear me, I began :—"Fellow-Communicants, 'Ye know the grace of our Lord Jesus Christ, that though he was rich, yet for your sakes he became poor, that ye through his poverty might be rich.' Having a vivid recollection of this well known passage, I had no difficulty in getting thus far. Then I continued :—'Fellow-Communicants, we have been solemnly pledging ourselves'—a pause and a clearing of the throat — 'My dear Fellow-Communicants' — I could get no further, but instantly took to my heels and ran, stopping not till I had got over a dyke, behind which I sank down, and roared and groaned under a burden of shame. 'Ma conscience, that it should have come to this!'" Ever afterwards, Anderson was a generous and indulgent critic of the sermons and writings of other men.

The following pithy and incisive advice given to the young scholar by his worthy grandfather is well worth repeating :—"Now, sir, I know you will be beginning to try and make fine sentences,—make them as fine as you can; but O, preserve simplicity in prayer! God does not need to be told that He made the constellations. Confess to Him your sins, and express your confidence in His Son." His grandson took the hint, and his prayers always avoided those tiresome and inflated laudations of the Deity in which many still indulge.

There was a great deal of obstruction raised to his ordination on the ground that he *read* his sermons—a heinous offence in those austere days—and fully a year elapsed between the time of his receiving the call and the time of his ordination, in consequence of this obstruction. The obstruction was almost entirely ministerial—the people were on his side. A blind woman had been praising one of his sermons, when a neighbour interposed—"But he was reading it." "I'm sure I did not *see* him," was the *naive* reply. At last after a hard fight, he overcame all opposition, and was duly ordained as stated above; and soon gathered round him a large and deeply attached congregation.

There was a tinge of romance about his first marriage. Two years before he was licensed, and when attending Mr. Barr's Church, Dovehill, he saw one day a young lady who seemed to him a vision of loveliness—tall, dark-haired, and handsome in form—and for whom he conceived an ideal passion. Mr. Barr had talked of introducing him to a young lady of his acquaintance who might suit him, but after that sight the proffered introduction was no longer desired. It turned out fortunately, however, that Mr. Barr's young friend and the creature of the day-dream were one and the same! Her name was Isabella Binnie, daughter of Mr. John Binnie, builder, Glasgow. They became acquainted, and found an extraordinary congeniality in their spiritual feelings. A courtship followed, which ended in a happy marriage in 1825.

Dr. Alexander M'Leod, his colleague, relates a story which he heard him tell in his own pulpit. He was expounding the words, "He that putteth not out his money to usury." "Does that mean," he said, "asking ten per cent or more? Not entirely. It means also the spirit in which the per cent is taken. There was once in this church a poor widow, and she wanted £20 to begin a small shop. Having no friends, she came to me, her minister, and I happened to know a man, not of this church, who could advance the money to the poor woman. So we went to this man, the widow and I, and the man said he would be happy to help the widow. And he drew out a bill for twenty pounds, and the widow signed it, and I signed it too. Then he put the signed paper in his desk, and took out the money, and gave it to the widow. But, counting it, she said, 'Sir, there are only £15 here.' 'It is all right,' said the man, 'that is the interest I charge.' And, as we had no redress, we came away. But the widow prospered. And she brought the £20 to me, and I took it myself to the office of the man who lent it, and I said to him, 'Sir, there are the £20 from the widow.' And he said, 'There is the paper you signed, and if you know any other poor widow, I will be happy to help her in the same way.' I replied, 'You help the widow! Sir, you have robbed this widow, and if you do not repent, you will be damned.' And, my friends, I kept my eye on that man. And before six months were over, God smote him, and he died." A correspondent in Edinburgh adds to this story the following:—"And when his will was produced and read, it appeared that on the very day Dr. Anderson had spoken to him, he had put to it a codicil leaving £50 to the poor. Poor deluded mortal, to think his soul's salvation could be bought for £50."

Although Dr. Anderson was an exceedingly popular preacher and lecturer, this was not because he said things merely to tickle or please his audience. On the contrary, he was a most faithful and fearless speaker, and came down very sorely upon the sins and follies of men. Here are one or two examples :—

Once lecturing in the City Hall, when he was reading Dr. John Brown on the Duties of Women, he said—"When a number of ladies meet and have nothing very edifying to speak about, what can they do but *bite?*" A titter was the reply to this home thrust.

On another occasion, when lecturing in the City Hall on the "Errors of Romanism," he had unearthed, in some way or other, the scapulary charms, which some earnest devotees of the Roman Church were said to wear upon their breasts at that time. He held up the charms themselves—pieces of calico shaped like hearts. He told his audience how, if they wished to be safe, they should buy one of these, and put it on the naked breast; but if they had plenty of means, and wished to be safer still, they should buy two, and put one on the breast above, and one on the back behind, the heart. Then came the climax. "We have heard of many ways and means of salvation. There is the oldest dispensation of all, salvation by *works;* and in the Mosaic dispensation salvation by *works of the law.* And in the new dispensation we have salvation *by grace;* and we have had, since that new dispensation was set up, many comings and goings between the old and the new—salvation by *pilgrimages,* salvation by *priests,* salvation *by the church;* but this is the first time in the history of the world that we have been offered *salvation by clouts.*" One is not surprised to learn that it was some time before the lecturer could proceed.

The story of the "brown bawbee" is well known. Speaking of the disproportion between wealth and liberality in giving, he described a fashionably dressed lady approaching the church, and after sailing along in all the majesty of crinoline and consciousness of position and cash, depositing from a white-gloved hand in the plate—what? Five pounds, or a sovereign, or even a shilling? No, but a brown bawbee! He is said to have added—"I stood beside the elders in the porch last Sabbath evening, and observed how the people cast their gifts into the Lord's treasury. I exclaimed, 'There they go! Three a penny, three a penny!'"

A great many other incidents characteristic of "Willie Anderson" could be related, but our space will only permit of other two of a more pathetic kind :—

When Dr. Anderson attended the Jubilee Soiree of his venerable father (who laboured as a minister in Kilsyth till his 92nd year) he stepped forward to him at the close of his speech, laid his hand on his head, then covered with silver hair, and broke out into the old song:—

> "John Anderson my jo, John,
>   When we were first acquent,
> Your locks were like the raven,
>   Your bonnie brow was brent;
> But now your brow is bald, John,
>   Your locks are like the snaw;
> But blessings on your frosty pow,
>   John Anderson my jo."

The effect is stated to have been indescribable, electrifying to all, and melting to many.

In March 1871, when his own Jubilee came round, he was entertained to a Soiree in the City Hall, and was presented with a Testimonial of £1,200 on a silver salver. In the course of his reply he delivered himself of the following apostrophe to the City Hall, endeared to him by so many varied reminiscences:—" Dearly beloved Glasgow City Hall!—I have had, or have, four homes on earth—the venerable home of my father's house; the sweet home, first and last, of my own house; that earnest, oft experienced, of the heavenly home, the church in John Street; and the joyous jubilant home of the City Hall. At our family reunions here, though the bigger brethren with their clarionets discoursed sweeter music, yet I am ready to flatter myself that the natural notes of my ram's horn sometimes excited to higher raptures the shout of liberty. At all events, your cheering response greatly animated myself. Good City Hall! you have proved a happy home to me. And when I feel as if this evening I were bidding thee farewell, it is with a heart overflowing with gratitude for the manner in which thou hast contributed to the joy, the honour, and the usefulness of my life."

It was characteristic of the unselfishness and generosity of the man that the £1,200 presented to him on this Jubilee occasion was devoted by him to the founding of "William Anderson Scholarships" in connection with the United Presbyterian Church. Altogether Dr. Anderson was a man of whom Glasgow may well feel proud; and it will be long ere his memory and the aroma of his beautiful life will pass away from us. (*Life of Dr. William Anderson*, by George Gilfillan.)

DAVID STOW—EDUCATIONALIST AND MISSIONARY.

One of the real benefactors of Glasgow in modern times, though his fame has not been blazoned over the country, as that of many a less worthy man has been, was DAVID STOW, an earnest Sabbath school teacher and reformer, and founder of the training system of education. He was born in Paisley on 17th May, 1793, and was educated at the Grammar School there. He removed to Glasgow at the age of 18, where he was engaged in a mercantile house. On his way to and from business, he required to pass through some of the lower localities of the city, and was deeply impressed with the misery and vice which abounded there. This led him to engage in the work of Sabbath school teaching, which was very little regarded in those days. The locality he selected for his labours was the Saltmarket, which was then densely populated. By constant visitation at the homes of about seventy families, he gathered around him a very needy but very attached flock of ragged children, amongst whom he laboured with great zeal and success. His labours attracted the notice of Dr. Chalmers, who was then organizing his parochial system of relief and education; and so struck was he with the excellence of Mr. Stow's system, that he established in his parish of St. John's this principle of Sabbath schools, by which the labours of each teacher was to be confined to his own appointed locality, so that not a family in it should be neglected. Such was the commencement of local Sabbath schools, a method to which Dr. Chalmers was enthusiastically devoted, and regarding which he said, "This is what I call preaching from house to house!" The Doctor got Mr. Stow elected one of his elders, an office demanding no small amount of time and labour.

But Mr. Stow soon perceived that the teaching of one short hour or so on the Sabbath day was not sufficient to meet the requirements of his neglected little ones. He wished to extend the benefits of his training from one day in the week to seven. In this work he would, doubtless, have had the approval and aid of Dr. Chalmers, but that eminent man had by this time removed to St. Andrews. He was, however, assisted by some of his former pupils who had grown up and became devoted to the good work. A great and beneficial improvement took place among the young people in the locality of their labours, and in course of time, a church and day school (afterwards named St. Luke's) were organized, so that these young people might carry on a systematic course of Christian work. Having formed his theory of the training system from his ten years of experience of Sabbath school teaching, Mr. Stow proceeded in the Spring of 1827 to reduce it to action, by adapting a house and garden in the Drygate as a school and playground for about 100 pupils, and a dwelling for the teacher. The Drygate was a poor densely peopled district, teeming with idle, unreclaimed children, and well fitted for his experiment. Devotional principle and moral practice, the chief essentials of human training, were inculcated during the whole week instead of a seventh of it. There was no corporal punishment; the only chastisement was the public opinion of the class. As for the playground, it was to form the children's world instead of the streets in which they had roamed at large. The morning lessons of the week-day training school were made the basis of the practice of the children each day, under the superintendence of an accomplished master trainer in-doors at lessons, and out-of-doors at play. The walls of the school were draped with illustrative pictures, and the whole system was conducted on the principles of *education, sympathy of companionship, practical application,* and *natural instruction,* instead of mere instilling of dry lessons, shorter catechism, and the *tawse.* A great outcry was made against this new fangled style of education, and the prejudices of many old-fashioned, orthodox people were aroused, but Mr. Stow persevered, and soon produced astonishing results. The pale, ragged, ignorant children became healthy, happy, and intelligent, and their answers in trying examinations produced approval and even wonder. To make the effects of the new system more widely known, the master and mistress of the Drygate School, with a dozen of their juvenile scholars, visited different towns from Rothesay to Stranraer in 1829; and so deep was the impression made by these visits, that similar schools were established in various towns in Scotland. A society was formed in Edinburgh, and Mr. Caughie, the teacher of the Drygate School, with twelve of his pupils, was invited to exhibit the nature of his teaching. They were conveyed by stage coach, and for three successive days the exhibitions were continued in the Waterloo Rooms, which were attended by the magistrates and many of the leading men of the city, and the result of their approval of the system was the establishment of the Edinburgh Model Infant School.

Meanwhile Mr. Stow was engaged in extending his operations in Glasgow. He obtained premises for the establishment of a new school in Saltmarket—upon the ground floor of a Wesleyan chapel—with the space in front for a playground; and here a fresh legion of young city pariahs was assembled, whose conduct soon justified the principles of their training. The flowers of their playground remained uninjured, and the tempting currants unplucked. Their new sense of beauty admired the former, and their adopted principles of honesty spared the other. The money they had formerly squandered was spent in the purchase of books, and in many cases their reckless parents were shamed or allured, by the example of their children, into more orderly behaviour. Mr. Stow subsequently proceeded to establish "graded schools," whereby the training of the children could be carried on from one stage to another; and finding it necessary for the full development of his system to provide for the training of teachers as well as of pupils, he originated the Normal School or College, which was inaugurated on 14th November, 1836. That was a happy day for Mr. Stow. Five hundred of the leading citizens—including the Dean of Guild, the members of the Trades' and Merchants' Houses, many of the clergy, the Professors of the Andersonian University with their distinguished President, James Smith, Esq., of Jordanhill, and the office-bearers of the Educational Society—walked in procession to lay the foundation-stone, and the Moderator of the General Assembly offered up the dedicatory prayer. This institution was fostered and nursed under the care of Mr. Stow, and was regarded in all quarters as a new era in the science of Education. Sir John Kay Shuttleworth, in his examination before a Select Committee of the House of Commons on the Education of the Poorer Classes—which sat in March, 1838, about fourteen months after the Glasgow Normal Seminary had been started—said it was "the most perfect school of this description with which he was acquainted." The merits of Mr. Stow as an educational reformer were now so generally recognized that the Privy Council Committee on Education offered him the first Inspectorship of Schools in Scotland; but after careful consideration he declined the honour. "I would not like," he said, "to be paid for services in any shape, although I consider it right and proper that all special services should be paid." Mr. Stow was much grieved when, in May, 1845, the Normal Seminary was transferred to the Established

Church, as he contended that it was a national, not a sectarian institution, and he subsequently transferred his own services to the Free Normal School, which was established a few months afterwards. Active and indefatigable to the last in this and other good works, Mr. Stow died at Bridge of Allan on the 6th November, 1864, in the 71st year of his age. (*Eminent Scotsmen.*)

Origin of the Foundry Boys' Society.

In these modern days the religious communities of Glasgow have developed an amount of activity in the direction of evangelization and the elevation of the masses that has not been surpassed by any other city in the United Kingdom. We have always had amongst us, in all the denominations, ministers of the highest ability and the most earnest zeal—men who have been not more profound and learned as scholars and theologians, and eloquent as preachers, than devoted and self-sacrificing in their personal labours amongst the poor and lapsed masses in the wynds and lanes and other densely populated parts of the city. But these ministers have been efficiently assisted and encouraged—indeed, in many cases they have been stimulated and shown the example—by the laity of all ranks and classes and of both sexes. Many of our most eminent merchants and professional men, as well as our high civic dignitaries, have been active workers in the Sabbath school, the mission field, and in general church enterprises; and in later years large numbers of ladies have joined in the work with the best possible results. One of the largest and most successful of these home missionary organizations, which is peculiar to Glasgow and unique in its operations, is the Foundry Boys' Society, which has been upwards of twenty-one years in existence, and has spread its ramifications over the whole city, and been greatly beneficial to the young and rising generation. With this society from the first the name of an esteemed citizen—Mr. John Burns, who stands at the head of one of our largest shipping firms, and whose fame in this connection has gone over the globe—has been closely associated, along with Mr. Richard Hunter and Mr. M'Keith, and it redounds greatly to their honour that, in the midst of their onerous duties, they have found time and opportunity for working in this excellent field. But it will be interesting to our readers to know that the pioneer in this good work was a poor factory girl, named Mary Anne Clough. This young woman had no position in society, so called, and no worldly means save that which she earned by her own industry, standing all day among flying spindles in a dense and dusty atmosphere; but she had a large heart and a deep compassion for the temporal and spiritual interests of her fellow-creatures. Seeing around her many poor boys employed in the foundries who were not only utterly neglected, but early initiated into lessons of vice, she had compassion upon them. " I am but a poor working girl," she said, " but I will try in a loving spirit if I can win them to God and what is good." This noble resolution she set about to carry into execution, asking and obtaining the use of a room below the factory where she wrought. She opened it on a Sabbath in June, 1862, and ere long had gathered in some forty lads, with ragged clothes and dirty faces, from smoking clubs and back courts where they were wont to spend their Sabbaths in gambling, rude play, and wild merriment. For two years she persevered in this course, nor did she abandon the work she loved so well till failing health compelled her to resign it into the hands of others. Nor were her efforts to bless and save these boys confined to Sabbath days. They engaged all her spare time throughout the week. This noble girl, abundant in labours in season and out of season, so soon as the day's work was over took her way to the homes of the boys—if homes many of their lodgings could be called. Many a night she might have been seen by the glare of the drinking shops that threw their lights into the thick air wending her lonely and weary way, an angel in disguise, on her errands of mercy, through the ruffian crowd of the city's darkest, foulest streets. God owned her labours. So distinguished, indeed, from others of the same class and calling, by their superior industry, decency, freedom from profane language, and general good account, were those under her training, that " Mary Anne's boys" became a proverb in the foundries. Some are now teaching Sabbath schools, and some in other ways doing good, and at the same time occupying positions as respectable citizens, who, but for this poor factory girl, might have been pests in the community.

Such was the labour which, as we have said, resulted in the foundation of the great Glasgow Foundry Boys' Religious Society, which, at first confined to those employed like Mary Anne's *protégees*, is now extended to working boys of every other class and working girls as well. Its operations are divided into four great branches : one, aiming directly and incessantly at the highest life of the rising race, for time and for eternity; the second, gathering the children together for gratuitous instruction, with sewing for the girls, and sometimes a drawing lesson for the boys ; the third, or social reform department, dealing with such matters as drill exercises, flute bands, singing classes, Saturday evening entertainments, excursions into the country on Saturday afternoons, and one great annual festival for a whole week at a time; while the last, or provident department, labours at such prosaic matters as savings banks, cheap clothing schemes, benefit funds, and the like, and by its excellent management secures that the popular and attractive parts of the Society's programme shall be actually more than self-supporting!

From the latest Annual Report of the Society, we learn that in December, 1887, the branches numbered 79, at which there was an average attendance on Sabbath forenoons of 15,633 lads and girls, and 2,052 workers; that the collections at the Sabbath forenoon meetings for the year, and which were devoted to the various benevolent schemes of the Society, as well as for foreign missions and charitable purposes, amounted to £1,130, 9s. 6d., and the contributions received from the public were £698, 0s. 2½d.; that in its 19 Penny Savings Banks £2,677, 15s. had been lodged during the year, the number of transactions being 69,955; and that the Fair week trip in the previous summer was successfully conducted, whereby 650 working lads and girls were taken from the temptations of the city at that season, and spent nearly a week on the shores of Lochfyne and in Ayrshire.

We regret that our space will not permit us to extend our references to the modern religious life of our city. There have been many other leaders in that sphere—both lay and clerical—worthy of honourable mention, the narrative of whose labours would be both interesting and instructive. In no city in the country, we believe, is there more earnest work on behalf of the lapsed masses being done than in Glasgow. Since the first visit of the American evangelist, Mr. Moody, about twenty years ago, this work has been taken up more than ever before, by ladies and gentlemen of the better classes, and numerous and varied are the schemes and organizations in operation for the social and spiritual elevation of the people. These comprise, in addition to ordinary mission services, free breakfasts, poor children's dinner tables, Dorcas societies, "Mizpah" bands, "Salvation Army" operations, and many others. Nor must we omit to mention the great and successful efforts put forth by Mr. William Quarrier and his co-adjutors, in providing homes and situations for the young waifs of our streets, efforts which have been generously assisted by our wealthy citizens, and which have resulted in the reclamation of many thousands of our city arabs, who but for them must have grown up in the midst of wretchedness and vice, and been added to our criminal population. The age of faith as well as that of money making in Glasgow has not yet passed away, for in connection with Mr. Quarrier's operations, the experiences of Mr. Müller, of Bristol, in former years, has been repeated in quite as wonderful and remarkable a manner in that of our Glasgow philanthropist.

CHAPTER XII.

SKETCHES OF SOME ODD CHARACTERS OF GLASGOW.

> "Oh, for the good old times! when all was new,
> And every hour brought prodigies to view;
> Full of their theme they spurn'd all idle art,
> And the plain tale was trusted to the heart."
> —*Gifford.*

A NOTABLE feature of most Scottish towns and villages, in the bygone days more than in the present, was the number of "queer" or "odd" characters that haunted or frequented them. These oddities were a never-failing source of wonder or amusement to the inhabitants, and their sayings and doings have been handed down to posterity with as much care and zeal, as if these characters were men and women of the highest genius, or had done great deeds of valour or benevolence in their day and generation. There is a strange fascination, to the common mind especially, for what is abnormal, grotesque or humorous, and although these characteristics are associated with much that is repulsive, degrading, and unsavoury, still they possess a wonderful power over the minds of the people. In the Waverley Novels, some of the best specimens of such oddities are to be found, and none of the Great Wizard's characters are more popular than, for example—Edie Ochiltree, Caleb Balderstone, Madge Wildfire, Nicol Jarvie, Dugald Dalgetty, Dandie Dinmont, and many others. But a sort of immortality has also been gained by some oddities of a far inferior stamp to any of these wonderful creations; and the student of Glasgow history is surprised to find what an amount of prominence is given to such questionable characters as "Bob Dragon," "Bell Geordie," "Hirstling Kate," "Hawkie," "Rab Hall," and several others who frequented our streets during the close of last and beginning of this century. Not only are these "queer folks" sketched and described in our imposing and dignified histories, but in several instances, separate books have been published regarding them, as for example—"Glasgow Characters" by Peter Mackenzie, and more recently the autobiography of "Hawkie" by John Strathesk. These works have been published at so low a price, that we feel it would be superfluous for us to rehearse the sketches of the "oddities" of our city in these pages; and we therefore content ourselves with a notice of one or two of the more notable amongst them.

It is perhaps not quite the proper thing to class amongst these oddities the renowned editor of the *Glasgow Herald*, Mr. Samuel Hunter, for although he was a man of jovial wit and humour, yet he was a gentleman of high standing in the community and undoubted ability. Still, as we do not intend to take up the rough and profane genius of the gutter here — with the notable exception of that of "Hawkie"—we may be pardoned for including in this chapter the worthy name of Samuel Hunter. He was born in the manse of Stoneykirk (of which parish his father was minister) on 19th March, 1769, and was educated at Glasgow University for the medical profession. At the close of the century, he served in Ireland as a surgeon, and subsequently as captain in the North Lowland Fencibles he took part in the campaign for the suppression of the Rebellion of 1798. Some time after his return from the Green Isle, he took up his residence in Glasgow, and almost immediately became a great favourite with the best society in the city, not more for his wit and humour, than for his innate principles of honour and gentlemanly deportment. He was a man of portly physical build, and his face was always beaming with kindliness and good humour. He became sole editor and part proprietor of the *Herald* in 1803, and occupied the editorial chair till 1837, when he was succeeded by the late Mr. James Pagan. His conduct of that journal was characterized by sterling good sense and sound judgment. His style of writing was terse, clear, and racy. There was no circumlocution about his articles, but he invariably went straight to the object he had in view. In the West of Scotland he was regarded almost as an oracle; and instead of asking at each other, "What are the news?" the gossips used to inquire, "What is Samuel saying to it to-day?" Mr. Hunter seems to have had a strong military bias, for shortly after assuming the control of the *Herald*, he was appointed major of the Gentleman Sharpshooters, and afterwards colonel of the 4th Regiment of Highland Local Militia.

Numerous anecdotes are told illustrative of his keen wit and caustic humour:—About the year 1810 a fire took place in the *Herald* office, and Dr. William Dunlop, a partner with Mr. Hunter in the concern, made great exertions to extinguish the flames. Next day the Doctor told his friend Samuel that while he was on the roof he lost his hold, and must have fallen to the ground and been killed had he not been fortunately arrested in his downward career by one of the rhones. "Aye," replied Samuel, "I dare say, thae rhones kep a heap o' trash."

Our worthy editor, though a bachelor, was celebrated for his hospitality. On Wednesdays, being the market day, he generally had a dinner party to bachelor friends from city and country at his residence in Madeira Court. His housekeeper was an excellent cook; but, like many of the culinary tribe, she was fond of a glass, which bronzed her face and made her hands unsteady. On one occasion the dinner hour, which was generally four o'clock, had arrived and passed, but no appearance of food. The host looked often at his large watch, and pulled away at the bell. At length the door burst open, and the old lady appeared carrying a large tureen of hotch-potch. She, however, tripped at the entrance, and the soup was spread over the carpet. Samuel, with the utmost gravity, coolly remarked—"Gentlemen, you have long been waiting for your dinner; you will all be glad to perceive that it is now *on the road!*"

This cook was rather celebrated for introducing rarities in her art. Pea soup was among the novelties of the time, and a bachelor friend, who had dined with Samuel, went home to his maiden aunt, who kept house for him in his large mansion, on the east side of Jamaica Street, full of the praises of pea soup. His aunt was willing to try the new dish, but was at a loss how to prepare it. "Nothing more simple," said the gentleman; "nothing surely but pease meal." The recipe was hastily adopted, and a party invited and assembled to enjoy the new soup. As might be expected, it turned out a failure. The guests were astonished to find only hot water instead of soup. Our host, somewhat annoyed, blamed his aunt for her unskilful handling of the ladle. "Stir it up; stir it up from the bottom, Effie; stir it up." But all in vain. The stirring process failed to make the dish more savoury.

Story of Robert M'Nair, Jean Holmes & Coy.

If not exactly entitled to be ranked among the *elite* of the Glasgow citizens of their day, Robert M'Nair and his worthy spouse, were certainly somewhat of notable *characters*, after a fashion; and were very fair examples both of the keen business talent and enterprise, and of the exuberant humour that distinguished the merchant class of Saint Mungo of a century or so ago.

Robert M'Nair, merchant and general dealer in Glasgow, was born about the beginning of last century, and died in 1779, at the ripe age of 76. He is said to have commenced business with a basket of half spoiled oranges. His partner in matrimony was also his partner in trade; and they seem to have been quite "birds of a feather" in business push and in humour. Their shop was situated at the head of King Street in the Trongate. It had a very gaudy appearance, being painted in bright green. The worthy couple were also conspicuous in their personal appearance, being gaily tricked out in antique frenchified style.

That Mr. M'Nair and his wife had a strong sense of humour and eccentricity, coupled with keen worldly wisdom, in their composition, may be seen from the following anecdotes :—

Amongst his other whims, Robert ordered the key-stones of the arches above the shops at the corner of King Street and Trongate, to be cut so as to represent ludicrous human faces, and each one to be different from the others. It was a source of amusement to him, on market days, to join the crowds of country folks who were gazing upon these faces, and to hear their remarks upon them. About the time he did business in Trongate, there was a rage for joint-stock companies and long worded firms, and not to be behind his neighbours, Mr. M'Nair assumed his wife as a partner, and had the name of the firm painted above his shop door, "Robert M'Nair, Jean Holmes & Co.," and the second member of the firm was quite as active a member as the other. She acted as cashier of the concern, and stood in the shop from morning till night, as we have seen, decked out in an antique costume. There happened one season to be a scarcity of oranges in Glasgow, and unfortunately for Mr. M'Nair, his stock was small, while a neighbouring grocer held nearly the whole stock of oranges in Glasgow. M'Nair, however, was not to be beat ; he told all his customers that he had a large cargo which he expected to arrive every hour. Meantime he made up apparently a barrow-load of oranges with his small stock, and employed a porter to wheel them past his neighbour's shop and deliver them at his own, as if he were getting in his cargo. Immediately afterwards, he privately sent the porter with his load well covered up by a back door and through cross streets, and made him return openly as before with his load exposed : and this was continued for several hours. Having thus, to all appearance, laid in a large stock of oranges, he engaged a person to call upon his neighbour grocer and buy his whole stock, which he did on very moderate terms, the grocer believing that Mr. M'Nair had received a large supply; and then, of course, M'Nair sold them at a handsome profit.

By such methods of business, and strict economy in all things, Mr. M'Nair and his partner acquired considerable means, and became very extensive proprietors of houses and lands. One of his purchases was a piece of land which was anciently termed "the little hill of Tollcross," for which he paid the sum of £100. When asked, at the sale, for a bond for the price, he pulled from his pocket a greasy leather bag, and replied, "Na, na, nane o' yere gauds for me, here's Jean's pouch, gie me my papers." On this ground, Mr. M'Nair built a two storeyed house, planned by the two spouses themselves, and, consequently, it was rather of a grotesque description, and created a good deal of merriment in the passers by. It was named after its fair mistress, "Jeanfield Mansion House," and the grounds now form the Janefield or Eastern Cemetery. Mr. and Mrs. M'Nair travelled daily between this house and their place of business in the city, in a small carriage or phaeton. At this time the Government laid a tax upon two-wheeled carriages, and to elude this obnoxious tax, Robert took off the wheels from his phaeton, and placed the body of it upon two long wooden trams, and on this "queer machine" the worthy couple drove to kirk and market, to the great amusement of all spectators.

But Mr. M'Nair's devices did not stop there; and by one of these he was the means of bringing about a much needed reform in the administration of justice in the country. It seems to have been the practice at this period in all Exchequer trials, for the Crown when successful, to pay each juryman one guinea, and give him a supper to the bargain. It happened that M'Nair had got into some scrape with the Excise, and an action was raised against him in the Exchequer Court at Edinburgh. When the case was called, the Crown Advocate, after narrating the facts and commenting on them, concluded his address to the jury by reminding them that if they brought in a verdict for the Crown they would receive a guinea each and their supper. Upon hearing which, Mr. M'Nair rose and asked the Judges if he might be allowed to speak a word to the jury. This liberty being granted, Mr. M'Nair addressed the jury as follows:—"Gentlemen of the jury, you have heard what the learned Advocate for the Crown has just said. Now here am I, Robert M'Nair, merchant in Glasgow, standing before you, and I promise you two guineas each, and your dinner to boot, with as much wine as you can drink, if you bring in a verdict in my favour:" and here Mr. M'Nair sat down. He obtained a verdict in his favour. After this trial, the Crown never again made any attempts at influencing the jury by this species of bribery.

It would appear that Mr. and Mrs. M'Nair had two buxom daughters, and as the parents were known to be wealthy, the young ladies had no lack of wooers. In order to prevent them making foolish matches with penniless young lads, the old couple inserted the following advertisement in the *Edinburgh Courant* of 26th October, 1758:—

"Glasgow, 23rd October, 1758.—We, Robert M'Nair and Jean Holmes, having taken into our consideration the way and manner our daughter Jean acted in her marriage, that she took none of our advice, nor advised us before she married; for which reason we discharged her from our family for more than twelve months; and being afraid that some or other of our family may also presume to marry without duly advising us thereof, we, taking the affair into our serious consideration, hereby discharge all and every one of our children from offering to marry without our special advice and consent first asked and obtained; and if any of our children should propose or pretend to offer marriage to any without, as aforesaid, our advice and consent, they in that case shall be banished from our family twelve months; and if they should go as far as to marry without our advice and consent, in that case they are to be banished from our family seven years; but whoever advises us of their intention to marry and obtains our consent, shall not only remain children of the family, but also shall have a due proportion of our goods, gear, and estate, as we shall think convenient, and as the bargain requires. And, further, if any of our children shall marry clandestinely, they, by so doing, shall lose all claim or title to our effects, goods, gear, or estate. And we intimate this to all concerned, that none may pretend ignorance."

It happened at one time that Mr. M'Nair required a quantity of copperas for his business, and accordingly he wrote to his agents in London to send him 2 cwt. of that article; but Mr. M'Nair was not very expert at either writing or spelling, and in the letter ordering the copperas he spelled the words "2 cwt. of capres." The agents in London, however, read these words "2 cwt. of capers," and it was with much difficulty that they could make up the order for such a large quantity. Upon the capers arriving in Glasgow, Mr. M'Nair was quite astonished, and immediately wrote back to his agents, saying that he ordered them to send "2 cwt. of capres," instead of which they had sent him a large quantity of "sour peas," which nobody in Glasgow would look at; therefore he was going to return them. The mistake, however, turned out better than Robert had expected, for capers in London (in consequence of the market being cleared) suddenly rose greatly in price, so that Mr. M'Nair re-sold his "sour peas" again to great profit.

Robert M'Nair, Jun., of Belvidere, was an extensive sugar refiner in Glasgow. He had been a partner with his father in the concern of Robert M'Nair & Son, of the Gallowgate Sugar Works. After his father's death he assumed his younger brother, James, as a partner, and the firm became Robert & James M'Nair. Mr. M'Nair continued to reside at Belvidere till about 1813, when he removed to Leith, on his appointment as Collector of Customs there, and Belvidere was sold in that year to Mr. Mungo Nutter Campbell. This Mr. Campbell was Lord Provost of the city in 1824-25.

ANECDOTE OF STIRLING OF KEIR.

The ancient family of Stirling of Keir was intimately connected with Glasgow in its later generations. From the middle of last century to the end of the first quarter of the present, different members of that family were extensively engaged in West India commerce as partners in the great house of Stirling & Gordon. The laird of Keir who lived in 1715 was a staunch Jacobite, and was compromised in the rising of that year. When brought to trial it happened that the indictment against him was limited to one point— viz., an appearance at a certain treasonable meeting. His life and fortune depended on this one fact: if he could prove an *alibi* he was safe, but otherwise he was sure to be condemned with little hope of mercy. The principal evidence was that of an old and attached servant, who had attended his master to the treasonable meeting. Keir knew that this man's evidence must be conclusive against him, and he resigned himself to his fate. His surprise, therefore, was great, and only equalled by the disappointment of the Lord Advocate, when the old steward, being put on oath, swore that his master was not at the Jacobite meeting, but that he was at the time at a place so far distant that his presence there was quite impossible on the day set forth in the indictment. This witness, when questioned and cross-questioned, maintained his statement with the most unblushing effrontery, and told his story with such wonderful consistency that nothing more could be said. Keir was acquitted, and instead of being shut up in a condemned cell, was allowed to depart in peace for Perthshire. When he and his faithful servant were fairly on the road, the following dialogue took place :—

Keir.—"Lord preserve us, John! How *could* you tell such an awful lie? You ken very weel that I was at the meeting, and you was riding ahint me."

John.—"Weel do I ken you was at the meeting, and frankly do I confess that I did forswear myself; but then I thought it far safer for me to trust my soul to the mercy of the Almighty than your Honour's life to the mercy o' the Whigs!"

Charles Stirling, the grandson of this old Jacobite laird, was one of the most distinguished and influential merchants in Glasgow during the first quarter of this century.

ANECDOTES OF WILLIAM CAMERON, *alias* "HAWKIE."

Among the odd characters who have in past times haunted and enlivened the streets of Glasgow, few have been so well known or so popular as "Hawkie." He was born of humble parents in the hamlet of Charter's Hall, in the parish of St. Ninians. After leaving school he was apprenticed to the tailoring trade, but was of too restless and roving a disposition to remain at so sedentary an occupation, and made such a wretched attempt at learning his trade, that his employer was only too glad as "Hawkie" himself says in his autobiography, to "run his shears through every stitch o' his indenture," and set him at liberty. After this he was sent to act in the capacity of dominie to some poor children in the outlandish district of Plean Muir Colliery, in the parish of his birth; but soon "the tawse were thrown aside, and the indomitable roving spirit of the unhappy orator threw him loose from every moral or relative restraint. He attached himself to a band of the most dissolute strolling players, and 'starr'd it' through part of the county of Fife. A toy manufacturer was the craft that Cameron next tried, but this was too laborious for him, and he then tried china-mending, and formed a connection with an itinerant cementer of crockery ware—but no cement could bind the unsettled changeling." He now settled down to the calling which he found to be really congenial to him, and which he followed till the end of his chequered life—viz., speech-crying; and "with a boundless range of imagination, a most minute knowledge of persons, places, circumstances, dates, and a most tenacious memory," he soon acquired a popularity amongst the common orders of society, which made his advent to any place he visited to be hailed with delight by old and young.

He wandered nearly over the whole country—notwithstanding that he was a cripple—but he had a great attachment to Glasgow, and there spent the later years of his life, earning a precarious existence by speech-crying; interwoven with original, shrewd and humorous remarks, on the manners and customs of the people who came under his observation. When he became old and frail in health, he was in the habit of betaking himself to the City Poor House during winter, and coming out—with the birds--in spring. His favourite beat in Glasgow was on the south side of Argyle street, and he had always a crowd about him whenever he opened his lips to speak.

On one occasion when he complained of infirmity, he was told by some one in his audience that he looked as well as he had done for years. "Hawkie" replied "Na, na, I'm a gone corbie this winter if I get'na some place to shelter me; I may look about my usual, but I often compare mysel' to the Briggate clock: it keeps a guid weel gilt outside, but the wark is sair gane within—it's chappin after three o'clock in the afternoon when it's only twal' o' the day.

"Hawkie" seems to have been at all times exceedingly fond of our national beverage—whisky, and never made any secret of this predilection. Food and clothing may have been matters of some consideration, but whisky was a *sine qua non.*

"Oich man, Willie," said a Highland benefactress of the street orator, "but it's a perfect vext to see you going about with a coat all broken out at every corner—deed is it. I'm sure there's plenty shentlemans in oor big toun o' Glasgow here, that will got you a gooder coat nor that— waur they couldna gie you, ay, just for a word to them." "Weel, lady," replied Will, "it wouldna be discreet if I didna thank you for the hint; and I think there's scores in Glasgow would gie Hawkie a coat—and they hac done't too—they're no to blame; but a coat that's worth a gill canna be aboon a day on my back, an' I'm no sure if I could succeed in my calling sae weel, in a better coat—it behoves a man aye to be like his profession."

On another occasion, a native of the Sister Isle, observing "Hawkie" draining off a glass of aqua, said to him, "Don't take any more of that vile stuff, Hawkie, it will kill ye man, every glass of it is just another nail to your Norway jacket, and the carpenter will be taken' ye're length very soon, at any rate." "Hech, man, Paddy," retorted "Hawkie," "your coffin would be as thick set wi' thae nails, if ye had the bawbees to pay for them, as the scales on a herrin'. Gae hame wi' you, our hangman can scarcely get time to tak' his denner for you bairns o' the Bog."

"Confound you Eirish," he said on another occasion, "we canna get the use o' oor ain gallows for ye, noo a days."

At the time of the first visit of Her Majesty to Glasgow in 1849, a grand triumphal arch was erected at the south end of the Broomielaw Bridge, in honour of the auspicious event. "Hawkie" asked the bystanders, one day, "Do ye ken the heicht of the arch at the Broomielaw?" No answer being forthcoming, he added, "Weel, if ye dinna ken, I'll tell ye; it's just the heicht of cursed nonsense."

Cameron derived his *sobriquet* of "Hawkie" in the following manner. An impostor, named Ross, was in the habit of gulling the mobs that collected around him on the street by predicting the destruction of the Briggate by a great flood, to which, no doubt, the floods of 1782 would give him the cue; and "Hawkie," not to be outdone, by Ross, and with much greater sagacity, set up a claim for prophetic vision also, and made his seer "Hawkie," a twa year 'l quey frae Aberdour, in the kingdom o' Fife, and sister German to Ross. "It is to be destroyed," said the Aberdour stirk, "by a flood o' whisky, and the wives will be ferrying in washing tubs frae ae door to anither, and mony o' their lives will be lost, that itherwise micht hae been saved, by louting ower their tubs to try the flood whether it was sky blue or the real Ferintosh." "Hawkie" found this prediction so profitable that he continued to cry it very frequently—and so the nickname became stereotyped.

Most of "Hawkie's" jokes were rather of the vulgar order, and showed more of cleverness of repartee than of refinement; but there was sometimes a good deal of shrewd mother wit in his remarks, and occasionally a spice of real truth and homely, telling, worldly wisdom. His speech on *Trial by Jury* is a fair specimen of his better style of address.

"Your jurymen," he says, "at least the maist o' them that I hae seen—and I'm thankfu' I was never before ony —micht hae been born and brocht up in a cabbage bed; ye may see, ony day, as mony sensible looking kail stocks, wi' their curly heads looking ower the creels in the green market—and your special jury are nae better—they only differ in the length o' their shanks. Every man worth twa hunner pounds is fit to sit on a man, and murder, transport him, or put him to gang up a wooden turnpike for a month, and get nae far'er up than twa or three steps; for though he's gaun up a' the time, he gets na oot o' the bit, which maks a perfect fule o' a reasonable creature. It's no the rent o' a house that a man lives in that should qualify him for the jury, for there's mony a twa-legged calf that owns a castle; it's no the number o' his acres, for mony o' your lairds are of as muckle value to the community aneath the earth as aboon 't. They cam' oot o' yird—a' they were worth was yird—they gaed to yird at last, when death had done his darg wi' them. It's no the claith that covers the carcass; the tailor wi' his shears, needle, and goose, can thus qualify for office, for if this be a' that's necessary, a cuddy ass can carry claes; nor is't being able to jabber

Greek and Latin—being brocht up at college; for they come oot wi' heads as naked as a sheep aff the shears. I wad advise a' thae numskulls to be made writers o', if they can sign their ain name; they'll tak' care o' themsells—and there's nae animal, that I ken, grips the grass sae near the grund as a goose. So it's nane o' thae possessions or adornments that, wi' justice and humanity to poor criminals, should ever determine between guilt and innocence; but it's the man that has heart an' head, that kens his ain heart, and what crimes are there, though uncommitted—depend on't it's no his faut that they wer'na—a man wha's tongue keeps within the teeth when he does guid to his neighbour—happin' the naked, an' fillin' the mouth o' the hungry—and instead o' wishing puir wretches on the tread mill, or to let hangie put a runnin' knot roun' their neck, would help to hide the puir wretch if they thocht that he wouldna do't again. Were such like fo'k to be set up as judges o' richt an' wrang, innocence and guilt, in oor kintra, from the Lord Chancellor, wha's head is whiles nae better filled than his seat, to a magistrate o' the Sautmarket—wi' some feasability, it micht be said, that justice and judgment had their place amang us."

Anecdotes of William Dunn.

William Dunn, of Duntocher, was one of our merchant princes who raised himself from extreme poverty in early life to great opulence by industry, sagacity, and parsimony, at least till his fortune was made. In his latter years he kept up a considerable style, and resided in an elegant mansion situated in St. Vincent Place. In this mansion he exercised considerable hospitality, and entertained some of the notable men of his day. On one occasion, it is said, one of the Judges of the Court of Session—Lord Robertson, a noted wag, and a boon companion of Mr. Dunn—officiated as a flunkey, and at another time as a cook, at Mr. Dunn's dinner table; for practical joking of this sort was a common amusement of the last generation. Mr. Dunn was fond of litigation, and, strange to say, his great opponent in the law courts was Lord Blantyre, whose son seems to have inherited the same litigious propensity in a remarkable degree. When Mr.

Dunn was ill and drawing near his latter end, his minister paid him a visit with the view of preparing his mind for that solemn event, for hitherto Mr. Dunn had not been noted for his piety. The minister found Mr. Dunn in great spirits, and he welcomed the minister with the following salutation :—" Come away, sir ; I am glad to see you, for I have at last conquered my greatest enemy." At such a moment the worthy minister could conceive of only one enemy that required to be conquered—viz., the great arch-enemy of mankind ; and after some further conversation with Mr. Dunn, he came away well pleased with his visit. On his way home he met a friend of Mr. Dunn, to whom he communicated the fact of his visit to the dying man, and joyfully informed him of the victory the latter had obtained over his greatest enemy. " His greatest enemy!" ejaculated his friend ; "do you know who his greatest enemy is ? He has conquered Lord Blantyre and the Duntocher Dam." The poor minister was sadly taken down by this intimation, and went on his way moralizing on the perversity of human nature.

It is of Mr. Dunn also that the following story is told, and of the same period—towards the end of his life. The minister of a church in his parish of Old Kilpatrick came to him one day to ask a subscription from him towards the erection of a new church. The sum required was a large one, for Mr. Dunn was wealthy, and it was expected he would be the principal contributor. On hearing the request Mr. Dunn made a wry face, as if it would be greatly against the grain to part with so much money. But a sudden idea struck him. "Do you think," said he to the minister, "that if I were to give you this large sum, it would be placed to my credit in the other world ?" The pawky minister, after a pause, replied, " Well, sir, I could not absolutely say; but I should think the experiment is one well worth the trying."

CHAPTER XIII.

MISCELLANEOUS STORIES AND ANECDOTES.

> " Langsyne ! how doth the word come back
>   With magic meaning to the heart,
> As memory roams the sunny track,
>   From which hope's dreams were loath to part ;
> No joy like by-past joy appears ;
>   For what is gone we fret and pine,
> Were life spun out a thousand years,
>   It could not match langsyne ! "
> —*D. M. Moir.*

ROMANTIC STORY OF GOVERNOR MACRAE.

THE well known statue to King William III at the Cross of Glasgow has stood for about a century and a half, the wonder and pride of all our youthful citizens, the trysting-place of many fond lovers and drouthy cronies; and the memorial of a brave, able, and distinguished prince, who was the instrument of one of the most important and beneficial revolutions that ever befel the British Empire. In all probability that statue will stand there for generations to come. No question of its removal to our storehouse of statuary in George Square can ever be entertained. It is sacred to the spot ; and we might as well abolish the time honoured Cross itself, as remove the figures of " Willie " and his noble steed. Could that silent and impassable warrior describe the strange kaleidoscopic scenes of human life that have passed before his view since he was mounted on his immovable charger, what wonderful, stirring tales could he relate! Before his fixed, stony gaze, how many actors have appeared upon life's chequered stage, and like puppets have played their little parts—some in tragedy, many in comedy, perhaps most in hideous burlesque—and then have passed away out of sight for ever. The grave, solemn procession of the Justiciary Lords, preceded by the town guard of halberdiers, and followed by the douce bailies of the burgh, has marched slowly along from the comfortable hostelrie of the Saracen head in the Gallowgate ; and within the adjoining Town Hall those judges have passed their solemn sentences over innumerable criminals, many of which sentences were carried to a completion on the scaffold, not very far distant; the tobacco lords in their cocked hats, buckled shoon, knee breeches, and cut-away coats with shining brass buttons, have strutted about on the neighbouring plainstanes with all the pomp, display, and arrogance that too frequently accompanies acquired wealth; the dashing mail coach with its team of smoking horses, its red-coated, white-beavered coachman and guard, have galloped past, bearing the news of stirring battles by flood and field; the fair dames of a century ago were borne along in their sedan chairs, or clattered on in their pattens, towards the ball rooms and concert halls, or their evening tea-and-scandal parties; the jovial frequenters of the clubs have reeled home from their orgies in the dread hour of midnight, shouting their bacchanalian songs to the Cross steeple and the unconscious equestrian, or playing their rude practical jokes upon the more simple or more inebriated of their companions. How often, as the Cross bell struck the knell of doom to the departing year, have the voices of thousands of the humbler citizens rung out the old and rung in the new, in boisterous greetings and noisy congratulations; while for ever and unceasing have crowded along, the great seething masses of pedestrians, in their pursuit of business, pleasure, virtue, or vice.

The theme were a strangely suggestive one, but we must pass on and tell the story of the remarkable man by whom this noble statue was bequeathed to the city.

Somewhere about the beginning of last century there resided in a small cottage, not far from the "auld toon" of Ayr, a poor but honest widow named Macrae, more familiarly known by her maiden name of "Bell Gardner." She had two sons, the eldest of whom, "Willie," was a bit of a musician, and when he grew up earned at least a portion of his livelihood by playing at penny weddings and other festive gatherings. He was greatly in demand all over the country side, and was much respected in his humble sphere. His younger brother was of a more restless and roving disposition, and while yet a mere lad disappeared from his native place, and no trace of him could be found. Long years passed away and no tidings of the long lost son ever reached the poor widow Macrae, and she died in the belief that her boy had preceded her to the other world. But about forty years after his disappearance an advertisement appeared in the Ayr papers to the effect that if there were any of the descendants of a widow Macrae who lived near the town of Ayr about a certain specified period, they would hear of something to their advantage by applying to the office of a solicitor in London. This advertisement caught the eye of a lawyer in Ayr, who asked his wife if she remembered of such a person as Widow Macrae who lived in that locality. After some reflection the lawyer's wife said that she did not recollect the widow, but possibly "Willie Macrae, the fiddler," might be some relation. The fiddler accordingly was sent for, and some inquiry was made as to his antecedents. He said that his mother had been a widow, and had at one time lived in the locality referred to, and he also stated that he had had a brother who had disappeared unaccountably about forty years before. This information the lawyer duly communicated to the address in London, and a reply came back inviting the fiddler and his two little daughters to come up to the great city. On arrival there the trio were taken to a splendid west end mansion house, and were there shown into the presence of a distinguished looking personage, and who was no less than Governor-General Macrae, of the Presidency of Madras. After some conversation had taken place between the grandee and the poor Ayrshire fiddler, it turned out that the former was no other than the long lost son of Widow Macrae, and the fiddler's own brother. This was an astounding revelation to the bewildered Willie, for it would appear he had entertained very little expectation of anything coming out of the advertisement and of the visit to London. But the Governor-General was delighted to meet with his brother and his two little nieces. He loaded them with presents, and ere he returned to India he made ample provision for the maintenance and education of the girls, and ordered that they should be brought up in a manner becoming his high rank. He was a bachelor and enormously rich, and he avowed his intention of leaving all his fortune to the daughters of his brother. Among his other benefactions Governor Macrae presented to the city of Glasgow the noble equestrian statue of William III, which, as we have said, forms so prominent and highly prized a monument in our principal thoroughfare. We are not sure what were the motives which animated the mind of the Governor in paying this compliment to our city; but doubtless he would, in his capacity as ruler over the large province of Madras, have had much correspondence with Glasgow merchants and their emissaries, and observed their extensive business relationships with India.

The governor having settled affairs in this satisfactory manner sailed for India and resumed the duties of his high office, while his two nieces were sent to a boarding school and were educated in all the branches and accomplishments necessary to fit them for occupying a position in refined and polite society. Some ten or twelve years elapsed when news arrived of the death of their distinguished uncle and, true to his promise, he had left the bulk of his immense fortune to the two daughters of his brother William. By this time they had grown up to be elegant and accomplished young ladies, had taken their place amongst the gentry of their native county, and were everywhere admired and esteemed for their amiable conduct and good manners. About this time the young Earl of Glencairn found his estates considerably embarrassed and burdened with debt, and in his trouble he had recourse to the advice of the same lawyer, who had been the means of introducing Willie Macrae and his daughters to their wealthy relative. After long deliberation this legal gentleman informed Lord Glencairn that there was only one way that he could see, by which the reduced fortunes of the nobleman could be retrieved, but he thought it would be thoroughly effective. Glencairn eagerly enquired what that way might be. "Marry a rich heiress, my Lord," replied the shrewd lawyer. "Aye," said the Earl, "but where will I find such an one?" "I can introduce you to one," said the lawyer, "who is at present resident in this county." "And, pray, who may the lady be?" queried the Earl. The lawyer replied, "Miss Macrae, niece of the late Governor-General of Madras, and an elegant woman."

The Earl was quite taken up with this flattering description, more especially as the wily lawyer had in the first instance omitted all reference to the poor widow and the fiddler. An introduction was brought about; the Earl was charmed with the appearance and bearing of the elder of the sisters, and in due time Lizzie Macrae, the daughter of Willie Macrae, the fiddler, and the school-fellow of the father of Charles Tennant, the founder of St. Rollox Chemical Works, was transformed into the Countess of Glencairn; and in course of time became the mother of James, Earl of Glencairn, the benefactor and friend of Robert Burns, who mourned the loss of his patron in that beautiful and pathetic lament with which we are all so familiar, ending with the couplet—

"But I'll remember thee, Glencairn,
And a' that thou hast done for me!"

Jenny Geddes Outdone in Glasgow.

It may not be generally known by our readers, that the spirit of the famous "Jenny Geddes" who flung her stool at the Dean of Edinburgh while he was attempting to introduce the Liturgy into the worship of the church in Saint Giles' Cathedral, also animated the "guidwives" of Glasgow, and took even a more violent and demonstrative form, than that of the East Country heroine.

In 1637, a Mr. William Annan preached a sermon before the Synod at Glasgow, in defence of the Liturgy. Baillie gives the following account of the result:—"Of his sermon among us in the Synod, not a word; but in the town among the women, a great din. To-morrow, Mr. John Lindsay, at the Bishop's command, preached. He is the new moderator of Lanerk. At the ingoing of the pulpit, it is said, that some of the women in his ear assured him, that if he should touch the service-book in his sermon, he should be rent out of the pulpit. He took the advice, and let that matter alone. At the outgoing of the church, about thirty or forty of our honestest women, in one voice before the Bishops and Magistrates, fell a railing, cursing, scolding with clamours on Mr. William Annan. Some two of the meanest were taken to the Tolbooth. All the day over, up and down the streets where he went, he got threats of sundry in words and looks; but after supper, while needlessly he will go to visit the Bishop, who had taken his leave with him, he is no sooner on the street at nine o'clock, in a dark night with three or four ministers with him, but some hundreds of enraged women of all qualities, are about him, *with neaves, staves, and peats*, but no stones. They beat him sore; his cloak, ruff, and hat, were rent; however, upon his cries, and candles set out from many windows, he escaped all bloody wounds; yet he was in great danger even of killing. This tumult was so great, that it was not thought meet to search for either the plotters or actors of it, for numbers of the best quality would have been found guilty. To-morrow poor Mr. William was conveyed with the bailies and sundry ministers to his horse; for many women were waiting to affront him more. Always at his on-leaping his horse unhappily fell above him in a very foul mire, in presence of all the company, of which accident was more speech than of any other."

ANOTHER SHAWFIELD RIOT.

The famous Shawfield Mansion in Glasgow, as is well known to all readers of the history of our good city, stood on the north side of the Trongate, next to what was then termed the West Port, at the head of the present Stockwell, or rather at the foot of Glassford Street. This house was for many years in the possession of the Campbell family, who became also proprietors of the Islands of Islay and Jura. A goodly portion of the price paid for these Islands had been received by Mr. Daniel Campbell, M.P., from Government, as compensation for the partial destruction of the Shawfield mansion by a Glasgow mob in 1725, in consequence of Mr. Campbell having made himself obnoxious to the citizens by voting for the Extension of the Malt Tax to Scotland. This affair is commonly known as "The Shawfield Riots." But the "Shawfield Riot," the story of which we are about to relate, though not so serious or historical as the other, was, nevertheless, of rather an interesting character, and gives a somewhat racy illustration of the manners of our go-a-head gentry of former days.

One of the descendants of the Campbell who had his mansion ransacked in 1725, was a Colonel John Campbell, a remarkably good looking person, upwards of six feet high, and possessing a fine figure, with the commanding military carriage of a soldier. In 1796 he married the celebrated Lady Charlotte Campbell, daughter of John, Duke of Argyll, and uterine sister of Douglas, Duke of Hamilton. At the time of his marriage, this John Campbell was only a Captain in the army, but was well known in London, in the circle of its bucks, by the name of "Handsome Jack of the Guards." Her ladyship at this time was about 21 years of age, in the full bloom of youth and beauty, and replete with life and sprightliness. She was said to possess the handsomest limbs of any lady at Court, and she was not sparing of exhibiting them, both there and elsewhere, to the greatest advantage. It was reported that Queen Charlotte desired one of her ladies-in-waiting to tell Lady Charlotte Campbell to take a tuck out of her petticoat the next time she appeared at Court.

"Senex," in his gossipy and interesting volume of "Loose Memoranda," tells us that one day he was passing the foot of Candleriggs when his attention was arrested by seeing crowds of people surrounding two ladies and a young gentleman who were walking eastwards towards the Cross along the Trongate. Like others, he ran forward to see what was going on, and then he beheld Lady Charlotte, dressed in the height of the then Parisian fashion, with petticoats almost as short as a Highlandman's philabeg, which dress exhibited the pretty little ankle and the beautiful contour of the calf to admiration. In an instant the word passed from mouth to mouth of the crowd, "It's Lady Charlotte Campbell! it's Lady Charlotte Campbell!" And then might have been seen a scampering of all classes from the four streets of the Trongate, King Street, Candleriggs, and Gallowgate, to get a sight of this celebrated beauty. The crowd now became so dense that her ladyship and party could no longer proceed along the Trongate, every one of the mob eagerly pressing upon them to have a sight of Lady Charlotte, who then became greatly alarmed lest she should be attacked by the mob. The party having in vain attempted to proceed, at last, in a state of great alarm, rushed into a shop nearly opposite the Tron Church, and begged the shopman instantly to shut his door till the mob dispersed, which he not only did, but also put up the shutters of his shop window. The mob, however, so far from dispersing, became greater and greater, for the word had passed on all sides that Lady Charlotte Campbell, dressed nearly half naked, had taken refuge in the shop; and so every one waited to get a peep at the half naked beauty on her exit from the shop. The shopman now became alarmed for the safety of his goods as well as for the safety of his guests, and therefore jumping out by the window of his back shop, he ran at full speed to the guardhouse (then situated in the Candleriggs opposite Campbell & Co.'s warehouse) and procured the attendance of a sergeant and a party of soldiers, who took their station at the shop door, which was still kept closely shut. In the meantime, Lady Charlotte, being at her wits' end how she was to escape the attack of the rabble, resolved to follow the example of the shopman, and accordingly jumped out of the back window, which brought her into a throughgoing close leading into the Candleriggs, and, without the crowd having observed her, she entered an adjoining house, where, upon explaining her situation, a carriage was sent for, which safely conveyed her ladyship to the Black Bull Inn. This Black Bull Inn occupied a site near to that of the former Shawfield Mansion. As soon as the shopman had seen Lady Charlotte fairly out of danger, he communicated the fact to the military who were guarding the shop door, and then under the protection of the soldiers, he threw open his door to allow the remaining lady and young gentleman to pass on their way. The crowd were sadly disappointed at seeing only the lady and young gentleman coming forth, as the lady was dressed in ordinary garb, and not at all remarkable. The mob, however, to their credit, behaved to them with great politeness, for the instant they made their appearance the crowd voluntarily separated, and left a clear lane upon the pavement to allow them to pass westwards without molestation, the mob neither hooting, hissing, nor behaving in any respect rudely towards them. "Senex" adds, " The times are now sadly changed, 'Handsome Jack of the Guards' has been gathered to his fathers ; and Lady Charlotte no longer bears the ancient name of Campbell. The beautiful and fascinating belle, whose name resounded throughout every corner of our island in her early days, is now the old, faded, and decrepit Lady Bury, bending under the load of fourscore years, and nearly forgotten by the world; while the princely estates of Islay and Woodhall have passed away to creditors. 'Vanity of vanities, saith the preacher, all is vanity!'"

A Deputation to London in the Olden Time.

In the present democratic days a good deal of grumbling takes place among the ratepayers in our good city at the cost of municipal deputations to London in the Parliamentary Session time, and we dare say there is more of that sort of expenditure sometimes than there is any need for. But it would appear that in the middle of last century a deputation to the great metropolis was a much more formidable and costly affair than it is at present. Here are some interesting details regarding one of those ancient deputations:—

During the Jacobite Rebellion of 1745, as is well known to readers of Glasgow history, Prince Charles Stuart paid a visit to Glasgow, which was anything but a welcome event to our Radical citizens. During his stay the Prince occupied the famous Shawfield mansion, at the corner of Trongate and Glassford Street. Here he held a kind of royal court, and endeavoured in various princely ways to ingratiate himself and his cause in the eyes of the inhabitants, but with very little success. Partly incensed at their indifference, and partly to equip his somewhat ragged soldiery, he imposed a very heavy levy upon the citizens of Glasgow. It is said that the demand made for broadcloth, tartan, linen, bonnets, and shoes amounted to nearly £10,000, besides which the rebels got a sum of money. At that time the entire revenue of Glasgow was only £3,000, and its expenditure was £3,081. It may well be considered, therefore, that this levy upon the citizens by Prince Charlie would be felt as a severe burden. But it was not till about three years after that—viz., in the end of 1748—that a representation was made to the Government for an indemnity for the loss that had been sustained. It was on this mission that Provost Cochrane and Bailie Murdoch were sent on the deputation referred to; and from the Council Records we are presented with the details of their expenditure. The minute is dated 28th January, 1769:—

"The which day Andrew Cochrane, Provost, and George Murdoch, late Bailie, gave in an account of their charge and expenses in relation to their late journey to and from London about the town's affairs, which is as follows:—

"To a chaise and maker's servant, £28, 2s. 6d. To John

Stewart, the servant, at several times on the road, £6, 7s. 2d. To ditto at London, to account, £5, 8s. To the servant, to carry him with two horses, £1, 10s. To charges at Whitburn and four days at Edinburgh, £8, 10s. To charges on road to London, 11 days, £28, 10s. To lodging at London, and house account for coals, candle, tea, sugar, breakfasts, &c., £61, 15s. 9d. To William Alloe, the servant, for wages, boarding, and incidentals at London, and for turnpikes and expenses on road down, £17, 13s. 3d. To shaving and dressing, £2, 7s. To Mr. Burden, for liqueurs to quarters, £4, 12s. To chaise mending, 10s. To post-hire from London to Edinburgh, £21. To hostlers, riders, horses, &c., £2, 2s. To charges on road from London, £5, 12s. 6d. To charges at Edinburgh and Whitburn, £2, 13s. 6d. To charges from Edinburgh home and the driver, £2. To extraordinary entertainments in London, £30. To writing copies petition and memorial, &c., £7, 11s. To expenses and incidentals, ordinary and extraordinary, at London—viz., By Andrew Cochrane, £125, 12s. By George Murdoch, £105, 4s. 0½d. To a writing master to come down (no doubt to improve the character of the city penmanship), £5, 5s. To charge of advertisements, 6s.—extending the said sums to £472, 11s. 8½d. sterling."

Perhaps the most interesting item in the foregoing account is the odd halfpenny charged in Bailie Murdoch's incidental account. It shows the worthy bailie to have been an extraordinarily conscientious man, determined not to charge the city a farthing more than he had actually expended. But some cynical people in these modern cheese-paring days may think that this odd halfpenny was intended to blind the eyes of the citizens to a multitude of peccadilloes committed by the douce bailie in the gay metropolis. It is satisfactory to learn, however, that this deputation was successful in its mission, and obtained from the Government no less than ten thousand pounds indemnity for the loss sustained by the city.

It may be interesting to our readers to learn that the forces of Prince Charles, on entering Glasgow, did not exceed 3,600 foot and 500 horse. To conceal their weakness, the prince caused his men, after passing from the Trongate into the gate of Mr. Glassford's house, to return to Queen Street and Ingram Street, to the front, and again march in as if they were fresh troops—a trick which reminds us very vividly of the similar one played by the enterprising firm of "Robert M'Nair, Jean Holmes & Co.," in the matter of the oranges. Verily human nature is very much alike, whether found in princes or in general grocers!

Gib, who acted as steward to the Prince's household, mentions that his master dressed more elegantly when in Glasgow than he did "in any other place whatsoever." This compliment to the ladies does not appear to have softened their political prejudices, or gained a smile from any fair lips, but those of his favourite and admired Clementina Walkinshaw, third daughter of John Walkinshaw of Barrowfield. Her beauty attracted the Prince, as his good looks, princely state, or interesting misfortunes attracted her; and she, at a later date, lived with him, sometimes in Switzerland and sometimes in Flanders, as his mistress, and bare him a daughter, who was legitimatized in 1787, and created Duchess of Albany.

Two Remarkable Coalpit Adventures.

It may appear rather curious to any of our readers who may reside in, or be acquainted with, the now populous squares, crescents, terraces, and splendid streets of that portion of Glasgow situated in the district of Woodside, at the north-west end of the city, to be told that not more than a hundred years ago, that district was the resort of the school boys of that period, in their more daring adventures after birds' nests, nut gathering, and other similar pursuits. There were few habitations near, and in former times there had been coalpit workings, and these pits had been only partially filled up. On Wednesday, the 13th of September, 1769, a strange thing happened to a gentleman residing in Glasgow named Lieutenant George Spearing. On that day, this person wandered into the little wood at North Woodside in the course of a walk, and while there he amused himself by plucking hazel nuts from the bushes in the wood. He had not been more than a quarter of an hour engaged in this pastime, when he fell into one of the partially filled coalpits to which we have referred. He fell to the bottom, a depth of about 17 yards, and for a short time he was rendered insensible through the violence of his fall. When he recovered his senses, he looked his watch, and found it was ten minutes past four in the afternoon, and thinking that as the wood was small, he would soon be discovered, he did not put himself greatly about. But hour after hour passed, and no one apppeared, while his cries for help were totally unheeded. He began to regard the situation in a more serious light. Night was approaching, and to add to his discomfort, the rain began to fall in perfect torrents, and now it was highly improbable that anyone would come near his place of confinement that night. He, however, was not greatly alarmed, and endeavoured to compose himself to sleep, with but indifferent success. The long, dark night passed away, and he was cheered by the approach of daylight, and by the cheerful song of a robin which sat on a spray overhead. About a hundred yards from the pithead there was a flour mill, and Mr. Spearing could hear the voices of the miller's family, the cackling of the fowls, and the tramping of horses on the road between the mill and the pit. But no one appeared to hear the loud cries of the imprisoned lieutenant. Hour after hour passed away. He grew faint with cold, thirst, and anxiety, but, strange to say, he felt none of the pangs of hunger. At the bottom of the pit large numbers of frogs, toads, snails, and slugs abounded, and frequently crawled over his person, to his infinite disgust. But amidst all this discomfort and suspense Mr. Spearing, who afterwards wrote out a lengthy account of his experiences, retained his self-possession, and never allowed hope to desert him. But all that day passed over, night again drew on, and still no human help came. Friday, the 15th, passed over slowly and drearily, and still no relief, the rain still falling heavily, and everything miserable and disheartening, but the sweet song of the red-breast, which, like an angel of hope, came every day to cheer him in his pitiable condition. On Saturday, the 16th, there fell but little rain, and he had the satisfaction of hearing the voices of some boys in the wood. He shouted to them with all his might, but they either did not hear him, or else they were possessed with an idle story of a wild man living in the wood, for the voices ceased, and no one drew near. On Sabbath, the 17th, he spent his 41st birthday in this miserable confinement, and no doubt his thoughts on that anniversary would be very bitter, but this day too passed away, and the next, and still no relief appeared. On Tuesday, the 19th, Mr. Spearman, who appears to have preserved his serenity of mind in an extraordinary degree, amused himself by "combing his wig on his knee, humming a tune, and thinking of Archer in the 'Beux Stratagem.'" At length, on Wednesday, the 20th September, the seventh of his confinement, his attention was aroused by a confused sound of human voices, which seemed to be approaching; immediately he called out, and most agreeably surprised some of his friends who had come out in search of him. They told him afterwards that they had not the most distant hope of finding him alive, but they were anxious to discover his body, that they might give it decent burial. As soon as they heard his voice, they all ran towards the pit, and he heard a well known voice exclaim, "Good God, he is still living!" Another of them, in surprise and joy, called out in true Irish fashion, "Are you really alive?"

After some difficulty Mr. Spearman was drawn up from the pit, and was carried to the house of the miller close by, where restoratives were applied and he was put to a comfortable bed. But his limbs were so benumbed with the cold and exposure, and want of circulation, that it was impossible for him to stand or walk. Medical aid was called in, but it would appear that the doctors bungled his case, and instead of getting better he grew worse. He lay in the miller's house for six weeks, and then, strange as it may now appear, the roads got so bad that the doctors could not come out from the city to visit him; and so he was brought home to his lodgings in a Sedan chair. But here the process of bungling and blundering went on, and at last on the 2nd May, 1770, he had to get his leg amputated below the knee, and after that he slowly recovered. The closing words of his narrative are interesting and pleasing. "Six weeks after the amputation I went out in a Sedan chair for the benefit of the air, being exactly nine months from the day I fell into the pit. Soon after I took lodgings in the country, where getting plenty of warm new milk, my appetite and strength increased daily, and to this day I bless God I do enjoy perfect health, and I have since been the happy father of *nine* children."

The other accident strangely enough happened in the

very same pit into which Lieutenant Spearman had been imprisoned, and the accident occurred to an honest washerwoman named Janet (surname not recorded), in the month of September or October, 1773. Janet had been in the city delivering some clothing which she had been washing and bleaching in the open field, and was returning to her home having been rewarded in addition to her wages, with a dram, a farl of oatcake, and a whang of cheese. Passing through the wood, she had strayed from the path to gather a few brambles, when unfortunately she fell into the aforesaid pit. This was on a Saturday evening, and poor Janet remained a prisoner in the pit till the following Tuesday. She suffered a good deal from her fall, her fright, and from her exposure. But the farl of cake and bit of cheese which she carried, stood her in good stead in allaying the pangs of hunger. On Sunday she heard the distant church-going bells of the city, and these, in her present circumstances, awakened within her thoughts of a more serious and solemn nature than she had ever been accustomed to. On Tuesday following, however, she was discovered and raised out of her perilous position by a working man, who had happened to pass that way and heard the cries of the distressed damsel. She was not much the worse of the strange accident which had befallen her, and it is related that she rewarded her deliverer by conferring upon him her hand and heart in marriage. But alas! for the "romance of real life" in this case, he turned out to be a drunken worthless fellow, who plagued her life and lived in idleness, upon the hard-earned fruits of her industry at the wash tub and bleaching green.

THE WAIL OF THE OLD CANAL.

(The Glasgow, Paisley, and Ardrossan Canal was commenced in 1807, and was finished as far as Johnstone in 1811, when the work of formation was stopped for want of funds. In the Session of Parliament for 1881, the proprietors, Glasgow and South-Western Railway Co., obtained powers to fill up the waterway of the canal and construct a railway upon it. The following lines were written just before these operations began.)

Last night in dreamy, careless mood, I wandered forth alone,
To muse by verdant field and wood, and breathe the pure ozone
That floated in the ambient air, far from the city's haze ;
While o'er my spirit, visions fair came back from other days.

I thought upon the ancient times, when Glasgow's sainted sire
First heard the soft melodious chimes fall from his chapel spire ;
By Molindinar's classic stream, sweet murmuring through the dell,
Their blended voices well might seem a tale of peace to tell.

"By preaching of the sacred Word, let Glasgow Flourish, sure,"
Was the refrain St. Mungo heard from chimes and streamlet pure ;
Then straightway on the city's scroll the mystic words he wrote,
And said, "While future ages roll, be this your guiding note."

Long dwelt the city, clear, serene, beneath its Bishop's sway,
Nor smoke, nor sewage marred the scene, or shamed the orb of day.
No din of foundry, car, or train, made hideous the night,
Nor piercing whistle racked the brain of weary labouring wight.

But ages passed, and other men appeared upon the stage :
A sordid, worldly race, and then, what changes did engage
Their scheming minds ! the peaceful town a Babel scene became,
The very heavens with angry frown seemed charged with smoke and flame.

The clank of hammer, roar of steam, resounded through the vale,
While rushing engines' fiendish scream made ev'n the rocks to quail ;
And still the town encroaching spread o'er Nature's fair domain,
Gaunt chimneys grew for fertile mead, and streets instead of grain.

Till now, alas ! for weary miles nought meets the troubled gaze
But brick and stone in shapeless piles, and smoke and dust and blaze ;
While from the city's ancient scroll the sacred motto's torn,
"Let Glasgow Flourish" is still the *rolé*—the Gospel is out-worn.

Thus musing, dreaming, on I strayed, and watch'd night's shadows fall,
Till the pale moonbeams rose and play'd upon an old canal,
That darkly lay beside the road my wayward steps had press'd,
And wearied with my anxious load, I sate me down to rest.

Upon the bank I watched the light fall on the dusky wave,
When lo ! a spectre rose to sight, like ghost from watery grave ;
It beckoned, and in eerie tones bade me to list its wail,
And then with heavy sighs and groans, unfolded this sad tale :—

"I am the ghost of this canal," the dusky spectre said ;
"Long seventy years, full numbered all, have passed since it was made,
Ah me ! what changes I have seen, since that eventful day,
To tell the half of them, I ween, would take till morning grey.

THE WAIL OF THE OLD CANAL.

" What stately barges o'er me sped, when first my waters sweet,
Were poured into their clayey bed—they were a goodly fleet;
With gaudy pennons streaming proud through the fresh morning air,
While decks and cabins bore a crowd of manly forms and fair.

" What merry bands of children dear, all dress'd in bright array,
Have passed along with many a cheer, bent on high holiday—
Perchance by Cruickston's ruins old, to sport themselves the while,
And with pranks, games, and stories told, the witching hours beguile.

" How cheerily they romped and laughed with heedless careless joy :
The pleasures that their sweet lips quaffed were pure without alloy ;
And when at evening's peaceful close, they rested on my braes,
Their simple hymn to Heaven arose, a song of grateful praise !

" And in the long bright summer days I've watched the sturdy boys
Who came to me in quick relays, with boisterous mirth and noise,
To plunge them headlong from the bank, with hearts devoid of fear,
I trembled often as they sank, lest death should meet them here.

" And when, alas ! some noble lad would sink, to rise no more,
My poor old heart, erewhile so glad, with grief grew vexed and sore ;
And I have heard the bitter cry, wrung from a mother's woe,
As to her heart she clasped her boy, and would not let him go.

" And I've beheld with wond'ring look the patient fisher stand
Long weary hours with baited hook, yet ne'er bring fish to land ;
It seems that once in long past years, one caught a poor lorn braise,
And ev'ry spring its ghost appears, the angler's hopes to raise.

" But to my eyes the sight most fair was when on summer eve
Fond lovers walk'd in mystic pair, their hopes and dreams to weave ;
Ah, me ! what vows, what melting sighs my greedy ears oft drank,
It seemed as if fair paradise dwelt by canal's plain bank.

" Oh, happy hours of love and youth, how radiant are ye !
How full seems earth of hope and ruth, the air with melody !
Alas ! that darker days must come to all those happy bands !
For some shall die of grief, and some by their own sinful hands.

" And I could tell full many a tale of horror, dark and drear,
Of grim despair I've heard the wail, and seen foul murder here ;
O, many a sweet babe newly born I've clasp'd to my cold breast,
And many a soul with anguish torn have 'neath my wave sought rest :—

" Aye, sought it, but hath found it not, for in the midnight lone
What shrieks ascend from each dark spot wherein foul deed was done.
For in that sleep of awful death, what dreams do nightly come
To those who die from want of faith in God's Truth, Love, and Home !

" And other sad sights I have seen increasing year by year,
Oh, that my voice had warning been to stop the wild career
Of those who, mad with demon drink, and brain aglow with fire,
Have staggered, cursing o'er my brink, and perished in foul mire.

" Thus, I, the humble dusky wraith of this despised canal,
Have gazed on scenes of life and death that might the hearts appal
Of men who by false science led, and of their scheming vain,
Have plotted to ride o'er my head with thundering railway train.

"Yes, I have heard the knell of doom pronounced o'er my poor wave—
'To progress thou must now make room, and hie thee to thy grave!'
Ah, woe the day! when heart of man with pride is lifted high,
And dares to fight 'gainst Nature's plan, the good old pathways fly.

"What progress to the human race can mortals ever see
In hurling men at headlong pace into Eternity?
For did mine old eyes not behold such scenes but yesterday
As made the city's heart grow cold with horror and dismay?

"By Pennilee's ill-fated box * what dreadful woes befel,
When train met train with frightful shocks, 'midst dying groan and yell,
Nor this alone; o'er all the land, the same wild cries ascend,
From River Tay's romantic strand to far off lone Land's End.

"But courteous stranger! who hast heard, so patiently my tale,
Let me bequeath one parting word, ere yet mine accents fail:
Beware this bastard ill-starred line, mark well the words I say,
This miry track shall still be mine, I'll haunt it night and day."

. . . .

I heard no more, for while he spake there came a rushing noise
A mighty wind the trees to shake, that drowned his feeble voice;
While o'er the moon-beams' radiant smile, that sweetly on me shone.
Dark gloomy clouds arose the while, and I was left alone.

* A serious collision took place shortly before this period at Pennilee Signal Box near the Arkleston Tunnel whereby several persons were killed and a large number injured.

GLASGOW: PRINTED BY ALEX. MACDOUGALL.

New Books and New Editions.

ANGLING REMINISCENCES OF THE RIVERS AND LOCHS OF SCOTLAND. By Thomas Tod Stoddart. Post 8vo. Price 3s. 6d.

If not the most useful, this is at least the most interesting of all Stoddart's angling works, of which there are three in number. The above is not to be confounded with "The Scottish Angler" on the one hand, or "The Angler's Companion" on the other, though from the same pen. The present work is colloquial throughout, and teeming with the richest humour from beginning to end.

THE WHOLE FAMILIAR COLLOQUIES OF ERASMUS. Translated by Nathan Bailey. Demy 8vo. Price 4s. 6d.

A complete and inexpensive edition of the great book of amusement of the sixteenth century. Probably no other work so truly and intensely depicts the life and notions of our forefathers 350 years ago, as does this inimical production of the great Erasmus.

There are 62 dialogues in all, and an immense variety of subjects are dealt with, such as "Benefice-Hunting," "The Soldier and the Carthusian," "The Franciscans," "The Apparition," "The Beggar's Dialogue," "The Religious Pilgrimage," "The Sermon," "The Parliament of Women," etc., etc. The whole work is richly characteristic, and is full of the richest humour and satire.

THE COURT OF SESSION GARLAND. Edited by James Maidment, Advocate. New edition, including all the Supplements. Demy 8vo. Price 7s. 6d.

A collection of most interesting anecdotes and facetiae connected with the Court of Session. Even to those not initiated in the mysteries of legal procedure, much of the volume will be found highly attractive, for no genuine votary of Momus can be insensible to the fun of the Justiciary Opera, as illustrated by the drollery of the "Diamond Beetle Case," and many others of an amusing nature, such as "The Poor Client's Complaint," "The Parody on Hellvellyn," "The King's Speech," "Lord Bannatyne's Lion," "The Beauties of Overgroggy," etc., etc.

ST. KILDA AND THE ST. KILDIANS. By Robert Connell. Crown 8vo. Price 2s. 6d.

"*A capital book. It contains everything worth knowing about the famous islet and its people.*"—The Bailie.

"*Interesting and amusing. It includes a lively description of the daily life of the inhabitants, the native industries of fishing, bird catching, and the rearing of sickly sheep and cattle, and gives a vivid picture of the Sabbatarian despotism of the Free Church minister who rules the small population.*"—Saturday Review.

THE PRAISE OF FOLLY. By Erasmus. With Numerous Illustrations by Holbein. Post 8vo. Price 4s. 6d.

An English translation of the "*Encomium Moriae*" which has always held a foremost place among the more popular of the writings of the great scholar. This work is probably the most satirical production of any age. It is intensely humorous throughout, and is entirely unique in character. This edition also contains Holbein's illustrations, attaching to which there is very considerable interest.

HUMOROUS AND AMUSING SCOTCH READINGS. For the Platform, the Social Circle, and the Fireside. By Alexander G. Murdoch. Second Edition. Post 8vo. Price 1s. Paper Covers.

Humorous and amusing Scotch readings, fifteen in number, and illustrative of the social life and character of the Scottish people, than which the author believes no more interesting subject can be found. Among other readings may be mentioned, "Mrs. Macfarlane's Rabbit Dinner," "The Washin'-House Key," "Jock Broon's Patent Umbrella," "Willie Weedrap's Domestic Astronomy," etc., etc.

ANECDOTES OF FISH AND FISHING. By Thomas Boosey. Post 8vo. Price 3s. 6d.

An interesting collection of anecdotes and incidents connected with fish and fishing, arranged and classified into sections. It deals with all varieties of British fish, their habits, different modes of catching them, interesting incidents in connection with their capture, and an infinite amount of angling gossip relating to each. Considerable space is also devoted to the subject of fishing as practised in different parts of the world.

THE DANCE OF DEATH: Illustrated in Forty-Eight Plates. By JOHN HOLBEIN. Demy 8vo. Price 5s.

A handsome and inexpensive edition of the great Holbein's most popular production. It contains the whole forty-eight plates, with letterpress description of each plate, the plate and the description in each case being on separate pages, facing each other. The first edition was issued in 1530, and since then innumerable impressions have been issued, but mostly in an expensive form, and unattainable by the general public.

THE LITERARY HISTORY OF GLASGOW. By W. J. DUNCAN. Quarto. Price 12s. 6d. net. *Printed for Subscribers and Private Circulation.*

This volume forms one of the volumes issued by the Maitland Club, and was originally published in 1831. This edition is a verbatim et literatim reprint, and is limited to 350 copies, with an appendix additional containing extra matter of considerable importance, not in the original work.

The book is chiefly devoted to giving an account of the greatest of Scottish printers, namely, the Foulises, and furnishes a list of the books they printed, as likewise of the sculptures and paintings which they so largely produced.

GOLFIANA MISCELLANEA. Being a Collection of Interesting Monographs on the Royal and Ancient Game of Golf. Edited by JAMES LINDSAY STEWART. Post 8vo. Price 4s. 6d.

A collection of interesting productions, prose and verse, on or relating to, the game of golf, by various authors both old and recent. Nothing has been allowed into the collection except works of merit and real interest. Many of the works are now extremely scarce and, in a separate form, command very high prices. It contains twenty-three separate productions of a great variety of character—historical, descriptive, practical, poetical, humorous, biographical, etc.

THE BARDS OF THE BIBLE. By GEORGE GILFILLAN. Seventh Edition. Post 8vo. Price 5s.

The most popular of the writings of the late Rev. Dr. Gilfillan. The author, in his preface, states that the object of the book was chiefly a prose poem or hymn in honour of the poetry and the poets of the Bible. It deals with the poetical side of the inspired word, and takes up the separate portions in chronological order.

ONE HUNDRED ROMANCES OF REAL LIFE. By Leigh Hunt. Post 8vo. Price 3s. 6d.

A handsome edition of Leigh Hunt's famous collection of romances of real life, now scarce in a complete form. The present issue is complete, containing as it does the entire hundred as issued by the author. All being incidents from real life, the interest attaching to the volume is not of an ordinary character. The romances relate to all grades of society, and are entirely various in circumstance, each one being separate and distinct in itself.

UNIQUE TRADITIONS CHIEFLY OF THE WEST AND SOUTH OF SCOTLAND. By John Gordon Barbour. Post 8vo. Price 4s. 6d.

A collection of interesting local and popular traditions gathered orally by the author in his wanderings over the West and South of Scotland. The author narrates in this volume, thirty-five separate incidental traditions in narrative form, connected with places or individuals, all of a nature to interest the general Scottish reader, such as "The Red Comyn's Castle," "The Coves of Barholm," "The Rafters of Kirk Alloway," "Cumstone Castle," "The Origin of Loch Catrine," etc., etc.

MODERN ANECDOTES: A Treasury of Wise and Witty Sayings of the last Hundred Years. Edited, with Notes, by W. Davenport Adams. Crown 8vo. Price 3s. 6d.

The Anecdotes are all authenticated and are classed into Sections—I. *Men of Society.* II. *Lawyers and the Law.* III. *Men of Letters.* IV. *Plays and Players.* V. *Statesmen and Politicians.* VI. *The Church and Clergy.* VII. *People in General.*

In compiling a work like this, Mr. Adams has steadily kept in view the necessity of ministering to the requirements of those who will not read anecdotes unless they have reason to know that they are really good. On this principle the entire editorial work has been executed. The book is also a particularly handsome one as regards printing, paper, and binding.

THE LITURGY OF JOHN KNOX: As received by the Church of Scotland in 1564. Crown 8vo. Price 5s.

A beautifully printed edition of the Book of Common Order, more popularly known as the Liturgy of John Knox. This is the only modern edition in which the original quaint spelling is retained. In this and other respects the old style is strictly reproduced, so that the work remains exactly as used by our forefathers three hundred years ago.

THE GABERLUNZIE'S WALLET. By JAMES BALLANTINE. Third edition. Cr. 8vo. Price 2s. 6d.

A most interesting historical tale of the period of the Pretenders, and containing a very large number of favourite songs and ballads, illustrative of the tastes and life of the people at that time. Also containing numerous facetious illustrations by Alexander A. Ritchie.

THE WOLFE OF BADENOCH. A Historical Romance of the Fourteenth Century. By SIR THOMAS DICK LAUDER. Complete unabridged edition. Thick Crown 8vo. Price 6s.

This most interesting romance has been frequently described as equal in interest to any of Sir Walter Scott's historical tales. This is a complete unabridged edition, and is uniform with "Highland Legends" and "Tales of the Highlands," by the same author. As several abridged editions of the work have been published, especial attention is drawn to the fact that the above edition is complete.

THE LIVES OF THE PLAYERS. By JOHN GALT, Esq. Post 8vo. Price 5s.

Interesting accounts of the lives of distinguished actors, such as Betterton, Cibber, Farquhar, Garrick, Foote, Macklin, Murphy, Kemble, Siddons, &c., &c. After the style of Johnson's "Lives of the Poets."

KAY'S EDINBURGH PORTRAITS. A Series of Anecdotal Biographies, chiefly of Scotchmen. Mostly written by JAMES PATERSON. And edited by JAMES MAIDMENT, Esq. Popular Edition. 2 Vols., Post 8vo. Price 12s.

A popular edition of this famous work, which, from its exceedingly high price, has hitherto been out of the reach of the general public. This edition contains all the reading matter that is of general interest; it also contains eighty illustrations.

THE RELIGIOUS ANECDOTES OF SCOTLAND. Edited by WILLIAM ADAMSON, D.D. Thick Post 8vo. Price 5s.

A voluminous collection of purely religious anecdotes relating to Scotland and Scotchmen, and illustrative of the more serious side of the life of the people. The anecdotes are chiefly in connection with distinguished Scottish clergymen and laymen, such as Rutherford, Macleod, Guthrie, Shirra, Leighton, the Erskines, Knox, Beattie, M'Crie, Eadie, Brown, Irving, Chalmers, Lawson, Milne, M'Cheyne, &c., &c. The anecdotes are serious and religious purely, and not at all of the ordinary witty description.

DAYS OF DEER STALKING in the Scottish Highlands, including an account of the Nature and Habits of the Red Deer, a description of the Scottish Forests, and Historical Notes on the earlier Field Sports of Scotland. With Highland Legends, Superstitions, Folk-Lore, and Tales of Poachers and Freebooters. By WILLIAM SCROPE. Illustrated by Sir Edwin and Charles Landseer. Demy 8vo. Price 12s. 6d.

"*The best book of sporting adventures with which we are acquainted.*"—ATHENÆUM.

"*Of this noble diversion we owe the first satisfactory description to the pen of an English gentleman of high birth and extensive fortune, whose many amiable and elegant personal qualities have been commemorated in the diary of Sir Walter Scott.*"—LONDON QUARTERLY REVIEW.

DAYS AND NIGHTS OF SALMON FISHING in the River Tweed. By WILLIAM SCROPE. Illustrated by Sir David Wilkie, Sir Edwin Landseer, Charles Landseer, William Simson, and Edward Cooke. Demy 8vo. Price 12s. 6d.

"*Mr. Scrope's book has done for salmon fishing what its predecessor performed for deer stalking.*"—LONDON QUARTERLY REVIEW.

"*Mr. Scrope conveys to us in an agreeable and lively manner the results of his more than twenty years' experience in our great Border river. . . . The work is enlivened by the narration of numerous angling adventures, which bring out with force and spirit the essential character of the sport in question. . . . Mr. Scrope is a skilful author as well as an experienced angler. It does not fall to the lot of all men to handle with equal dexterity, the brush, the pen, and the rod, to say nothing of the rifle, still less of the leister under cloud of night.*"—BLACKWOOD'S MAGAZINE.

THE FIELD SPORTS OF THE NORTH OF EUROPE. A Narrative of Angling, Hunting, and Shooting in Sweden and Norway. By CAPTAIN L. LLOYD. New edition. Enlarged and revised. Demy 8vo. Price 9s.

"*The chase seems for years to have been his ruling passion, and to have made him a perfect model of perpetual motion. We admire Mr. Lloyd. He is a sportsman far above the common run.*"—BLACKWOOD'S MAGAZINE.

"*This is a very entertaining work and written, moreover, in an agreeable and modest spirit. We strongly recommend it as containing much instruction and more amusement.*—ATHENÆUM.

PUBLIC AND PRIVATE LIBRARIES OF GLASGOW. A Bibliographical Study. By THOMAS MASON. Demy 8vo. Price 12s. 6d. net.

A strictly Bibliographical work dealing with the subject of rare and interesting works, and in that respect describing three of the public and thirteen of the private libraries of Glasgow. All of especial interest.

THE LIFE OF SIR WILLIAM WALLACE. By JOHN D. CARRICK. Fourth and cheaper edition. Royal 8vo. Price 2s. 6d.

The best life of the great Scottish hero. Contains much valuable and interesting matter regarding the history of that historically important period.

THE HISTORY OF THE PROVINCE OF MORAY. By LACHLAN SHAW. New and Enlarged Edition, 3 Vols., Demy 8vo. Price 30s.

The Standard History of the old geographical division termed the Province of Moray, comprising the Counties of Elgin and Nairn, the greater part of the County of Inverness, and a portion of the County of Banff. Cosmo Innes pronounced this to be the best local history of any part of Scotland.

HIGHLAND LEGENDS. By SIR THOMAS DICK LAUDER. Crown 8vo. Price 6s.

Historical Legends descriptive of Clan and Highland Life and Incident in former times.

TALES OF THE HIGHLANDS. By SIR THOMAS DICK LAUDER. Crown 8vo. Price 6s.

Uniform with and similar in character to the preceding, though entirely different tales. The two are companion volumes.

AN ACCOUNT OF THE GREAT MORAY FLOODS IN 1829. By SIR THOMAS DICK LAUDER. Demy 8vo., with 64 Plates and Portrait. Fourth Edition. Price 8s. 6d.

A most interesting work, containing numerous etchings by the Author. In addition to the main feature of the book, it contains much historical and legendary matter relating to the districts through which the River Spey runs.

OLD SCOTTISH CUSTOMS: Local and General. By E. J. GUTHRIE. Crown 8vo. Price 3s. 6d.

Gives an interesting account of old local and general Scottish customs, now rapidly being lost sight of.

A HISTORICAL ACCOUNT OF THE BELIEF IN WITCHCRAFT IN SCOTLAND. By CHARLES KIRKPATRICK SHARPE. Crown 8vo. Price 4s. 6d.

Gives a chronological account of Witchcraft incidents in Scotland from the earliest period, in a racy, attractive style. And likewise contains an interesting Bibliography of Scottish books on Witchcraft.

"Sharpe was well qualified to gossip about these topics."—SATURDAY REVIEW.

"Mr. Sharpe has arranged all the striking and important phenomena associated with the belief in Apparitions and Witchcraft. An extensive appendix, with a list of books on Witchcraft in Scotland, and a useful index, render this edition of Mr. Sharpe's work all the more valuable."—GLASGOW HERALD.

TALES OF THE SCOTTISH PEASANTRY. By ALEXANDER and JOHN BETHUNE. With Biography of the Authors by JOHN INGRAM, F.S.A.Scot. Post 8vo. Price 3s. 6d.

"It is the perfect propriety of taste, no less than the thorough intimacy with the subjects he treats of, that gives Mr. Bethune's book a great charm in our eyes."—ATHENÆUM.

"The pictures of rural life and character appear to us remarkably true, as well as pleasing."—CHAMBERS'S JOURNAL.

The Tales are quite out of the ordinary routine of such literature, and are universally held in peculiarly high esteem. The following may be given as a specimen of the Contents:—"The Deformed," "The Fate of the Fairest," "The Stranger," "The Drunkard," "The Illegitimate," "The Cousins," &c., &c.

A JOURNEY TO THE WESTERN ISLANDS OF SCOTLAND IN 1773. By SAMUEL JOHNSON, LL.D. Crown 8vo. Price 3s.

Written by Johnson himself, and not to be confounded with Boswell's account of the same tour. Johnson said that some of his best writing is in this work.

THE HISTORY OF BURKE AND HARE AND OF THE RESURRECTIONIST TIMES. A Fragment from the Criminal Annals of Scotland. By GEORGE MAC GREGOR, F.S.A.Scot. With Seven Illustrations, Demy 8vo. Price 7s. 6d.

"*Mr. MacGregor has produced a book which is eminently readable.*"—JOURNAL OF JURISPRUDENCE.

"*The book contains a great deal of curious information.*"—SCOTSMAN.

"*He who takes up this book of an evening must be prepared to sup full of horrors, yet the banquet is served with much of literary grace, and garnished with a deftness and taste which render it palatable to a degree.*"—GLASGOW HERALD.

THE HISTORY OF GLASGOW: From the Earliest Period to the Present Time. By GEORGE MAC GREGOR, F.S.A.Scot. Containing 36 Illustrations. Demy 8vo. Price 12s. 6d.

An entirely new as well as the fullest and most complete history of this prosperous city. In addition it is the first written in chronological order. Comprising a large handsome volume in Sixty Chapters, and extensive Appendix and Index, and illustrated throughout with many interesting engravings and drawings.

THE COLLECTED WRITINGS OF DOUGAL GRAHAM, "Skellat," Bellman of Glasgow. Edited with Notes, together with a Biographical and Bibliographical Introduction, and a Sketch of the Chap Literature of Scotland, by GEORGE MAC GREGOR, F.S.A.Scot. Impression limited to 250 copies. 2 Vols., Demy 8vo. Price 21s.

With very trifling exceptions Graham was the only writer of purely Scottish chap-books of a secular description, almost all the others circulated being reprints of English productions. His writings are exceedingly facetious and highly illustrative of the social life of the period.

SCOTTISH PROVERBS. By ANDREW HENDERSON. Crown 8vo. Cheaper edition. Price 2s. 6d.

A cheap edition of a book that has long held a high place in Scottish Literature.

THE BOOK OF SCOTTISH ANECDOTE: Humorous, Social, Legendary, and Historical. Edited by ALEXANDER HISLOP. Crown 8vo., pp. 768. Cheaper edition. Price 5s.

The most comprehensive collection of Scottish Anecdotes, containing about 3,000 in number.

THE BOOK OF SCOTTISH STORY: Historical, Traditional, Legendary, Imaginative, and Humorous. Crown 8vo., pp. 768. Cheaper edition. Price 5s.

A most interesting and varied collection by Leading Scottish Authors.

THE BOOK OF SCOTTISH POEMS: Ancient and Modern. Edited by J. Ross. Crown 8vo., pp. 768. Cheaper edition. Price 5s.

Comprising a History of Scottish Poetry and Poets from the earliest times. With lives of the Poets and Selections from their Writings.

*** These three works are uniform.

A DESCRIPTION OF THE WESTERN ISLES OF SCOTLAND, CALLED HYBRIDES. With the Genealogies of the Chief Clans of the Isles. By SIR DONALD MONRO, High Dean of the Isles, who travelled through most of them in the year 1549. Impression limited to 250 copies. Demy 8vo. Price 5s.

This is the earliest written description of the Western Islands, and is exceedingly quaint and interesting. In this edition all the old curious spellings are strictly retained.

A DESCRIPTION OF THE WESTERN ISLANDS OF SCOTLAND CIRCA 1695. By MARTIN MARTIN. Impression limited to 250 copies. Demy 8vo. Price 12s. 6d.

With the exception of Dean Monro's smaller work 150 years previous, it is the earliest description of the Western Islands we have, and is the only lengthy work on the subject before the era of modern innovations. Martin very interestingly describes the people and their ways as he found them about 200 years ago.

THE SCOTTISH POETS, RECENT AND LIVING.
By ALEXANDER G. MURDOCH. With Portraits, Post 8vo. Price 6s.

A most interesting resumé of Scottish Poetry in recent times. Contains a biographical sketch, choice pieces, and portraits of the recent and living Scottish Poets.

THE HUMOROUS CHAP-BOOKS OF SCOTLAND.
By JOHN FRASER. 2 Vols., Thin Crown 8vo (all published). Price 5s.

An interesting and racy description of the chap-book literature of Scotland, and biographical sketches of the writers.

THE HISTORY OF STIRLINGSHIRE.
By WILLIAM NIMMO. 2 Vols., Demy 8vo. 3rd Edition. Price 25s.

A new edition of this standard county history, handsomely printed, and with detailed map giving the parish boundaries and other matters of interest.

This county has been termed the battlefield of Scotland, and in addition to the many and important military engagements that have taken place in this district, of all which a full account is given,—this part of Scotland is of especial moment in many other notable respects,—among which particular reference may be made to the Roman Wall, the greater part of this most interesting object being situated within the boundaries of the county.

A POPULAR SKETCH OF THE HISTORY OF GLASGOW:
From the Earliest Period to the Present Time. By ANDREW WALLACE. Crown 8vo. Price 3s. 6d.

The only attempt to write a History of Glasgow suitable for popular use.

THE HISTORY OF THE WESTERN HIGHLANDS AND ISLES OF SCOTLAND,
from A.D. 1493 to A.D. 1625. With a brief introductory sketch from A.D. 80 to A.D. 1493. By DONALD GREGORY. Demy 8vo. Price 12s. 6d.

Incomparably the best history of the Scottish Highlands, and written purely from original investigation. Also contains particularly full and lengthened Contents and Index, respectively at beginning and end of the volume.

THE HISTORY OF AYRSHIRE. By JAMES PATERSON. 5 Vols., Crown 8vo. Price 28s. net.

  The most recent and the fullest history of this exceedingly interesting county. The work is particularly rich in the department of Family History.

MARTYRLAND: a Historical Tale of the Covenanters. By the Rev. ROBERT SIMPSON, D.D. Crown 8vo. Cheaper Edition. Price 2s. 6d.

  A tale illustrative of the history of the Covenanters in the South of Scotland.

TALES OF THE COVENANTERS. By E. J. GUTHRIE. Crown 8vo. Cheaper Edition. Price 2s. 6d.

  A number of tales illustrative of leading incidents and characters connected with the Covenanters.

PERSONAL AND FAMILY NAMES. A Popular Monograph on the Origin and History of the Nomenclature of the Present and Former Times. By HARRY ALFRED LONG. Demy 8vo. Price 5s.

  Interesting investigations as to the origin, history, and meaning of about 9,000 personal and family names.

THE SCOTTISH GALLOVIDIAN ENCYCLOPÆDIA of the Original, Antiquated, and Natural Curiosities of the South of Scotland. By JOHN MACTAGGART. Demy 8vo. Price raised to 25s. Impression limited to 250 copies.

  Contains a large amount of extremely interesting and curious matter relating to the South of Scotland.

THE COMPLETE TALES OF THE ETTRICK SHEPHERD (JAMES HOGG). 2 vols., Demy 8vo.

  An entirely new and complete edition of the tales of this popular Scottish writer.

GLASGOW : THOMAS D. MORISON.
LONDON : HAMILTON, ADAMS & CO.

www.ingramcontent.com/pod-product-compliance
Lightning Source LLC
Chambersburg PA
CBHW032110230426
43672CB00009B/1697